Steve Palmer

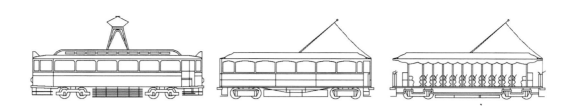

BLACKPOOL & FLEETWOOD

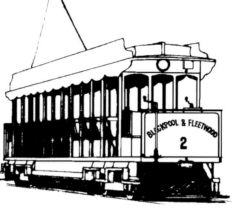

100 YEARS BY TRAM

Steve Palmer

PLATFORM
5

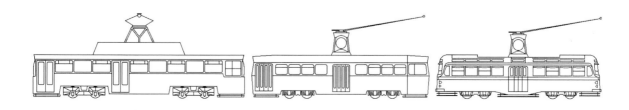

1st July 1898: the first tram to make the complete trip from Blackpool to Fleetwood, poses in Lord Street admired by the watching locals, undoubtedly enhancing the street. **Gus Kenderdine**

CONTENTS

Published by Platform 5 Publishing Ltd., Wyvern House, Sark Road, Sheffield, S2 4HG, England.

Printed in England by B.R. Hubbard Printers Ltd., Callywhite Lane, Dronfield, Sheffield, S18 2QX.

ISBN 1 902336 02 X.

FOREWORD

The phrase "design life" has come to mean how long we can expect to use something before it is time to replace it. What "design life" did the Directors of the Blackpool & Fleetwood Tramroad Company plan for their line? It is interesting to speculate whether they were looking at the short, medium or long-term. For a tramway, 20 years is not such a long time: so far as the original company was concerned, the Blackpool and Fleetwood Tramway was a medium-term investment, as the owners passed the business to Blackpool Council within 22 years. The Council owned and operated it for another 66 years, until the operation passed to Blackpool Transport Services Limited in 1986. The Council has kept the job of maintaining and replacing the track and electrical equipment, with Blackpool Transport running the service. Steve Palmer's book traces the history of the Blackpool & Fleetwood Tramway from Mr Camerson's original line right up to the present day. These pages tell the story of one of the best-known light rail lines in the world.

I am proud to be part of the team that runs the Blackpool & Fleetwood Tramway in its Centenary Year. Celebrating a centenary is a chance to look back at the achievements of the past. It is a time to celebrate the vision of those who knew that they were not building a system for 20 or 30 years, but were setting out to create a transport link that would survive for as long as people want to travel between Blackpool, Bispham, Cleveleys and Fleetwood.

Those of us who are responsible for the future of the line know that our job is to make sure that we offer an attractive service and adapt it to changing times. The route has continued through one hundred years of changes in the way we live, that would astound the original promoters, if they could see them now. These changes have radically altered our demands for personal mobility. Increasing environmental awareness has started to alter the balance in favour of public transport. In 1898, trams provided the only realistic way for most people to travel any distance in urban areas. In the future, buses and trams will become more important, as public transport is recognised as part of the solution to the challenges that traffic congestion, pollution and sustainable development bring.

As stewards of the Blackpool & Fleetwood Tramway, we aim to hand it on to those who will come after us, as an essential part of the public transport network of the Fylde Coast, with a renewed relevance for a modern world and in good shape for the start of its next hundred years.

Tony Depledge
Managing Director
Blackpool Transport Services Limited

ACKNOWLEDGEMENTS

As always, I would like to express my thanks for all the assistance I have received in compiling this book, particularly in supplying useful illustrations.

Especially I would like to thank Terry Daniel, who has provided the excellent fleet drawings for this – and the previous book – and Ian McLoughlin, who has drawn the map and checked the fleet details. Also special thanks are given to people whose photographs have been used in this book and enhanced it: R. P. Fergusson, Anthony Stevenson, Roy Brook, Fred Holland, Philip Higgs, Terry Daniel, Eric Berry, Ian McLoughlin, Ted Lightbown, Stuart Ibbotson. Photographs used and acknowledged: E. Fielding, J. Joyce, Alan A. Jackson, R. R. Clarke, Bert Ball, R. Wilson, W. G. S. Hyde and A. D. Packer Collection.

The National Tramway Museum – Historical Collection of Photographs by: Maurice O'Connor, H. B. Priestley, W. A. Camwell and John Price – NTM.
Ralph Smedley – for the use of his postcard collection.
Mrs Masters – for the use of the late Mr F. Wohrman's pictures.
Peter R. Burton for the later Frances Burton's photograph – of 200.
The Gazette, Blackpool – Editor David Todd - use of historic photographs.
Blackpool Transport Services – photographs and facility for information.
Blackpool Central Reference Library – Mrs P. Hansell & Miss G. Marsland.
Blackpool Department of Tourism – Jane Seddon & George Hill.

Credit for the Cover Illustrations: Eric Bottomley G.R.A., who has made excellent contributions to this book by paintings showing early days on the Cliffs and a post-war scene at North Station – also reproduced commercially.

CHAPTER 1

CAMERON'S KINGDOM 1898–1919

The link between Blackpool & Fleetwood was planned in 1895, when John Cameron, the Secretary and Manager of the Manx Northern Railway, was employed as a consultant to the Blackpool & Fleetwood Syndicate. He walked along the coast between the two towns several times and so planned the exact route of the line. Above all, it was Cameron - who in March 1898 became the Secretary and Manager of the Blackpool & Fleetwood Tramroad Company - who was its driving force. Together with his large family, notably his brother Angus who became the Chief Engineer, he ruled the line with a rod of iron. It was said that his staff swore by him, and sometimes he swore at them!

John Cameron's experience of constructing and operating railways was second-to-none: he had worked as a ganger on the Settle–Carlisle railway, and went to the Isle of Man in 1878 as a sub-contractor for the Manx Northern Railway. He became Secretary and Manager for this, the cheapest-operated railway in Britain, and so it was fitting that he should have been consultant for the construction of the Douglas–Laxey and Snaefell Mountain Railways. His credentials for managing the Blackpool & Fleetwood line were impeccable: an experienced contractor and operator of great character and efficiency, just what the new line needed! When he came to Blackpool in March 1898, it is said that 43 Manxmen followed him, and were employed by the Company for many years. Indeed there were still Manx names at Bispham Depot until its closure in 1963.

Cameron became so identified with the Company that its telegraphic address was 'CAMERON – BLACKPOOL'. He had a large family of 15 children, several of whom were involved in public transport in places as far apart as Northampton and South America. Your author had the pleasure of meeting one of them, T. Donald Cameron in 1963, whose memories of his father and the Company are included in this book, and which give an interesting insight to those far-off days.

A Brief History of the Concern

"The history of the Blackpool & Fleetwood Tramroad Company reads almost like a romance, more particularly in these days of modern industrial enterprise. In spite of the unaccountable lack of local interest in the concern in the early days of its inception, it has developed into one of the most successful Tramroad companies in the Kingdom, and its shares, which now yield a substantial dividend each year to its fortunate shareholders, are very properly regarded as a real gilt-edged security. In addition to this, the constructing of the line has been wholly responsible for opening up and developing in the most remarkable manner, the whole of the intermediate countryside along the coast, linking-up the popular resort of Blackpool with the important seaport of Fleetwood."

"Confidence of the Promoters"

This professional perspective from the Tramway & Light Railway Association in 1913, may give the reader some idea of the esteem in which the Tramroad was held amongst professionals, bringing visitors from all parts of the world.

"When the scheme was first proposed to construct a Tramroad along what was then, in the early part of 1897, regarded as the bleak and rugged cliffs of Bispham and the wild and desolate stretch of flat uninteresting country at Norbreck, it was looked upon locally with complete indifference, apathy, and even suspicion, to the extent that not a single share was taken up in Blackpool. This shortsightedness and want of spirited enterprise not often associated with the residents of Blackpool have subsequently caused a considerable amount of regret. Those who invested their capital in the Company at the outset had trust and still continue to hold an instinctive confidence in the concern, and is most strikingly shown in that the original Board of Directors still control the destinies of the Company as does Mr. Cameron, the Secretary and Manager."

"Not only has the Company done well for its loyal and enterprising shareholders by providing them each year with a gratifying dividend of 6½%, but it has conferred incalculable benefits upon the owners and land all along its route. Where formerly there were only a few old-fashioned buildings, and hundreds of acres of purely agricultural

Left: The Board of the Blackpool & Fleetwood Tramroad Company, including the legendary John Cameron, Secretary & General Manager.

land, there has now sprung up palatial hydros, and hotels, model garden cities, and charming private residences, which it is no exaggeration to say would not be there had it not been for the Tramroad."

"Construction of the Line"

"The Tramroad, which is in effect a light railway, with fixed stopping places and picturesque wayside stations, is 8½ miles in length and was completed in the record time of eleven months. That it hit the popular taste and supplied a much needed want was conclusively shown in the fact that from the day the line was opened, on 13th July 1898, up to June 30th in the following year, almost a million and a half passengers were conveyed over the system. For the first three months the whole of the traffic was conducted with ten cars, whilst at the present time (1913) there are 37, and even with this, their resources are greatly taxed during the summer season."

"Under the provisions of their 1896 Act, the Company may hold their line in perpetuity with the exception of the tramway in Fleetwood which may be purchased in 30 years by the UDC, and the tramway in Blackpool, which is held on 21 years' lease from the Corporation of Blackpool. The work of the construction, which was commenced in July 1897, was arranged in two contracts. Messrs Dick Kerr & Company became responsible for the construction of the permanent way and buildings, and Messrs Mather & Platt were entrusted with the complete equipment of the power station, overhead work and rolling stock. The contract for the permanent way and buildings was carried out under the supervision of Messrs Garlick & Sykes, engineers to the Tramroad Company, who were also architects of the power station."

"Financial & Legal"

"The original capital of the Tramroad Company was £120,000 in £10 shares and £40,000 in Debentures, but the share issue has been increased to £150,000."

"The Company has spent an enormous amount of time and care in litigation in establishing that the line is a Light Railway. Its character, with its fenced-in line, the sleeper-laid track, the crossings with pointsmen on duty, and the ornamental wayside stations, establish this clearly. The struggle was between the Company on the one hand and the three local authorities through whose territory the Tramroad ran, on the other. (These were Bispham-with-Norbreck UDC, Thornton UDC, and Fleetwood UDC). These local authorities insisted that the system should be rated in full as a tramway, and pay rates."

"So important was the matter to all parties concerned that it was carried from court to court and eventually to the House of Lords, where it was definitely decided that the undertaking was a railway entitled to a quarter rating. The decision has since proved of immense value to other systems in the United Kingdom."

However we must return to the beginning and the construction of the line.

Construction of the Line

Construction of the line commenced at the Fleetwood end on 19th July 1897, and there were some 400 navvies engaged on the work. At Copse Road, next to Riley's Saw Mill, work on the depot commenced without planning permission having been granted. Plans were informally approved by the Council Surveyor, and all was well. The provision of a railway link behind the car shed was significant in enabling a small locomotive to be used in ferrying equipment and materials forward as the line progressed towards Blackpool. The largest civil engineering project was carried out between Anchorsholme and Little Bispham, where there was a deep cutting, and similarly at Tom's Cabin where there were cuttings up to 16 feet deep. Despite this, by November 1897 there was a single line from Fleetwood to the Cabin. It was only at this stage that Blackpool Corporation stirred itself into action and commenced its portion of the route from Talbot Road Station to the boundary at King Edward Avenue (The Cliffs).

At a January meeting of the Directors in Manchester, the Chairman George Richardson said that it was hoped to open the line in May, and that a number of people had been over the line from Cabin to Fleetwood. He announced that the Company was promoting a Bill which would give it powers to construct an alternative line into Blackpool, although what they really wanted was running powers over Corporation lines. This dispute arose from the Corporation's insistence on a 'back road' route into town, rather than along the Promenade through Claremont Park. This was all connected to the Corporation's own plans to extend its tramway from Cocker Square to the Gynn. About this proposition, there

Left: The official party on the first ride, including Alderman Cocker 'Father of Blackpool', seen on the right - with white beard.

Right: A busy scene at the Gynn c. 14th July, when the regular service started from here to Fleetwood, and the crossbench car is besieged by passengers who board from both sides and fill the seats. In the foreground are the familiar landaus which have brought people here from the town centre. Notice the close proximity of the cliffs, before the Promenade was built in the twenties.
Gus Kenderdine

was a disagreement as to whether or not the tramway should be constructed along the Middle Walk. A town meeting threw out this proposal, and when the tramway was eventually constructed to the Gynn in 1900, it was along the Upper Promenade.

The 'Fleetwood Chronicle' of 18 February 1898 gave an interesting insight into the Progress of the Tramroad:-

"A sort of Yankee enterprise has possessed us. Only 8 months ago the contractors got to work, and today we are amazed to find that the line is almost complete. A double line has been laid to Uncle Tom's Cabin from Fleetwood, the portion within Fleetwood is one-third finished and the contractor hopes to have this complete by the end of March. The generator station is finished, despite a storm which blew down the buildings. The 180 feet chimney is 20 feet from completion, the boilers and economisers are fixed and the building of the engines is soon to be completed."

"Electric distribution equipment is in place at Fleetwood. The progress made has been prodigious, and not always easy. On the Gynn Estate, an 8-10 feet cutting for 2,000 feet has involved the removal of 15,000 cubic yards of material."

At a half yearly meeting of the Company, it was announced that £82,000 had been expended up to January 17th: "the only works which were not progressing were those the Corporation has in hand." At the Fleetwood end of the line, all was not plain sailing. The construction of the line along the main street and the laying of the power cables created considerable disruption. Correspondence between the Dick Kerr Company and Fleetwood UDC, indicates that the Council Surveyor had been using libellous language! However, good relations were restored by an invitation to the Council for a run on the tramway on 16th April, following lunch at the Mount Hotel. This excursion was by steam-hauled wagon, which took only eight minutes to reach Rossall. The estimated running time between Blackpool & Fleetwood by tram was to be 25 minutes.

A report appeared in the 'Gazette News' regarding a ride over the Tramroad from Fleetwood to Blackpool using wagons drawn by one of the steam engines.

"A party of seven were comfortably seated on chairs placed in a wagon to be drawn by an engine called the 'Fleetwood'. It was not exactly an up-to-date corridor train, and although the wind blew in pretty piercing blasts we were quite comfortable deep down in the "Pullman car." We left Fleetwood at about 2.15, amid affectionate leave-takings and were soon well in sight of good old Rossall. Rapidly we steamed through fields, crossed bridges and skimmed between budding hedgerows and in the short space of twenty minutes we were actually in breezy Blackpool. After a look round Blackpool we started our homeward journey, this being a little before five, just to give the engine breathing space – not in order the satisfy any desire of our own – we were at home in Fleetwood ready for church, having spent a pleasant Sunday afternoon by rail."

An article in the 'Fleetwood Chronicle' on May 10th 1898 indicated the importance of the new line to the development of the Fylde Coast.

"The time is fast approaching when the Fleetwood to Blackpool tramway will be completed. The rails have been placed in position, and in a few weeks time the first cars will run between the two watering places. The occasion will be an important one, for the opening of the tramway will mark a definite epoch in the progress of this part of the Fylde. For years past, inter-communication between the towns of Fleetwood and Blackpool have been of a very inconvenient character and now that the promised improvement is to take place, the result is bound to be seen in a more rapidly advancing development. Even at Bispham, which was never regarded as a particularly enterprising place, the inhabitants are mak-

ing a spirited endeavour to secure the full advantages of the new car line, and streets are being laid out to such an extent that practically a new town is starting up, and the truly rural aspect of the village is seriously threatened. The hamlet promises to become a flourishing suburb."

"At Fleetwood, too, transactions in the local property market show that the establishment of the improved means of communication has put an enhanced value on property and land. In fact, in several respects the district is being developed by the new tramway, and greater things are looked for in the near future. This being the case, should not the public of Fleetwood make the arrival of the first tram an opportunity for showing their appreciation of the public spirited and far-seeing policy which has characterised the Tramway Company? The tram line will in all probability be opened at Whitsuntide. The public of Fleetwood should certainly show their appreciation in some tangible way to give the tramway a good send-off."

By June, when eleven cars had been received and several trial runs made on the Tramroad section, the press was speculating that the new line: "Will become as popular as that from Douglas to Laxey (Isle of Man)." The first passenger journey over the whole system took place on July 1st, when Crossbench Car 4 travelled to Talbot Road Station to collect a distinguished party of Blackpool Councillors, officers of the Tramways Department and the press. The party included Alderman Cocker, 'Father of Blackpool', whose pronouncements at the opening of the Blackpool Tramway in 1885 that it would be a short-lived novelty, had proved wide of the mark. To R. C. Quin and J. Lancaster of the Tramways Department, whose trials and tribulations with the conduit system in Blackpool are well-known, the ride to Fleetwood must have been a revelation! This is how the press recorded the event:

"Experimental Opening – An Exhilarating Ride"

"A large number of people crowded the street in front of the Talbot Road Station and gave a hearty send-off to the party, starting at 3.10 p.m. The youngsters were the most demonstrative and cheered heartily. Stops were made for inspection by the Borough Engineer and the Town Clerk. The metals were filled with grit and the ride through the streets was anything but smooth. Alderman Cocker commented: "You cannot have smooth sailing on the first trial." The sensation was different outside the boundary, as one of the occupants commented: "The feeling was grand."

"The View is Magnificent"

"On Friday afternoon the atmosphere was clear and the sea was only gently rippled by a north-westerly breeze; the Isle of Man and Barrow could be clearly seen. We were taken to the Company's premises: some deep cuttings have been made to get there. The Company has 30 motor-cars and 30 trailers (sic) and 2 accumulator stations. The car barn is capable of holding 12 cars, and close by are a number of houses for officials and workers of the Company which are not yet complete."

"The general appearance of the whole system is undoubtedly pretty and so it appears to be in the estimation of the Fleetwood public, judging by their enthusiastic turnout to see the arrival of the car and the cheery welcome of the children." (The author's grandmother was one of those flag-waving children who lined the track at Ash Street, and she remembered it well as one of the highlights of her childhood). "The return journey was started at thirteen minutes to five, and at Cleveleys the party adjourned to the Cleveleys Hotel with the Mayor, who was seen driving in his carriage. Alderman Cocker proposed a toast to the success of the Company, and the journey was resumed, arriving at 6 p.m."

The Board of Trade Inspection took place on July 13th, when there were two cars at the Talbot Road terminus waiting for Major Marindin and Major Cardew to arrive by train from London. The former was to inspect the tramway generally, and the latter the electrical aspects. The event was characterised by protests along the line, especially by the bus proprietors, who parked one of their buses at the kerb of the Park Hotel, where the road was narrow in order to demonstrate the dangers. The Inspector's reaction was that the road would have to be widened or the track interlaced. Nearer the Gynn, a furniture van was loading and obstructing the track. An impatient Mr. Cameron called to them to remove the van, to which they replied that he must wait until they had finished. The Inspector saw the funny side of it, and called out: "You cannot place a furniture van in front of an Act of Parliament." The result of this protest was that the approval was given for the opening of the Gynn to Fleetwood part of the line, but that the street section in Blackpool could not be opened until the streets had been widened. Service commenced on the next day, using the ten available cars, augmented in August by trailers 11–13. The formal opening took place on Saturday 30th, when a special car carried the Directors from Talbot Road Station to Fleetwood and back. The town was en-fete, and in the evening there was a banquet at the Imperial Hotel, where a specially-composed song was rendered by Mr. Harrison Hill, the music of which does not seem to have survived. The lyrics were somewhat banal, but reflected the problems and exhilarations of the line's opening:

"The New Electric Car"

The cars don't run in Blackpool,
So we started just outside.
For the Blackpool streets are narrow,
And the Blackpool buses wide.
But they're going to widen all the streets,
Of Blackpool just for fun.
And when they've widened all the streets,
Why then the cars will run.

Chorus:

Now roit you are for Blackpool,
For Fleetwood roit you are.
And Dolly and me sat viz-a-vee,
On the new electric car.

The line was now truly launched! From the first it proved popular, and the landaus did good trade in bringing people to the Gynn to be whisked along the coast to Fleetwood. As the Autumn nights drew in, the need for closed cars was met by the delivery of five Saloon cars 14–18. Work also began on building a small depot at Bold Street in Fleetwood, which would house four cars, the first and last of each day and thus avoid dead running to Bispham. Blackpool Corporation completed the required work on Dickson Road, and regular service to the station began on 29th September 1898.

BLACKPOOL & FLEETWOOD TRAMROADS
Tramway No. 3.
Schedule of Quantities and Prices

Of the various Works and Materials required in the construction and laying of double line of Tramways in Fleetwood, from the junction of Tramroad to the terminus at Euston Barracks.

The Contractor is to provide all Labour, Horses, Carts, Machinery, Tools, and Tackling of every description, and all Water which may become necessary to the full and complete execution of the several Works in all their parts, and he is to set out and be responsible for the correct setting out of the several Works, and for the accuracy of the depths, widths, gauge, and levels of any and every part of the same.

From the commencement to the completion of the Works, and until the same shall have been formally delivered over to the Corporation the care and risk of the same shall be entirely with the Contractor.

The attention of the Contractor is called to the Specification attending to this Contract, so that he may allow in his estimate and prices for all the stipulations and requirements therein contained.

Each price must include for providing all materials and all loading of materials to, from, and about the works.

15

Yds.	Feet	No.		@	£	s.	d.
2770			Cube, excavation of road metal, clay, gravel, sand, &c., including carting surplus away.	3/-	415	10	0
1385			Cube, Portland cement concrete, mixed as specified and laid in foundations, including prepared cement surface as specified, and preparing bed for concrete. Contractor to find all materials.	15/6	1073	7	6
Tons	**Cwts.**	**Qrs.**					
177	2	0	Steel rails in 30ft. lengths, weighing 81lbs. per lineal yard, holed at each end for fishplates, including drilling for tie bars.	£7/-/-	1239	14	0
3	16	2	Steel fishplates, weighing 18lbs. per pair.	£7/-/-	26	15	6
1	9	3	Fishbolts, weighing ·875lbs. each.	£10/-/-	14	17	6
5	0	0	Tie bars and nuts, weighing 14lbs. each.	£10/-/-	50	0	0
Yds.							
2380			Lineal, laying single line of Tramway (both rails) on concrete foundations, making joints with fishplates and bolts complete, accurate to gauge and levels, including all bends in rails along the route.	1/2	138	16	8
			Cutting rails to lengths required.		40	0	0
Tons							
188			Carting Tramway Rails, points, crossings, tie rods, bolts, &c., from the nearest Railway Station per ton.	3/-	28	4	0
		No.					
		797	Tie Bars, fixing only with bolts and nuts complete, each.	3	9	19	3
		2	Providing spring points and fixing complete.	£30/-/-	60	0	0
		2	Providing neutral points and fixing complete.	£20/-/-	40	0	0
		2	Providing Tramway Crossings, fixing complete.	£10/-/-	20	0	0
			Carried Forward...................£		3157	4	5

16

Yds.	Feet	No.		@	£	s.	d.
			Brought forward............................£		3157	4	5
1133			Lineal, making good Macadam road adjoining new sett paving (both sides), labour and material per yard.	4	18	17	8
8311			Super., providing and paving with 6in. granite setts, including all the cutting required for points, crossings, tie bars, manhole tops, and the serrating of the outer edge of the paving on each side of the Tramways as shown on drawings.	11/-	4571	1	0
8311			Super., forming and supplying bed of sand for paving 1 inch deep.	1	34	12	7
8311			Super., racking joints of paving with ½-inch limestone chippings and running thoroughly with pitch and tar.	2/-	831	2	0
		2	Raising or lowering manhole tops and ventilators £1 per set.		2	0	0
		70	Forming islands 6ft. by 3ft. at Electric Poles 12in. by 6in. tooled curbs raised 6in. above level of rails.	£5/10/-	385	0	0
			Carried to Summary ....£		8999	17	8

A scene of the ancient Gynn Inn with the passing tram track in cobbles and an empty Crossbench car 1, followed by box car 19. **Sankey Collection**

ELECTRIC RAILWAYS & TRAMWAYS : BLACKPOOL AND FLEETWOOD TRAMWAY
Mather & Platt Ltd

Mechanical, Electrical & Hydraulic Engineers, Manchester

The new tramroad, or to describe it more accurately, the new railway between Blackpool & Fleetwood completes the facilities for local communications along the coast of Lancashire, between Lytham and Fleetwood, a distance of about 19 miles. Although the last completed, the tramroad is by far the most important link of the system, which consists of the following sections, with an aggregate track length of 30 miles:-

Length of Route & Track Lytham to South Shore (gas traction) 4 miles... 8 miles South Shore to Blackpool (electric conduit)   3 miles... 6 miles Blackpool to Fleetwood (overhead trolley wire) 8 miles...16 miles

The first mentioned section was opened in 1896, and is owned and worked by the Blackpool, St Annes, and Lytham Tramway Company; the second section is owned and managed by the Blackpool Corporation, and although at present an electrical conduit tramway, it is shortly to be converted to the overhead trolley wire system. This line is especially interesting as the first electrical tramway constructed along a highway in England, and has a somewhat varied history. Originally laid down by a private company, it proved for some years a profitable undertaking, but in 1893 it was sold to the Corporation, and subsequently became unremunerative, and has been largely subsidised from the Corporation rates. During the past year however, it has shown a small profit. The conduit system as used on this line is now antiquated, and the Corporation has decided to reconstruct the line on the overhead trolley system, with the consent of the Local Government Board and a loan for this purpose. The existing line meets the Lytham tramway at its southern end and a short extension will connect it at Blackpool (Gynn Inn) with the new line to Fleetwood.

The distance from Blackpool to Fleetwood is eight miles, and hitherto the only regular public means of travel has been the joint line of the Lancashire & Yorkshire and London & North Western Railways. This line runs inland to Poulton, where it joins the railway from Preston, and passengers from Blackpool to Fleetwood generally have to change here.

The result is that the average journey between the two towns requires over half-an-hour and trains are not frequent. In these circumstances there could be little question that an electric railway constructed directly along the coast, and providing frequent and rapid service, would not only be of great benefit locally, but would prove a profitable enterprise. Under the provision of their 1896 Act, the Company may hold the line in perpetuity, except the tramway in Fleetwood which may be purchased in thirty years by the Urban District Council, and the tramway in Blackpool which is held on a twenty-one years lease from the Corporation.

(Undoubtedly the subsequent acquisition by Blackpool Corporation proves beneficial financially to them, while serving the population)

Construction was begun in July 1897. The work was arranged in two contracts: Dick Kerr & Co became responsible for the construction of the permanent way and buildings, and Mather & Platt were entrusted with the complete equipment of the power station, overhead work and rolling stock. The contract for the permanent way and buildings was carried out under the supervision of Garlick & Sykes, Engineers of the Tramroad Company, who were also architects of the power station.

LIGHT RAILWAY BETWEEN BLACKPOOL & FLEETWOOD

The accompanying map and plans show the situation of the line and the gradients, none of which are severe. The terminus at Blackpool has been conveniently placed at Talbot Road, adjacent to the joint station of L & Y and L & NW Railway Companies. From this point the tramway extends along Dickson Road to Warley Road where there is a falling gradient of 1 in 26.5 to the Gynn Inn. Here is the northern end of the Blackpool marine promenade, one of the finest in the country, and at this point the sea comes within view. The line crosses the street to the seaward side of the new road recently made by the Corporation along the cliffs. At this point, on the right, is one of the accumulator stations to which reference will again be made. At a distance of about 1 1/8 miles from the Blackpool terminus, the line crosses the Borough boundary, and here the ordinary form of tramway construction gives place to a light railway type of roadbed. Just before the boundary there is the commencement of a long incline, with a gradient which brings the line to its highest point at an elevation of 95 ft above the sea level (at Uncle Tom's Cabin). For the next mile and a quarter the gradient falls gradually until at a distance of 3½ miles from Blackpool, the line is only 13 ft above sea level (Little Bispham).

From this point to the terminus at Fleetwood the gradient is practically level. The generating station and principal car shed is situated at Bispham, about two miles from Blackpool, a short distance from the line with a siding leading down to the car shed. All cars stop near the station and at various fixed stopping places along the route. Some distance beyond the power station is the village of Norbreck. Up to this point there are fine views of the sea, but the line now strikes inland, passes through Cleveleys, and follows alongside the main road to Rossall, at the well-known public school. At this point the tramway turns well to the north-east, and runs with a few easy curves direct to Church Street in Fleetwood, passing the second accumulator station and car shed in Copse Road. Here the light railway type of construction terminates at the main street, and for the remainder of the distance is similar to that in Blackpool, conforming closely to the best designs for tramway permanent way. The terminus is near the railway station and the landing stage of the steamers to Belfast, Douglas and Barrow. As already mentioned, the distance between the termini is a little over 8 miles, and the time occupied by the journey is under 25 minutes. The speed is limited by official regulations, or the journey could be performed in much less time, as the motors are capable of attaining a speed of 30 m.p.h.

PERMANENT WAY

The track is of standard gauge and double throughout, except in Blackpool where passing places are provided. As we have stated, the permanent way includes both tramway and light railway forms of construction. From Talbot Road terminus to the Blackpool Borough boundary and again from Church Street Fleetwood to the terminus, the line is a tramway. However the intervening section, about 6½ miles in length, has all the characteristics of a light railway, the line being fenced and the road being designed for comparative high speeds.

As regards the tramway construction, there are no novel points to note, except that the groove of the rails is made slightly larger to suit the thicker flange required for running on the Vignole rails. The roadway was excavated to a depth of 12 ins for the full width of the track and for 18 ins on each side of the outside rails. The rails used in Blackpool weigh 98 lbs per yard, those in Fleetwood 83 lbs. They are tied to gauge by steel bars at intervals of 9 ft and the sets which bring the roadway up to the rail level are of granite. On the tramway sections the electrical connections between each rail ends consist of two copper bonds of the 'Daniel' type.

On the tramroad the form of construction is entirely different. The route lies across fields and, as the roadbed had to be made throughout, it will be readily understood that the work could not be carried out as rapidly as in the case of a tramway. In the latter, materials can be deposited all along the route, and several gangs of men can be simultaneously employed at intervals along the route. There was no roadway by the side of the route of the tramroad and ballast, sleepers, rails etc. had to be carried forward on the rails as the line was prepared, the contractors using small steam engines for hauling material and for inspection. A large amount of excavation (123,000 cubic yards) was required, the cuttings ranging up to about 16 ft in depth (e.g. Anchors-holme). The great bulk of the material excavated was hard and tough red clay - very difficult to work - in fact the cuttings had to be blasted out, as in heavy rail construction. In building these, close poling and pumping was required, the material met with being 'quick' clay and running sand. There are ten level crossings on the line, seven of which are on public roads, and all are provided with cattle guards to the track. On this section the track consists of Vignole rails - 56 lbs per yard - and are laid on transverse sleepers with centres 3 ft 6 3/4 ins apart. The rails are spiked directly to creosoted redwood sleepers (9 ft x 9 ins x 4½ ins), chairs not being used, and the sleepers are embedded in 12 ins of ballast in the usual way.

A feature of special interest, since it is wholly new in this country, is the 'Plastic rail bond' (see drawing). This bond has been used with what appears to be great success in America. It is composed of two portions - a plastic or putty-like metal compound - which makes contact between the rail and the metal of the joint, and a flexible elastic cork case to hold the plastic part in position. The fish plate is bolted down and as the bolts are tightened, the cork case is compressed to half its former thickness, giving an electrical connection between the rails of low resistance. The bond is thus entirely concealed from view, and is protected by the cork case from injury arising from movement between the rail and fish plates.

GENERATING STATION

The whole of the electrical equipment has been designed and executed by Messrs Mather & Platt Ltd of the Salford Iron Works.

The generating station and principal car shed is situated about two miles from the Blackpool terminus, and a quarter of a mile from the line, with which the car shed is connected by a spur track. All the buildings, including a lofty chimney, are constructed of brick.

The whole installation is compactly and conveniently arranged. The boiler room measures 66 ft by 33 ft, and the engine room 76 ft by 28 ft. Three Lancashire boilers, constructed by Galloways Ltd of Manchester, form the steam raising plant: each boiler is 30 ft long x 8 ft wide and the steam pressure is 120 lbs. Water is obtained from a reservoir adjacent to the engine room, which is filled by surface water collected from surrounding fields and springs. If required, water can also be drawn from the local supply, the reservoir is expected to supply all requirements. After passing through the hot well, the water is fed to the boilers through two sets of economisers of 96 tubes each. Two direct steam-driven feed pumps are employed.

All steam and exhaust pipes are placed in a basement beneath the engine room, giving easy access to all parts: the steam pipes are arranged in the form of a ring. The main pipe and the branch to each engine are fitted with a steam separator. A water gauge indicates the amount of water collected, and by means of a valve the attendant may clear the separator of water when required. After leaving the engine room the water passes down a wooden troughing, and for some distance around the reservoir before entering it. The water for the condensers is pumped up by circulating pumps driven by Mather & Platt's high-speed engines.

There are four open marine-type vertical compound engines of 200 horse-power each, running at a speed of 165 revolutions per minute. Three boosters have been included in the equipment of the station. They stand along the wall beside the switchboard, and occupy little space. The engine room is provided with a five ton travelling crane, which is also designed for use in the adjacent car shed, which has space for twelve cars and pits for four cars. The trolley wires are brought into the shed so that cars can be conveniently shunted. At one end of the shed is an eight horsepower Mather & Platt 'Manchester' motor, which drives a shaft for operating tools required for repairs. The whole of the station buildings are lit by incandescent lamps controlled from one central distribution board.

DISTRIBUTING SYSTEM

Current is conveyed from the generating station to the line by four feeders, each consisting of copper cables, lead-covered and armoured and laid in trenches along the trolley line. The feeders are taken into cast-iron section boxes, which are placed at intervals of a half mile along the line, and are then connected with the trolley wire through four wedge switches placed in the section boxes. One feeder cable runs direct to each of the two accumulator stations, which are situated in Blackpool (Gynn Cliffs) and Fleetwood (Copse Road depot). At each of these stations there are batteries of 250 cells, each battery having a capacity of 300 ampere hours at a voltage of 500. Usually the batteries will be in parallel with the trolley wire, as their principal function is to steady the voltage on the line and supply sudden demand for currents, thus relieving the generating plant from undue strain. Another important use of the accumulators is to provide power independently of the generating station for early morning or night cars, thus allowing the generators to be shut down over longer periods than would otherwise be the case. The two batteries at Blackpool and Fleetwood will provide sufficient current for 100 car miles, or six return journeys. This use of batteries for traction, was first introduced by Mather & Platt on the Douglas and Laxey electric tramway, and is now frequently employed. Mather & Platt have since made use of batteries on the Snaefell Mountain Railway, and the system has also been adopted at Leeds and Halifax. In all these installations the Chloride cells have been used with results that appear to be very successful.

ROLLING STOCK

The rolling stock ordered have been delivered and the Company have sixteen open cars, eight closed cars and three trailer cars. Each open motor car is 34 ft 6 ins long, and is mounted on two bogie trucks with 28 ins wheels, There is a seating capacity for 48 passengers and the car weighs 12 tons - when loaded. On each bogie is mounted an iron-clad motor, rated to give about 35 horsepower. The motor is geared to the axle through a single reduction cut gear - enclosed in an oil bath - the ration being about 4:1. The controllers are of the series parallel type, as there are no outside seats the trolley pole is of the ordinary swivel type and the cars are lighted with incandescent lamps.

TRAFFIC ARRANGEMENTS

The tramway was opened to the public on 14th July. A timetable had been arranged, but it was not been adhered to, as the traffic exceeded anticipation. In fact, the cars which were almost always full were run as often as possible. On August Bank Holiday, and other special occasions, the rolling stock available proved insufficient to carry the crowds that besieged the Blackpool terminus, and the eagerness of visitors to try the new electric cars must have been gratifying to those directors and share holders who attended the formal opening of the undertaking on 30th July. The occasion was marked by an enjoyable dinner given by the directors at the Imperial Hydro Hotel, Blackpool, after an inspection of the line and the power station. Their satisfaction with the excellent manner in which the contractors, both for the permanent way and electrical equipment, have further increased by the excellent receipts of the tramway. From 14th July to 22nd August the total mileage amounted to 52,965 miles, 288,930 passengers were carried and the receipts amounted to £6,096-17s 10d. Therefore the average earning for forty days was £152-8s. These figures are a record of the busy season at Blackpool, when the town is thronged with holiday-makers eager to experience all the novel sensations which the watering place can offer. The low capital cost of the undertaking is a gratifying feature. The total amount of the contract for the construction and equipment of the line, including the purchase of the line, was £156,500. The authorised capital of the Company consists of £120,000 in £10 shares, and the directors are authorised to borrow £40,000. The Chairman of the Company, Mr George Richardson, is known to every tramway man as the experienced Chairman of the Belfast Tramway and several other successful tramway companies.

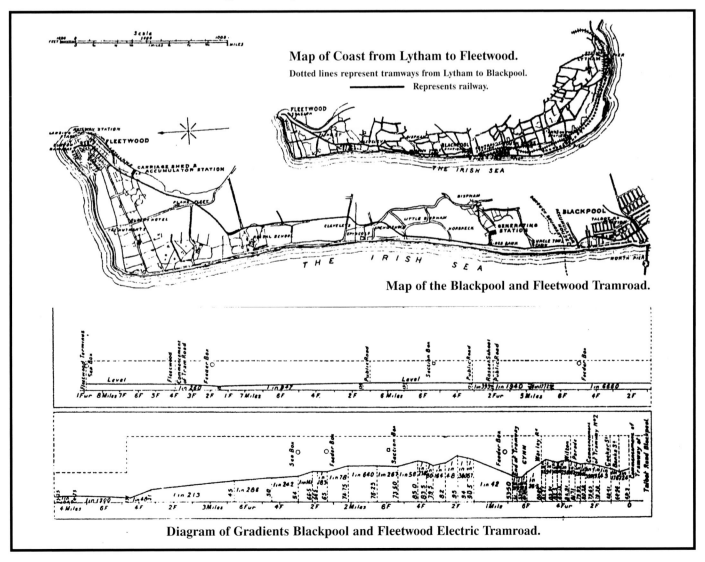

Map of Coast from Lytham to Fleetwood.

Dotted lines represent tramways from Lytham to Blackpool.

———— Represents railway.

Map of the Blackpool and Fleetwood Tramroad.

Diagram of Gradients Blackpool and Fleetwood Electric Tramroad.

Above: A lively scene outside Talbot Road Station in 1913, with a Vanguard tram waiting at the terminus and the line terminates at Queen Street. Judging by the pedestrians in the street, there were more horses and less traffic in those days.
Sankey Collection

Left: Looking from the cliffs at Bispham station with the Yank in the foreground and groups of houses behind. Looking towards Blackpool are open fields used by the farmer. **Commercial**

Bottom Left: Cleveleys Square with crossbench car 13 – formerly a trailer – and waiting passengers at the station, with the Victoria Cafe behind – today the National Westminster Bank – and traffic lights. **Author's Collection**

Right: An interesting view down West Street – today Lord Street – with Box car 15 on the reservation at Ash Street, today the location of Fisherman's Walk. Alas, the centre poles are no longer in place, but the terraced houses are shops today. **Author's Collection**

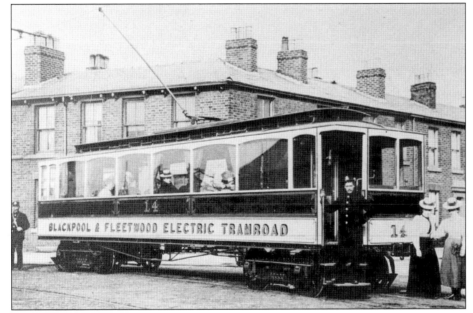

BLACKPOOL & FLEETWOOD ELECTRIC TRAMROAD

Above: In Pharos Street the funnel of the Belfast boat is seen between the Box car and the arriving Yank composite car.
Author's Collection

Top Left: A busy scene at the Fleetwood terminus in North Albert Street, as the passengers jostle for seats in both directions, before the crew have turned the trolley. The position of the crossover is shown by a lady pedestrian, and there is a busy row of shops, doubtless helped by the tramway. **Commercial – NTM**

Left: A delightfully posed new car in 1898 with its uniformed crew and elegantly dressed passengers. For the sunny weather, the saloon has curtains and opening quarter-lights.
Author's Collection

A Tramroad Worker Remembers

A worker's perspective on the Tramroad Company is provided by this transcription of a conversation with the late Jim Whiteside made in 1965.

"My father and I both worked for the Blackpool & Fleetwood Tramroad Company at Bispham depot, and this is how it happened. One day, my father saw an advert in the newspaper for a blacksmith at Thornton windmill. He walked from Lancaster to Knott End in 1897 and at that time there were men at work digging on the line of the Tramroad. After twelve months he sold the blacksmith's shop. I remember his saying, "I've been to Cleveleys and met some men working on the tram line. They said, come with us, our boss wants a jobbing blacksmith who can make anything." So he walked up the tram track and met John Cameron – who was very Scottish – and who gave him a job. He came home to our cottage near the windmill, delighted with his new job.

So he started working for the Blackpool & Fleetwood Company. Every morning he walked to Cleveleys for the 7.00 a.m. tram to Bispham. He often worked till 10.00 p.m.

at night: it was overtime after 5.30 p.m. Once on his lonely walk home from Cleveleys to Thornton - there was not one house between the two places – he was attacked by two men who were after his wages. Being a blacksmith, he was pretty strong, and managed to beat them off. Father worked with Angus Cameron in the Depot, where he examined the brakes of every tram. Most of the employees were Manx, several were Scottish and a very few were locals. Two trams were kept at Fleetwood, which were first out in the morning. Eight men worked there, four on each shift.

When I was fifteen, I went to work at Bispham Depot. In those days, if there was a job there were fifty for it. I worked in the depot at night servicing the cars. One man had to clean the motors, another chap had to brush out the trams and sprinkle sawdust, while another washed the panels of the car, dusted outside and cleaned the windows. There were 8–10 service cars, and a team of three worked on each car at a time. Young Angus Cameron worked in the electricity engine shed with two men, and nobody else

was allowed in there. When they shut down the power at night, all the lights went dim. Cleaners were told not to touch the switchbox, not even with a duster. Once a young cleaner touched the main switch and he was hurled out of the car door full-length down the pit. He came round several hours later! A painting firm (Preston's of Fleetwood) had a contract with the company to paint the cars in the depot. They used to pile empty cans and bottles in a corner of the depot. One day, a young man was looking for a bottle in the pile while smoking, and there was suddenly a tremendous noise. It blew off his moustache and eyelashes and some of his hair, and left him white as a sheet!

Sometimes I worked on the line and was paid £1-3s-6d on a Saturday. We had to pack the sleepers tightly, and this was very strict so that the cars could run as smoothly as a railway carriage. Every Sunday morning John Cameron toured the system, standing next to the driver whilst inspecting the track for any flaws. Fine shingle was used for packing the track and it was delivered by railway wagon. There was a permanent staff of about a dozen drivers plus the depot staff. In the winter season, conductors were sacked at the end of September. You had to work for several years until a permanent position occurred. It was the duty of the last driver at night to put out the lights on each of 45 poles along the route: the last tram leaving College Farm at 10.45 p.m.

Racks which were not used a great deal, were used to pull wagons, no more than two at a time. They were shunted across at Bispham and pushed down to the depot siding nearest the boilers. The coal was shovelled out and the trucks wheeled away. Latterly two carts with big horses would come to Bispham. They were two tons apiece and painted on each side was: 'Mary Malone, Carting Contractor, Layton, Blackpool.' When they got to Bispham, they would run up a ramp backwards, and after a bolt was pulled out, the coal shot into the boiler house. Parcels were carried on the front platform of cars, and when we went into the greengrocery business we used to get sacks of rhubarb carried from Blackpool to Cleveleys.

In the early days, the trailers were used regularly. Although they helped the service card, they were a menace at the terminus where the towing car had to run round them. The trailers became known as 'Powerful', 'Dreadful' and 'Dreadnought' after they were motorised about 1905. This work was done in Bispham depot by the staff. I helped to make them longer by extending the frames to make driving platforms. Trams not needed in winter were stored in Copse Road depot at Fleetwood, to make more room in Bispham.

A regular place for derailments was Rossall curve, because of the single running rail with no guard rail. This also used to happen at Cleveleys Hydro curve. I remember an open tram derailing there and ploughing two feet deep into the ground. The service was held up, including cars running to meet the Isle of Man boat. Cameron and his workmen came down from Bispham, and he was clearly vexed. A dozen men put jacks on the line and lifted the wheels, meanwhile Cameron was walking up and down the line with eyes like an eagle.

Left: The interior of Bispham depot, as extended over the power station cooling reservoir in 1914. Workshops were housed through the doorway to the left of the wheelsets. The saloon car appears to have an electric headlamp, and some sort of freight car stands at the back of this track. **Author's Collection**

An interesting situation developed at Cleveleys, where the landaus wanted 2/0d or 2/6d for a journey to Thornton Station. Mr. Parker of 'The Corners' owned a Toastrack bus, which he stored at Thornton Gate, but many-a-time it would not start. The bus would hold about six, and run down in time for the 8.16 a.m. train every morning, and at night meet the business train. The fare was 3d each way, but Cleveleys Hydro had its own bus with two horses. During the First World War, surveyors arrived to plan a railway line from Thornton to Cleveleys, but Blackpool opposed this and said that they would provide a bus when they took over the Tramroad in 1920. Sixty to seventy trains per day stopped at Thornton Station in those days."

Author's Note: Jim Whiteside's memories are confirmed by fact, for in 1918 the Railways were promoting a Parliamentary Bill to construct a branch line to Cleveleys, with a station to the east of Victoria Square. The Bill was withdrawn in 1919 when the Corporation successfully bid for ownership of the Tramroad, and promised to operate a bus service from Cleveleys Square to Thornton Station.

Tram Workers' Troubles

On the face of it, the company had a trouble-free existence, but there was another side to the coin. On July 10th 1901, a branch of the Amalgamated Association of Tramways, Hackney Carriage employees and Horsemen was formed for the employees of the Blackpool & Fleetwood Tramroad Company. On behalf of the men, the branch wrote to the Company requesting them to reduce weekly hours to 60 per six-day week and to guarantee a standard wage of 28 shillings for drivers and 24 shillings for conductors. (1 shilling = 5 new pence). The Company responded that it would increase wages to 29 s and 25 s respectively, if the working week was only reduced to 65 hours. This offer was accepted.

However relations deteriorated when a request for an interview with Mr. Cameron to discuss wage structures and working conditions, was rejected. At a union meeting held at the Hippodrome in Blackpool, it was alleged that 'old hands' who had joined the union were being laid off at the end of the season. At this meeting it was alleged that the union, "had never been so scurvily, miserably and contemtuously treated as by the manager of the Tramroad Company, Mr. Cameron, who had avoided the union representatives in every possible way." One speaker alleged that he had spent 109 hours on a tram during one week, and that it was to improve such conditions that the union had been formed. A boycott of the company's cars was urged, but had little effect. Mr Cameron denied all the allegations against him.

Fatalities in the Early Years

Deaths did occur on the Tramroad in the early years, showing the unfamiliarity of the victims with the nature of the trams and their location. Each of the press accounts show the circumstances and the inquest states the verdict – generally the fault of the deceased. In subsequent years deaths did not occur again, proving that the Tramroad was established with the local population, the track was fenced and lighted, with signals at the crossings.

'Killed by an Electric Tramcar – September 1898'

A fatal accident occurred at Fleetwood when a man – an Octogenarian – was killed by being run over by an electric tramcar. The man being elderly and very deaf did not notice the approach of the car, and whilst the driver rang the bell, switched off the current and applied the brake, unfortunately the man did not have time to get out of the way. The tramcar, which was one of the new covered-in type, had no protection at the front and the man was seen to be caught by the wheels and thrown underneath the car, the front wheels passing over both his thighs. The car was brought to a standstill and with the aid of planks it was prized up and the man extracted. He was conveyed to the Fleetwood Cottage Hospital but was past all medical assistance.

The police report of the accident was that while the man was crossing East Street – in the vicinity of St Peter's Church - no. 15 tramcar came along on the up-line in the direction of Blackpool, and ran over him, causing his death almost immediately. The accident occurred on the bend of the road and the tramcar was travelling slowly at the time. At the inquiry it was stated that there had been one or two accidents of a minor character since the cars commenced running two months ago, and considering the speed at which these travelled it is a wonder there had not been more. It was also stated that the car had only been in use a week or so, but was not fitted with lifeguards at the front as were the older cars. If such had been fitted the accident would not have happened.

The driver stated that the maximum permitted speed through the town was 8 m.p.h. He also stated that orders were issued to drive from the first notch which is equivalent to 3 m.p.h., but owing to a slight incline the speed of the car was only 4-5 m.p.h. at the time of the accident. According to an eye witness the car was moving only at walking pace when the accident happened. In summing-up the Coroner stressed that the driver was in no way to blame and passed a verdict of accidental death.

'The Second Fatal Accident'

This occurred at Bispham on the 15th November 1898, when a car ran over a man and killed him instantly. At the time of the accident the car was travelling at 14-15 m.p.h. and there was a lifeguard fitted under the front of the car, standing 3 inches from the rail. The accident happened at night, it was dark and wet and there was insufficient evidence to show just how it happened. The man was trespassing on the track and it was questionable whether he was drunk or not! He sustained multiple injuries, with his head almost severed from his body.

The jury found that there was not the slightest blame attached to the driver of the tram, but recommended that the line be fenced in places where it was now unprotected.

Clearly in this case, there could have been danger where the track was not fenced – as it is today – and the pedestrian was incapacitated.

'December 1898 – A Third Man'

A man met with his death on the track, close to Uncle Tom's Cabin at a crossing near Snape's farmyard. No. 3 tramcar from Talbot Road was laden with firebars - for the company power station - and no passengers. The tram was running down a slight incline at 8 m.p.h., and upon approaching Snapes crossing a man suddenly appeared from behind a pole in the permanent way. When the tram was within five yards the man appeared to reel the time was 4.45 p.m. and it was dark.

At the Inquiry the driver of the tramcar stated he was driving in the direction of Fleetwood at a speed of 8 mph. He had been ringing his bell after leaving Uncle Tom's Cabin, for the workman who he was going to pick up at Snape's Farm. On approaching the crossing there, the deceased who was walking in the direction of Fleetwood, appeared to stagger in front of the car. From application of the brakes, it was 40–50 yards before the car was brought to a standstill. The driver, on being asked how soon he could pull-up the car stated, "in 1½ lengths and the tram is 33-feet". In that vicinity the track was well-protected by fencing and gates.

A verdict of accidental death was brought in and the jury commented that the Tramroad was insufficiently lighted or protected at the crossing, and some drivers approach there at too rapid a rate.

It must be clear to the reader that today the Tramroad is brightly lit by the new street lamps, fenced on both sides and has sprung gates. In 1898 however the Tramroad was in open territory – with no houses!

Expansion & Growth 1899–1914

The continued growth in popularity of the line meant that by Easter 1899, the fleet totalled 27 cars, including 13 Crossbench cars, 3 Crossbench trailers and 11 Saloon cars, which had all been built by Milnes of Birkenhead. However the remaining 14 cars were built at Preston by the United Electric Car Co, and its predecessors. The first of these, 28-34 known to the staff as 'Yanks', because of their Brill bogies and American-type equipment, were delivered in 1899. The greater number of cars led to an increase in the capacity of the power station by the installation of an additional boiler and generating set early in 1900. This enabled the company to supply power to a beleaguered Corporation Tramway for a period of seven weeks, following a breakdown at its power station in Shannon Street. This proved possible by means of a jumper cable at the Gynn, where the two systems' lines were now only yards apart, following the municipal extension here on May 25 1900.

The effect of the Tramroad on Fleetwood is reflected in newspaper reports of the period. In 1901, the Manchester Evening Chronicle recorded, "one of the biggest and most successful land sales, which took place at Fleetwood, where 100 lots of freehold land were sold by auction. The auctioneer alluded to Fleetwood's phenomenal growth and said that the electric coast tramroad which now runs through the estate, conveyed nearly 2 million people from Blackpool to Fleetwood in that year." There followed the construction of a large park and pleasure ground by the Fleetwood Estate Company, which involved the laying-out of 40 acres of land, with a large lake and recreation facilities. One of the entrances was adjacent to the tram terminus, "which has been such a boon to Fleetwood".

The successful pattern of growth was reflected in the half-yearly reports of the Tramroad Company, its meeting being held alternately in Manchester (February) and at the Bold Street offices in Fleetwood (August). In 1910, three new cars built by UEC at Preston were paid for out of depreciation accounts, and became Vanguards 35-37. Effectively these were modernised Crossbench cars seating 64, with roller shutters and windscreens upon which the recent replica 619 was loosely based. After the company gained the status of a fully-fledged railway company in 1913, only one board meeting was held annually in February. In the 1914 Annual Report, reference is made to, "purchase of new locomotives – £1,260 and new carriages – £2,191," which is taken to mean the equipment and bodies of the four new Box cars 38–41. Readers will recall that the company had fought in the courts for the right to be recognised as a railway, and pay only a quarter rating to the local authorities concerned.

A poster produced by the Blackpool & Fleetwood Tramroad Company advertising excursions by tram and boat.

A Cameron Remembers

Author's Note: Mr T. Donald Cameron, one of the manager's sons who had worked in South America, came to see me in 1963 and I recorded his memories of the company, which form this part of 'Cameron's Kingdom'.

During the First World War, the Tramroad Company reached its maximum size, with 41 cars and three depots. in fact there was room for many more cars after the 1914 extension at Bispham, and no doubt more would have been built if the company had remained in existence longer. We lived at Bispham, in a large house called 'Pooldhooie' near to the depot and power station. (This is still standing today as the Bispham Conservative Club). The depot, as constructed was an imposing-looking building with a six-track fan, but capacity of only twelve cars. I remember an extension being built c. 1902 which doubled its size, and my father sternly warning me to keep off the building site. In those days, Red Bank Road certainly did not exist, and our house was one of only three or four which stood in this area. The cars approached the depot from Bispham Top, through a cutting. Below the depot was a clay track known as 'The Lane' and at the back were open fields. Angus Cameron, my uncle was the engineer of the tramway in charge of the depot and power station.

With regard to the other two depots, Copse Road which could accommodate about 18 cars was never used as a running shed in my recollection, but chiefly as a store. In fact I remember some cars on the Lytham Tramway Company being driven over Tramroad tracks at the end of the 1903 season and being stored there. This operation was completed at night, and it was certainly a good thing, because most of them derailed at Rossall Curve, due to their narrow tyres and the spread of the track at this point. This unusual concession to the Lytham Company was largely due to their manager being a personal friend of the family. The third depot and the smallest, was situated at the end of the line in Bold Street, and a waiting room and office adjoined it. The small shed would only house four cars, and was used to house the last two cars to Fleetwood at night which became the first two cars in the morning. This eliminated a great deal of dead mileage by cars running back to Bispham. There were two cleaners at Bold Street, but their job comprised not only the cleaning but also the maintenance of the cars.

Of the cars themselves, I will make little mention, since the details are given elsewhere. Generally the open-sided cars were known as 'Old Opens' (1–10), trailers 11–13 were rarely used (in 1905 it was said they could be operated in neither Fleetwood nor Blackpool) and later were equipped as normal cars and were curiously named 'Powerful', 'Dreadful' and 'Dreadnought' by the staff. Winter Saloons 14–24 gained the name 'Box Cars' from their angular appearance. 25–27 were 'Old Opens' like 1–10, built by Milnes in 1899. However 28–34 were known as 'Yanks', possibly because of their Brill bogies, although they were built at Preston in 1899. We called 35–37 'Vanguards', which had the distinction of having windscreens, and finally 38–41 became 'New Boxes'. A prominent feature of all the cars was the huge oil lamp which hooked on to the dash. This had to be carried because of a regulation which stated that the external lights must be independent of the traction power supply. These huge lamps were paraffin-burning and were kept in a special lamp room at Bispham Station. When the cars went into the depot at night, the lamp trimmer would be busily at work, so that the last car into the depot would take all the newly-trimmed lamps to Bispham Top for storage in the lamp room until they were needed at dusk on the next day.

The terminus at Talbot Road Station in fact was on a level with Queen Street, and the Dickson Road track was single, with passing loops at only three places. The first of these was opposite Springfield Road, next was Pleasant Street, where the trams came within sight of the Promenade and then curved inland again, along what was then Warbreck Road. Because the Park loop was thus situated before the curve, it was not possible for drivers to see if there was anything coming along the single track. They therefore used to stop the cars on the loop, jump down from their platform and see if there was anything coming before proceeding. There were occasions when two cars met, in which case one car had to reverse to the nearest loop. The third loop was at Wilton Parade, which was extended to take two cars in 1903, and a fourth loop added near Warley Road at the same time. At the top of the Gynn Hill there was a compulsory stop, where the double track commenced but was not wide enough for two cars to pass. The driver had to push a button on the adjacent pole which rang a bell in the Inspector's office at the Gynn. If the line

In Gynn Square showing Blackpool & Fleetwood cars 3 and 13 passing, together with a Municipal Dreadnought at the new terminus of 1900.
Author's Collection

A busy scene at Bispham Station in company days, with Yank 34, Box car 18 and Crossbench 3, seen from the site of today's Highfield Hotel.   **Commercial – Studio D**

was clear, the Inspector would signal back, and the car could proceed down.

Having passed the terminus of the Corporation cars (from 1900), the company cars would climb the hill to the Cabin, passing on the right a large grey building which was the accumulator house, for emergency power supply. Uncle Tom's Cabin was on the seaside of the track originally, but erosion of the cliffs made it precarious and in 1902 a new Cabin was built on the landward side of the track, where it stands today. The track was enclosed by a 'unclimbable' metal fence along the cliff tops, punctuated only by neat little stations at Bispham and Norbreck.

From Little Bispham the line ran in a deep cutting to Anchorsholme and curved into what is now Cleveleys Square. Here was a brick station where Victoria Road led down to Thornton, and there were a few houses in the vicinity. Just north of Cleveleys, at West Drive, there was a concealed road crossing. After an accident at this point, a skate was fitted in the overhead which operated an alarm bell and a red light when the trolley passed under it. There was a small station at Rossall Grange (now known as Rossall Beach), after which the line headed for the gates of Rossall School, where there was another station. This station building is still in use today, having been moved when the track was diverted in 1925 for the construction of Broadway. From the school gates, the track followed the line of an embankment which can still be seen today along the edge of the playing fields, before turning sharply towards Fleetwood Road (Broadwater). There was always trouble with the trolleys getting blown off in gale force winds at this curve, which was steeply banked. New rail was stored near to Rossall Station and my father had an allotment there, where he could keep an eye on the passing trams!

At the Fleetwood Road crossing – which was the only road into the town – there was a small wooden hut for the cross-

ing keeper. The only other stopping places were at the engine sheds and Riley's Sawmill next to Copse Road depot, before the track left the Tramroad and passed along West Street, then the main street of Fleetwood. Ornate bracket poles stood in the centre of the street, but these were later removed when they proved an obstacle to motor traffic. At the terminus in front of Bold Street depot, there was always a crowd waiting to board and a mad scramble to get a seat as soon as the cars came to a halt. There were two crossovers to facilitate motor cars running round their trailers, although this practice was discontinued after accidents here.

It was always said of John Cameron that he never wasted a penny, and certainly the shareholders rejoiced in their regular dividend of 6½% with a bonus of 2% in some years. The secret of his success was that he supervised operations personally, and was not averse to taking his turn at the controls when there was a shortage of drivers during the First World War. Indeed during that time all of his family had to help out. Those children who were of age were put to tram driving, while women were employed to guard the trams. I recall one occasion when I was taking the last car from Talbot Road Station to Bispham Depot on a Saturday night during the war. The last Fleetwood car had left at 10.15, and when we arrived there was an angry crowd of trawlermen waiting to get back to Fleetwood. When they found out that we were only going to Bispham, they threatened reprisals if we didn't go through. So I was forced to take the car on to Fleetwood!

Our house in Bispham was so situated that my father could sit in the upstairs bedroom window and watch the cars pass the top of the cutting. He could then see when business was slackening-off in an evening, and listening-in to his inspector's conversations on the internal telephone system, offered advice in no uncertain terms as to whether a car should do another trip or be sent to depot. "Shed the beg-

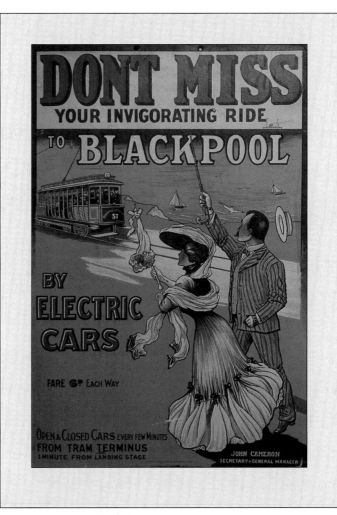

Top left: The family of three generations seen on a crossbench car with a sea view depicting the temptation of such a ride.

Top right: A couple in Edwardian dress have just missed Yank 32 along the coast – a warning by Manager John Cameron.

Left: A delightful poster showing Yank car 34 advertising a 9 mile ride for sixpence every few minutes – with closed cars used if it was raining!

Above: A small advertisement shown in magazines.

gar", was usually his advice! During track relaying, J C was always here supervising operations, and even had his lunch sent out so that he would not miss any part of the work. The track was of a very high standard at that time, largely due to the fact that my father used to ride around the system at least once a day, and would send the track gang to any place where improvement was called for.

As for the staff, there were about 80 on a permanent basis, with more employed in the summer. The permanent way men were all trained drivers, and during the summer peak were used either as drivers or guards. The platform staff wore uniforms of dark blue with red piping, and these lasted after the Corporation take-over because the Company staff were prudently allowed to wear them out before getting new ones. Each driver had a staff number and two licence numbers, which stemmed from the fact that separate licences were needed to drive in Blackpool and Fleetwood. The Fleetwood badge was a metallic colour and issued permanently, where as the Blackpool badge had to be issued each year. I stayed on for only a short while after the Corporation take-over, and remember its traffic manager coming up to Bispham, where there were three clerks and the engineer. The Company went out of existence on December 31st 1919, and my father, after calling to see if there was any mail for him on January 1st, never went near the offices or depot again. So Company days, with their personal family associations were over, and the Tramroad set out on a new chapter of its history under municipal ownership.

Above & Below: Postcards produced by the Blackpool & Fleetwood Tramroad Company, advertising rides on the trams along the coast and char-a-bancs into the country over the Wyre.

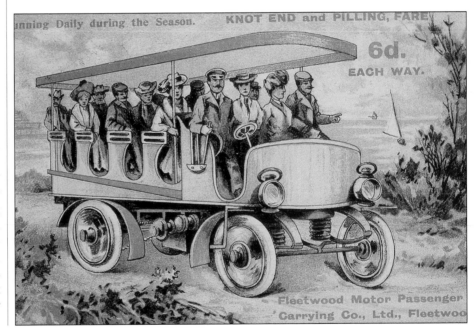

BLACKPOOL AND FLEETWOOD TRAMROAD FLEET LIST

Company Nos.	Year	Builder	Type	Seats	Trucks	Title	B.C.T Nos.
1–10	1898	G.F. Milnes	Crossbench	48	Milnes plate-frame	Old Open	126–135
11–13	1898	G.F. Milnes	Crossbench	48	"	Trailers	136–138
14–19	1898	G.F. Milnes	Saloon (6)	48	"	Box-car	106–111
20–24	1899	G.F. Milnes	Saloon (8)	48	"	Box-car	101–105
25–27	1899	G.F. Milnes	Crossbench	48	"	Old Open	139–141
28–34	1899	E.R.T.W.	Composite	55	Brill 27D type	Yanks	116–122
35–37	1910	U.E.C.	Crossbench	64	Preston MG McGuire	Vanguard	123–125
38–41	1914	U.E.C.	Saloon (6)	48	Preston MG McGuire	New Box	112–115

Notes:

Trailers 11–13 extended & motorised c. 1905, became known as Powerful, Dreadnought & Dreadful by the staff.
(6) denotes six-window saloon; (8) eight-window saloon.
E.R.T.W. = Electric Railway & Tramway Carriageworks Ltd Preston.
U.E.C. = United Electric Car Company Preston.
Company cars 2 (127) & 40 (114) survive today.

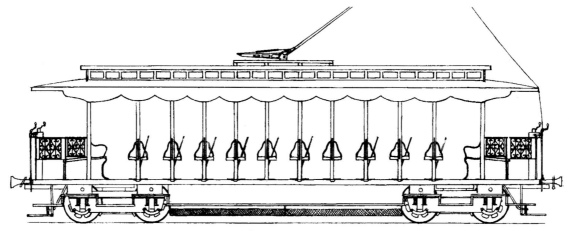

1898 Crossbench Car

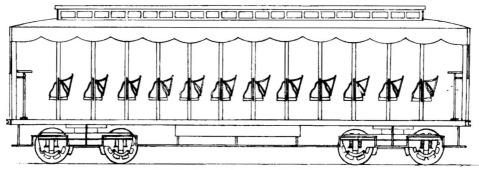

1898 Crossbench Trailer

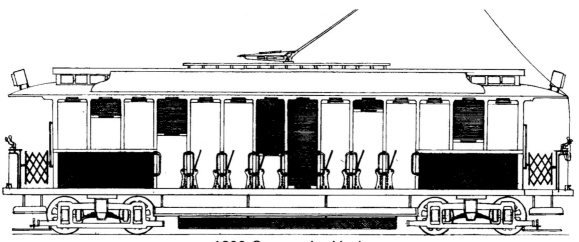

1899 Composite Yank

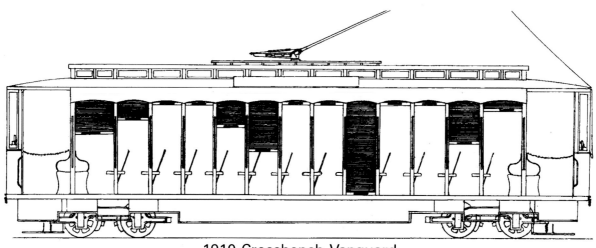

1910 Crossbench Vanguard

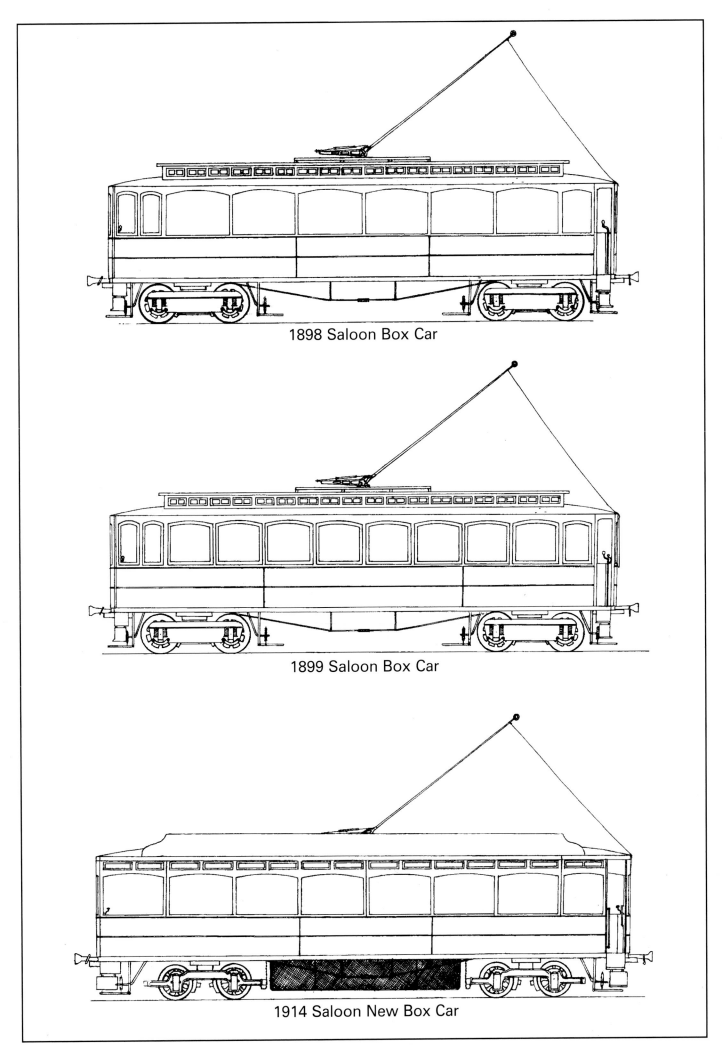

1898 Saloon Box Car

1899 Saloon Box Car

1914 Saloon New Box Car

A postcard of Gynn Square looking towards Uncle Tom's Cabin, with the Company cars loading separately from the Municipal Dreadnought and shelter.

Norbreck Tram Station with Crossbench car 4 loading, these buildings are still intact today!

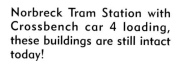

Crossbench car 6 with its side balustrade lowered, passing St Peters Parish Church in Fleetwood.

Looking northwards from the Cabin circa 1912, with the Yank car heading along the tramroad and the public relaxing on the Cliffs. Property is developing and the carriageway following the Tramroad.
Commercial

LOVE TO MOTHER

A charming card with a view towards Gynn Square, with the cliffs now protected by a sea wall under construction. Notice how close the Tramroad was to the cliff-edge for future safety. **Commercial**

LOVE TO MOTHER FROM BLACKPOOL

Blackpool from the Cliffs

Straight from the fresh sea breezes
And the sunkissed sandy shore,
I am sending this with a loving wish
And kisses by the score.

Gynn Inn, North Shore, Blackpool.

Gynn Inn where two tramways meet without contact, emphasised by the B&F Box car and the Borough Dreadnought. Notice the ticket booth for Tramroad journeys at the curve and Uncle Tom's Cabin on the seaside.
Commercial

Tramroad Finale

The demise of the Tramroad Company was fairly predictable, given that the operating lease on the Corporation-owned part of the line was only 21 years, terminating in 1919. In addition, a further three miles of the Tramroad fell within the Borough of Blackpool following its amalgamation with Bispham-with-Norbreck UDC in 1917. The Borough was anxious to extend its Promenade service from the Gynn to Bispham, but had no powers to do so. Faced with a somewhat bleak future, the Company decided to get the best deal it could for its purchase. Secret negotiations took place between John Cameron and Albert Lindsey Parkinson, Mayor of Blackpool and self-made millionaire.

As we have already seen from Jim Whiteside's memories, the railway companies were also interested in the Tramroad, although they may have had in mind a different

outcome to that subsequently provided by Blackpool. A handwritten minute of the Tramroad Board dated 5th March 1918 resolves, "That the undertaking be offered to the Lancashire & Yorkshire Railway Company for £225 000, the Company to retain its outside assets and cash to pay its obligations. This offer to be made subject the consent of the Company in the General Meeting." The minute is signed by the Directors and John Cameron, Secretary & Manager. This may have been a tactical move to force up the price, because Blackpool's offer was £284 000 including £4000 for the Directors and £10 000 for John Cameron, backdated to 1st January 1918. Should Blackpool Council refuse to back the deal, then Parkinson was prepared to take-over and operate the Tramroad himself. In the event, the Council approved the deal, viewing the prospect of ownership more favourably than either of the two alternatives.

The takeover was effected by the Blackpool Improvement Act of 1919, and in the interim period the Company continued the operation of the line, paying the shareholders their customary 6½% and the Corporation a profit of £3,000 for 1918. Opposition from the Railways and Thornton Council was silenced by the promise of a tramway or bus service between Thornton Station and Cleveleys for passengers and a goods service over the Tramroad to Cleveleys. Fleetwood UDC was given the right to purchase the part of the Tramroad within its boundaries after 21 years. So the way was cleared for Blackpool's takeover on New Year's Day 1920, and the Blackpool & Fleetwood Tramroad became part of the Corporation's town system, almost doubling its track mileage, and adding a power station, three depots and 41 cars to the inventory. The shareholders received roughly £16 for each £10 share, and John Cameron was £10 000 better off. He continued living at 'Pooldhooie' at Bispham, which did not form part of the deal, until his death on 5th March 1921.

Right: Saloon car 15 passing Fleetwood Parish Church, carrying a huge oil lamp on its front dash ready for running along the tramroad in the evening and at night. **Author's Collection**

Centre right: The Fleetwood terminus looking towards the Bold Street depot and offices in the background, along with the North Euston Hotel. In 1925 the Ferry terminus was created with a single-line here, as it is today. **Commercial**

Top left: An interesting view at Broadwater in the early days, with Box car 15 and its crew together with the described 'temporary' station of 1898. Behind the tram can be seen Rossall School and the track curing towards it across the farming field. **Commercial**

Bottom left: At the Blackpool end of the line, the terminus was at Queen Street near to Talbot Road Station, where crowds eager to get a seat on a saloon car pushed their way through the narrow entrance, before the trolley had been turned! **Lantern Slide**

Below: A view down North Albert Street, showing the centre poles and Box car 14 heading for the terminus, while Yank type 32 approaches with a roof headlight. **Commercial**

CHAPTER 2

TRAMROAD TO TRAMWAY 1920–1939

The annexation of the Blackpool & Fleetwood tramroad to the Corporation tramway happened at a difficult time for Blackpool. The First World War had just ended, leaving the tramway with a legacy of run-down cars and track in need of renewal all over the town. Maintenance of the Blackpool cars had suffered as a result of shell manufacture in a large part of Blundell Street tram depot, while painting had been transferred to Marton depot. There was a chronic lack of enclosed cars: from a fleet of 84 cars, 24 were toastracks, to which were now added 41 ex-Company cars. Of these no less than 26 were semi-open crossbench types. There was clearly much work to be done by Mr Charles Furness, the grandly-named Borough Electrical Engineer & Tramways Manager.

The first task, to physically join the tracks by curves at the Gynn and Talbot Road Station, was undertaken by a gang of men almost immediately. A double track curve was laid at the Gynn and a single track 'Y' junction with the Layton route at Talbot Road station. The purpose of this curve was revealed in the press when it was stated that it was proposed to run the Fleetwood cars down Talbot Road during the 1920 season, pending the construction of a line in Queen Street for which powers had been granted by the Blackpool Improvement Act of 1919. (After five years the powers lapsed and the line was never constructed). The condition of the track in Dickson and Warbreck Roads demanded urgent attention, repairs having been postponed

Fleetwood Ferry, Pantograph Car, 1928.

Above: A Fleetwood poster of 1928 depicting the striking Pullman car enhanced by a tall tower and pantograph, seen at the Ferry with people in the style of the Twenties.
Author's Collection

Above: A nostalgic scene of the National Tramway Museum in 1983, B&F Tramroad Crossbench 2 – with indicator box and headlamp of the Twenties – and Toastrack 166 in the Municipal livery of that time showing PROMENADE. **Author**

Right: The electric locomotive of 1927 at the National Tramway Museum in the original fleet livery with lettering and Municipal badge with red garter. Since here it is used for shunting trams, it has lost the buffers and the hook and chains used for wagons, but it is fitted with fenders to protect people from the wheels. **Author**

Left: The new Pantograph cars justified a coloured postcard like this, showing 175 at Bispham bound for Talbot Road Station. **Author's Collection**

Left: Cars were soon repainted in the Corporation red-and-white livery, in the style seen on Box car 109 at Gynn Square. It is interesting to see the saloon partition between smokers and non-smokers.
The Gazette, Blackpool

Below left: Doubling the track on Dickson Road – then Warbreck Road – was an early priority for Blackpool. Here shows the demolition of a projecting building, looking north towards the Imperial Hotel. **The Gazette, Blackpool**

Right: Vanguard 123 passes the Savoy Hydro and the new sunken gardens in the Twenties. Hotels finish with the Cliffs and Uncle Tom's Cabin stands alone.
Commercial

Below right: The Tramway Station at Bispham, showing the Dreadnought unloading, while the Box car traditionally proceeds to Fleetwood. **Commercial**

during the tenure of the Company. Readers will recall how the single track and passing loops hindered the efficiency of the route between the Gynn and Talbot Road Station.

Apart from the new junctions, early signs of the new ownership were seen on the cars, which were renumbered from 101–141 in the Corporation fleet. They were grouped by type, with the Saloons becoming 101–115 and the open cars following in sequence from 116–141. To increase the number of enclosed cars, it was proposed to rebuild six of the Yanks (116–122) as Saloons. At first the renumbering was carried out with the large Company numerals, but in March 1920 the first Box car appeared in corporation red and white with the addition of dash-mounted headlamps in place of the oil lamps. The local press, infused with civic pride, commented: "Particularly trim and smart in appearance is the first of the newly decorated Fleetwood cars turned out from Blackpool Corporation's tram depot. All advertisements have been removed and both the interior and exterior have received artistic treatment from the hands of the decorators. The lighting has also been improved."

Any idea that the Corporation had acquired by the Company take-over, a crock of gold at the end of the rainbow was dispelled by the March 1921 figures which showed only £114 profit. It fell to an increasingly beleaguered Charles

Furness to explain that, in acquiring the tramroad, the employees had all benefited by an improvement in their conditions of employment. Also considerable financial commitments were involved in restructuring the tramroad as part of the Promenade line. The increase in the basic Fleetwood service to a 10-minute frequency on 1st April 1920, and the proposed future operation of the Promenade tramway to Bispham, would need an improvement in the electrical distribution system. An early priority was to lay a main feeder cable along the tramroad from Cabin to Rossall, avoiding the reduced power which had previously affected the cars on the northern part of the line. It was proposed to close the Bispham power station and replace it with new equipment at the Corporation's own power station in Shannon Street.

What of the former Company employees? It is known that Angus Cameron and Tommy Cameron continued in charge of the depot and power station at Bispham for a time; heavy maintenance work on the ex-Company cars continued there until the new Rigby Road tram works was completed in 1923. However all was not well with those drivers who lived in Fleetwood, after the Corporation closed Bold Street and Copse Road as running sheds. There was much discussion in the Fleetwood Council Chamber, where it was said: "It is very galling to see the trams running through the street painted BLACKPOOL & FLEETWOOD, and Fleetwood men who have served faithfully for a number of years disbarred from serving in them." The clerk wrote to Charles Furness on the matter, and in his reply he indicated how the dispute had arisen. Since the take-over he was operating the Fleetwood line from Bispham Depot. This meant that the Fleetwood motormen were not able to continue in that capacity as there were no means for them to get home after finishing work. He had offered them alternative work in the depot as night clean-

SAVOY HYDRO AND GARDENS, BLACKPOOL.

ers on the same rate of pay: seven out of ten men had accepted the offer, but the other three declined. The Tramway Committee did not agree that there had been a victimization of Fleetwood employees, and there the matter rested, but it left a lingering resentment on Fleetwood's part that it was getting a raw deal from big brother in Blackpool.

As we have seen, by 1920 much of the Blackpool system needed relaying and a three-year programme was to be completed by 1923. This work was to include the relaying of the Marton route, removing some of the single track sections, and the doubling of the Talbot Road Station to

Gynn tracks, at a combined cost of a quarter of a million pounds. Added to this was the cost of the proposed mineral sidings at Cleveleys, which would fulfil a commitment in the take-over deal. Negotiations were also in progress with the Fleetwood Estate Company in November 1921 for an exchange of land at Rossall, so that the sharp curve here could be straightened out.

By the 1922 winter season, relaying of the track had started in Dickson Road, and a circular system was operating for the Fleetwood cars which were proceeding inbound to the station and then turning right down Talbot Road, through Talbot Square and on to the Promenade. This cre-

TRAMWAY STATION, BISPHAM

BISPHAM

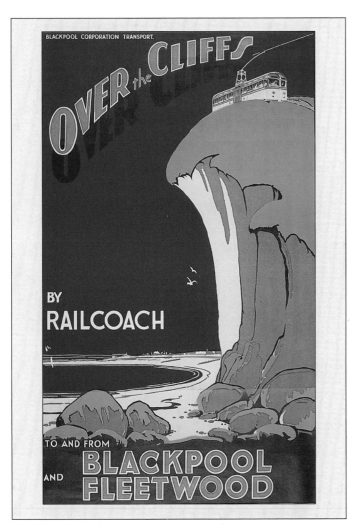

This page: Posters of the Thirties depicting the new railcoaches as 'a luxury' and the three internal display cards also used in post-war years.

Right: Cleveleys Square in its traditional style, with 108 loading for Fleetwood at the edge of the reservation, before re-aligning the track in 1924. **Author's Collection**

ated a considerable upheaval on the Layton route with its six-minute service and passing loops. When the Warbreck Road track was being doubled in 1923, the experiment was not repeated, and a bus service was run from the station to Gynn Square, while the Fleetwood car operated to North Pier for the first time.

Meanwhile work was in progress to cantilever the footpath along North Promenade over the Middle Walk, thus creating space for a reserved track tramway alongside the road. This would be joined to the track from Warbreck Road in a new layout at Gynn Square, which was opened in April 1924. Here it would be possible to reverse cars while a siding was provided for the through south-bound cars. This represented the physical integration of the two systems, as did the paving of the reserved track up to the Cabin. A new Cabin & Squires Gate service with double-deckers, started at Easter that year. To enable the ex-Company cars with their larger tyre profiles to operate down the Promenade, the new track was laid in bullhead rail on sleepers with angled check rail providing the groove. Conversely the same method enabled double-deckers to reach the Cabin.

At the northern end of the line, significant changes were to bring operating improvements there. In Cleveleys Square, the march of progress meant re-aligning the track in September 1924, in keeping with the development of the Square as a busy crossroads. Cleveleys had been the scene of Blackpool Corporation's first venture into bus operation in July 1921, when two Tilling Stevens petrol-electric buses began a service to Thornton Station, as pledged in the take-over agreement. Charles Furness was convinced that the buses would never pay, and their slack headway encouraged that view. However a precedent had been set, which would encourage demands for Blackpool to operate buses in other parts of its own territory.

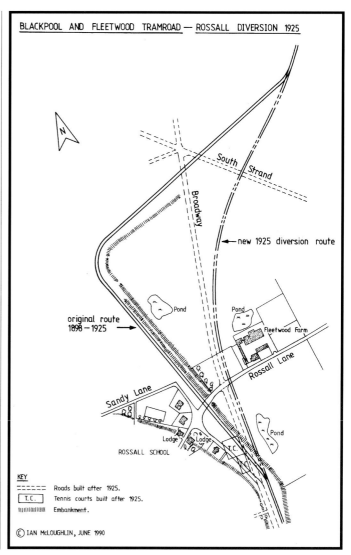

BLACKPOOL AND FLEETWOOD TRAMROAD — ROSSALL DIVERSION 1925

new 1925 diversion route

original route 1898 – 1925

South Strand

Broadway

Pond

Pond

Fleetwood Farm

Rossall Lane

Sandy Lane

Pond

Lodge   Lodge

T.C.

ROSSALL SCHOOL

KEY
------ Roads built after 1925.
T.C.   Tennis courts built after 1925.
|||||| Embankment.

© IAN McLOUGHLIN, JUNE 1990

Tram Station, Cleveleys.

Above: Lord Street after 1926, with the track relayed and the span-wires replacing the centre poles, showing the crossbench cars and the Tilling Stevens bus on Blackpool route 11. **Author's Collection**

Left: The new Bispham Station was built in 1926 and double-deckers arrived, like Deluxe car 66 here establishing Municipal development.
Commercial

Right: A shortage of enclosed cars led to the conversion of six Yanks to saloons, becoming known as Glasshouses. The 'before and after' is encapsulated here with cars 121 and 122 seen in Red Bank Road, Bispham. The cars are linked for multiple-unit operation using experimental English Electric equipment intended for export. The cars did not run together at Blackpool.
GEC Traction

Left: An interesting scene at Bispham Depot, as Works car 139 removes the boiler from the defunct Bispham power station in 1925. Seen in the background is 'Pooldhooie' the former Cameron family house.

The next improvement concerned the Rossall curve, which was to be replaced by straight track, cutting 300 yards from the route length. The track was constructed east of Rossall School gates in a direct line with Broadwater: the southbound track being connected on Sunday May 10th, while the northbound line had to wait until July 5th. The old track bed was now abandoned and the track lifted; unfortunately the brick shelter remained outside the school gates, until rebuilt in its present position in 1925. Construction of a terminal loop at the Ferry which was opened on 20th May 1925, was originally intended to facilitate trailer operation, but in the event this had to wait until 1958! However passengers found the new terminus much more convenient to reach the station, Knott End Ferry and the steamer quays. A special Boat tram was now operated each day at 09.45 from North Pier to connect with the 10.30 Isle of Man steamer from Fleetwood. The new line also provided the unique sight of trams passing the foot of the Pharos lighthouse, which they do to this day. Elsewhere in Fleetwood there was concern about the centre poles in Lord Street, which now were proving hazardous to motor traffic. In 1926 work started to relay the track and remove the poles, the overhead then being supported by span wires. This work was carried out jointly by Blackpool and Lancashire County Council, since the main street was scheduled as a trunk road.

Further integration of the tramroad occurred when the Cabin to Bispham tracks were reconstructed with bullhead and check rail in the winter of 1925/6, allowing double-deck cars to reach Bispham for the first time at Easter 1926.

The comment of an American visitor that the new Promemade at the Cabin, "is the most beautiful slab of concrete I have ever seen," perhaps deterred the corporation from treating the Bispham cliffs in the same way! 1926 also saw the arrival of the blue cars from Lytham St. Annes at Gynn Square, which became their northern terminal. It now became possible to travel the length of the Fylde Coast from Lytham to Fleetwood with only one change of tram. This in turn enabled Blackpool to operate a Fleetwood service from a siding in Manchester Square during August. Advertised as an excursion at a fare of 9d, it was a penny dearer than the traditional Fleetwood cars from Talbot Road Station. A Fleetwood–Pleasure Beach service followed during the short-lived autumn illuminations which were affected by the Miners' Strike. This meant that Blackpool, Fleetwood and Lytham cars shared the same tracks along the Promenade, providing a fascinating panorama for those early pioneer tram enthusiasts who were there to capture the scene.

At the southern end of the Promenade, the line was extended in 1926 to Clifton Drive along the New South Promenade, a distance of c.1½ miles. This involved a new sea wall and an elaborate terminus outside the Pleasure Beach, which had secured an interesting agreement in return for the right of way. In future, all trams passing the Pleasure Beach must show its name on their indicators. Lord Derby opened the new line with a pair of golden scissors at 11.15 on October 2nd: the same day that he opened the new Stanley Park. In many ways 1926 represented the logical conclusion of the integration process, but more was to come!

The Goods & Mineral Services 1927–1949

The provision of a Goods & Mineral Service on the tramway arose from Blackpool Corporation's acquisition of the Tramroad in opposition to the offer by the Lancashire & Yorkshire Railway. Thornton Cleveleys UDC was keen on a connection between Thornton Station and Cleveleys, being two miles from the railway. To pacify the Council, Blackpool would provide a bus service for passengers and augment a mineral traffic, in the form of a branch-line along the Tramroad. Thus the Blackpool Improvement Act of 1919 stated: "Council consent to carriage of goods and construction of sidings". It was not until 1926 that Blackpool received from LMS Railway terms for the Corporation's use of: "The present sidings at Fleetwood for transport of goods to the Corporation's new sidings at Cleveleys". Blackpool had to pay the estimated cost of £1300 to lay a connection between the railway and the sidings link-line behind the Copse Road Depot. Thus the essential delivery of wagons filled with coal could be shunted here each day, and collected by Blackpool's electric locomotive. The site of the sidings for delivery was created at Cleveleys Park - to be known as 'Thornton Gate' -appropriate for the delivery to the inland area in Thornton!

Since this became an unwanted burden upon the Tramroad, several years delayed the instigation of a mineral service, as promised by Blackpool Corporation to Thornton Cleveleys Council. Following the agreement of the connection to the railway at Copse Road depot, in March 1927 a tender of £1146 was accepted from the English Electric Company for a ten-ton electric locomotive with trolley. The loco arrived in summer that year in the red fleet livery, and the first wagons of coal appeared at Thornton Gate sidings on 23rd September. At this stage finishing was still taking place by a steam roller working on the cobbles, making a road between the rails of the sidings. This enabled access to the coal merchants' wagons for collection and they had set-up their offices here, while a weighbridge enabled their loads to be recorded and charged. The two-track layout of the sidings enabled up to 45 wagons could be stored there, while each train of six wagons were towed from Copse Road by the locomotive, which returned with six empty wagons. With its two 50 h.p. motors, the locomotive could cope with pulling trains of 150 tons in weight.

Of course the locomotive was permanently based at Copse Road depot, where a driver and guard – in uniform – would collect the delivery of wagons from the sidings behind the depot regularly. It is recalled – by the author – how the locomotive and train would follow a service car on each occasion, and could always be heard, by the clanking of its buffers, by the people en-route. Since the train travelled at a slow speed, in the season several trams could be seen following it. On reaching Thornton Gate, the train was drawn across Cumberland Avenue, then being pushed into the sidings by the locomotive. Once some wagons were empty, they were extracted from the sidings at either the north or south end and pushed back to Copse Road by the locomotive. It is true that wagons which stayed for more than 24 hours would be subject to a demurrage charge by the LMS. At this time, a crossover beyond Westmoreland Avenue enabled the train to leave the sidings at the north-end and thus traverse to the north-bound track. Since the locomotive pushed the wagons back to Copse Road during the afternoon, the guard travelled on the front wagon signalling to the driver with red and green flags, hence the safety of the crossroad at Broadwater. Certainly this was an unusual sight on the Tramroad, mixing with the modern railcoaches – and the more contemporary Pantographs – until 30th April 1949, when coal deliveries were diverted to Thornton and Layton railway goods delivery yards. Thus an interesting and all-too-brief episode in the history of the Tramroad took place, lasting for only twenty-two years.

Top left: The electric locomotive together with its uniformed driver on Thornton Gate sidings, with its train of wagons of London & North Western Railway. It is here in a traditional red livery, as seen today at the National Tramway Museum.

Left: A scene with Thornton Gate sidings full of railway wagons, and in the foreground the uniformed crew of the locomotive, train-driver and guard complete with a shunting pole. The railway wagons unload directly onto the coal-merchant carts, like the horse-drawn one seen here. **F. Wohrman (2)**

THE GREAT STORM OF 1927

The storm of 28th and 29th October 1927 was one of the worst that the Fylde Coast had ever experienced, with winds blowing up to 90 m.p.h. Fleetwood was the worst affected when the raging sea broke through the half completed sea defences. The torrent swept through the streets of the town, leaving it cut-off without electricity or transport. Between Rossall and Fleetwood the tram track was submerged and the ballast washed away for 150 yards. Six people were drowned when caravans were swept away during the night. To help rescue those marooned in their houses, a fleet of boats was brought from Stanley Park Lake at Blackpool on tramcar bogies and floated into the waters at Rossall! The tramway was under water along Radcliffe Road, and thousands of logs were washed out of Riley's Sawmills next to the tram depot. These filled Lord Street, making rescue work difficult.

At Blackpool, the wind created the worst effect, and people had difficulty reaching their trams at North Pier compelling them to make inland detours. The tram service continued: "Goggled tram drivers fight their way through the hurricane" was the Gazette headline. One did not make it: "Blackpool corporation tramcar 28 of the latest type, which left Bispham for the Pleasure Beach at 10.14 p.m. was blown over opposite Richmond Place, North Shore, while travelling slowly along. Fortunately there were no passengers and the driver, Joseph Walsh and the conductor Ernest Smith, escaped injury. The car was blown over on the footpath, bringing down the railings on the east side of the track, and the whole of the tram traffic from Fleetwood was stopped."

Standard car 28, which was only a few weeks old when if suffered its contretemps, was carted back to the depot in several pieces and was soon re-assembled and in service again. However the impression of that night remains vividly in the memories of those who lived through it!

Above: Floods in Cleveleys Square, in the aftermath of the storm there is much clearing-up to do! In the foreground is the local bus with a Blackpool tram and bus behind.
Ralph Smedley

Below: The bottom deck of Standard 28 on its side after overturning in the Great Storm of 1927. The bottom deck and seats have already been removed and taken back to the depot. Amazingly nobody was injured and the car was rebuilt.
The Gazette, Blackpool

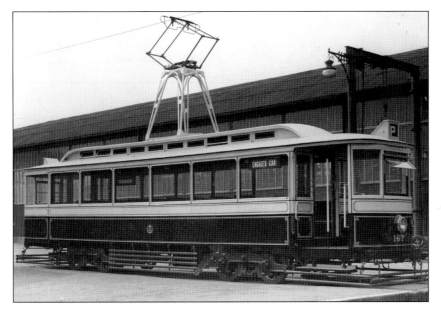

Left: The delivery of the first Pullman car 167 in the yard of Rigby Road Works, showing the elegant livery and lining, the tall tower with the pantograph, and the open platform.
The Gazette, Blackpool

Enter the Pullman Cars

All the work which had been done on the Fleetwood route prepared the way for much-needed new cars. A by-product of the inter-running of the Fleetwood and Lytham cars, was an unfavourable comparison drawn by the travelling public between the wooden seats of the former and the plush blue leather ones of the latter. It was time for a new Fleetwood car which would give the travelling public a comfort they felt entitled to expect. It was planned that the new cars would have 50 h.p. motors, and following experiments with Fischer bow collectors and pantographs in the years 1925–7, it was decided that the new cars would be fitted with pantograph collectors. This bold step is remembered by contemporaries, who recall the trials and tribulations which followed. Luckily the tramroad had been fitted from the outset with flexibly-suspended ears which would enable pantographs to be used. Two men were employed to grease the sliding plates, and it was said that the grease

was carried by the trolley wheels of other cars all the way to Lytham.

It was announced in September 1927 that ten new Pullman cars were to be purchased from English Electric at a cost of £2000 each. When delivered in 1928, the new cars (167–176) proved to be wide and spacious, with large platforms for carrying luggage as befitted the operation of a station route. The driver was given the protection of a windscreen, although no wipers were fitted! The Saloon seated 44 on upholstered double seats and there were two seats on each platform. The interior of the Saloon was light and airy with six large picture windows at each side, with opening ruby clerestory lights for ventilation. Essentially they were all-weather cars, highly suitable for operation on the exposed coastal route to Fleetwood, and somewhat reminiscent of American inter-urbans of the same period. Externally, their clean handsome lines were dominated by a tall pantograph tower amidships, which eventually christened them Pantograph cars rather than Pullmans. This started the Blackpool tradition of roof-mounted towers on the single-deck fleet, which is perpetuated in the Centenary cars today.

167 arrived at the end of July 1928 and on the 30th was towed from Rigby Road works to the Fleetwood route, to avoid the unsuitable Promenade overhead line which was

Below: An aerial scene of a Pantograph car passing the Norbreck Hydro in the early Thirties, shortly after the new road was opened, and with large farming fields in the hinterland – today built upon. **Aerofilms Ltd**

suspended by bracket arms. The car then gave a demonstration run from Fleetwood to Rossall for the licensing committee there. It was planned to introduce the new cars on the winter service that year, but there were teething problems with the first two cars in service: 172 & 175 which had trouble with their pantographs and had to return to depot. By 31st October, seven of the new Pantograph or Pullman cars took over the 12-minute Fleetwood route, which they continued to operate for the rest of their lives. They were unique in being built for, and exclusively operating their own route from which they rarely strayed, and then only on private hire.

The old Company Box cars survived in service for some years, operating short workings on their old route during the season, and along the Promenade in the winter, when traffic was light. The Crossbench cars were seen increasingly on the Promenade route in the season, and by 1931 all the ex-Company cars were fitted with proper destination boxes instead of the ubiquitous route letters. Most of the ex-Company cars, together with the Pantographs were based at Bispham Depot, retaining a distinctiveness which was known in the Department for years as 'The Other Firm'. Increasingly the Box cars compared unfavourably with the new cars on the Fleetwood service, which in the season required 14 cars with 4 short-workings. The order for the ten new cars should have probably been for twice that number had not political considerations in the twenties meant that there was considerable hostility to the tramways in general and Charles Furness in particular.

As the decade closed, the first stage of integration between the two systems was complete, but more was to follow. In 1930, the new Broadway was opened alongside the tramroad from Cleveleys to Fleetwood, and in 1932 the completion of the Norbreck to Anchorsholme section, meant that there was a direct road from Blackpool to

Top: Cleveleys owed its existence to the tramroad, and here the passengers wait for Pantograph car 176 which contrasts with Box car 111 loading for Fleetwood. **Author's Collection**

Above: Pantograph 170 is seen in North Albert Street, making an impact upon the street scene and followed by a Ribble bus, en-route for the Ferry terminus. **S.L. Smith**

Fleetwood. This encouraged motorcoach traffic along the Fylde Coast, and there was fierce competition from private operators for the Fleetwood excursion trade. A deal struck in 1931 between the Ribble Bus Company, LMS Railways and Blackpool Corporation, confirmed a monopoly of stage carriage operation along the tram route for Blackpool while relinquishing to Ribble the Cleveleys-Thornton bus service. The increasing development of motorbus services within the Borough (by 1926 there were eight routes) and the establishment of a Transport – as opposed to Tramway – Department, marked the need for a new Transport Manager. In 1932, it was decided that Mr. Furness was to become Borough Electrical Engineer with special responsibility for the illuminations, but that he was to relinquish responsibility for transport. A new era was about to dawn.

The Tramway Revolution 1933–39

The years since the Municipal take-over in January 1920 had been marked by an improvement in the infrastructure of the tramroad, with the doubling of the Dickson Road track and improvements at The Gynn, Rossall and Fleetwood, and of course the new Pullman cars. Despite the extension of Blackpool's Promenade service to Bispham, the main Fleetwood service was still operated by Bispham Depot along the original route from Talbot Road – now North – Station. 36 of the 41 ex-Company cars were still in operation, now showing their age, particularly when compared with modern motor-coaches. Clearly sound foundations had been laid for the revolution initiated by the new manager, which was to follow.

When the short-list for the new manager's post was drawn-up in September 1932, it included one John F. Cameron of Northampton. However Blackpool did not want a Cameron now, but rather an accountant which they got with Walter Luff, formerly Commercial Manager for West Riding. Following his arrival in January 1933, no time was lost in reviewing the undertaking and identifying priorities. There were 167 tramcars of a dozen different types, 39.6 miles of track and 62 motorbuses. Luff saw the need for rationalisation to make the transport system more efficient and profitable. By March, the Transport Committee had approved his Five Year Plan, which included some key provisions:

1. To centralise operations on Rigby Road by building a central office and depot, which would make possible a daily output of 100 vehicles with a staff of 700. All summer vehicles would be stored at Marton and Bispham depots, which would be closed in winter.
2. Purchase new tramcars for the Fleetwood route which would enable the journey to be completed between the two towns in 30 minutes.
3. Transfer of the permanent way maintenance from Highways to the Transport Department.
4. Losses at Thornton Gate sidings should be investigated and reduced.
5. Check rail should be extended to Cleveleys facilitating double-deck operations.
6. Inclusion in the next Parliamentary Bill, application for omnibus and trolley bus running powers in place of tramcar services where necessary.

Luff identified the Fleetwood tramroad, together with the Promenade route, as being especially suitable for tramway

operation, unlike some of the Blackpool town routes which presented operational problems. He was determined to introduce a new form of tramcar which would be able to compete on the Fleetwood route with motorcoaches which were now taking away some of the business. A change in livery from the traditional red and white to ivory and green was planned for trams on the Fleetwood route and buses, which would herald the new era. The first of the new railcoaches, designed by William Lockhart (Mac) Marshall of English Electric, was approved in model form in February 1933. The design exhibited all the features of current motor-coach practice: a streamlined exterior, roof windows, twin sliding sunshine roofs, and a centre entrance. The central entrance was a key part of Luff's philosophy for stage carriage vehicles: it provided rapid loading from its low-level platform and the passengers had only half the distance to come and go inside each Saloon. The conductor could get his fares in more quickly and

Top: While not showing its fleet number, 200 is seen in a rural setting, albeit in the grounds of English Electric Works, Strand Road, Preston. The Streamliner style was very modern in the Thirties, establishing a new tradition for the Blackpool fleet. **Official**

Bottom: In Blackpool, 200 carrying the pantograph, went on display at Gynn Square siding for the Annual Conference of the MTTA here. **Frances Burton**

easily reach the centre doors at stops, thus contributing to better safety and less claims. For the passenger, he had a comfortable upholstered seat, electric heaters by his feet, good visibility in all directions and a smooth ride. If he wanted sea breezes, he could lower the drop windows, or ask the conductor to wind open the roof, and if he wanted to know the time, there were two electric clocks, one in each saloon! The new car was to be the last word in tramway comfort, and far removed from those old ex-Company leviathans, so despised by Walter Luff. The objective was simple: first to attract the passengers to travel by tram, give them a good ride for their money and thus make them want to ride again.

The new car was to be revealed at a very special occasion: the Annual Conference of the Municipal Tramways and Transport Association, to be held in Blackpool on 21st June 1933. This was particularly important for an English Electric hungry for orders, and the deadline was achieved when a trial run was made along the Promenade, after dark on July 19th. The Conference was being held at the Imperial Hotel, and the new car, numbered 200 and sporting a Pantograph, was displayed on the siding at Gynn Square. This has recently been confirmed by a family snapshot which has come to light, taken of 200 while being inspected at the Gynn. The new car went into service on 23rd June and caused a sensation: its comfortable interior was such that passengers took off their hats upon boarding and looked round for a mat to wipe their feet! By this time the pantograph was replaced by a trolley arm: unlike the tramroad the Promenade line was suspended from side brackets, creating a potential hazard for a fixed collector. Significantly the decision was made shortly after, that the Pantograph cars 167–176 should be equipped with trolley arms. The pantograph era was temporarily ended, at least until 1974.

Trials with 200 proved that it had a running speed of 31 mph and could travel the 8.16 miles from North Station to Fleetwood, with stops, in 30 minutes. This represented an improvement in running time over existing cars of 20%, and an average speed of 16.3 m.p.h., which was high for a stage carriage vehicle. With this evidence, Walter Luff presented a satisfactory report to his committee in late June, together with a tender from English Electric for a further 24 cars, which was accepted. Having secured a fleet of railcoaches for the Fleetwood route, Luff turned his attention to the Promenade, where the bulk of passengers in the season was transported by the twenty Dreadnought open-toppers, which he described as 'monstrosities.' A bemused committee were shown models of a 92-seat streamlined open-topper and a modern version of the toastrack, 'without the objection of running boards.' English Electric offered to build a car of each type by the end of the year and quoted a price for building a further 25 of each type before the 1934 season! Even an enthusiastic manager could not push them this far, and only the prototypes were ordered by a more cautious committee.

Above: Grouped in front of the Cenotaph are the four types of the streamlined fleet, contrasting with the small open-top Lytham St Annes car and even a solitary Toastrack! The Boat is on the siding loading for the Circular Tour, and a track into Talbot Square for Layton trams is shown.   **Commercial**

Below: In the 1934 season, the Railcoach contrasts with the Dreadnoughts in their final year, together with the Lytham St Annes open-topper at North Pier.   **Commercial**

Above: An interesting scene at Gynn Square in 1934, showing five generations of the Blackpool fleet: Dreadnought, Box car, Pantograph, Standard and Railcoach, together with a Lytham St Annes Pullman car.
Author's Collection

Right: Contrasting types at Bispham in the 1930s with a vintage Crossbench car, a Pantograph car and a new Railcoach.
Commercial, Author's Collection

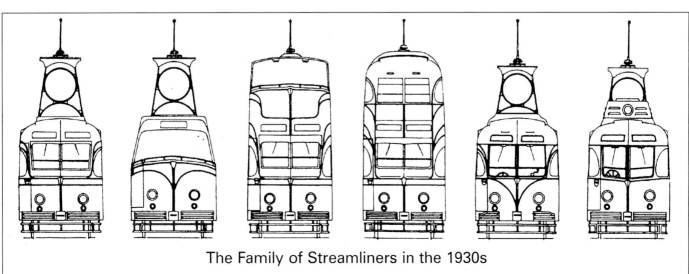

The Family of Streamliners in the 1930s

Meanwhile, the arrival of the first of the new railcoaches in December enabled some of the old Box cars to be broken up. By 6th January 1934, a railcoach service was in operation from Starr Gate to Bispham, and the next batch of new cars was used on the North Station to Cleveleys route. On 31st January, the new open cars 225 and 226 were in Blackpool and were soon displayed on the street siding at North Pier for public viewing: The Evening Gazette reported: "There was a rush to see the new Blackpool trams in Talbot Square today. The first two editions of the new types were open for public inspection, and in an hour considerably more than a thousand people passed through them. The seats possess the comfort of a Chesterfield, complete with luxurious footwarmers. The driver is the luckiest in the world, with a cosy little compartment for himself, plus a seat. Schoolchildren were drawn as if by a magnet, while old ladies and gentlemen rhapsodised on the fittings. Then the Councillors came: they asked questions and wholeheartedly expressed their praise." By Easter 1934, 25 cars had been scrapped to make way for the new railcoaches in the confined space of Blundell Street Depot.

Following the enthusiastic response to the new cars by the public, the Transport committee ordered eleven more of the open 'Toastracks', twelve more open-top cars and fourteen double-deckers with railcoach features. These would effectively replace the Dreadnoughts and provide streamlined double-deckers for the Lytham Road route, which was then operated by Standards. With a fleet of new cars in prospect, a new depot was planned on space at Rigby Road. Plans were prepared by February 1934 and work started in that year on the depot costing £35 000. This depot, which was to have nineteen roads accommodating about 100 trams, included separate road access from Kirkby Road, so that it could be used as an exhibition hall if required. For this reason the inspection pits only extended for half the length of the tracks, a fault later rectified. The new depot was to mark the end of Bispham depot as a running shed, for at the end of the Lights, the Pantograph cars ran into Blundell Street Depot ready for the winter service on the next day. The old Box cars returned to Bispham Depot, which was closed as a running shed until 1940. This marked the final stage of integration of the tramroad.

In 1935, when the new depot opened, all Dickson Road services were operated from there as part of the centralisation plan. By this time, the permanent way along the Promenade and the Tramroad was in the hands of the Transport Department, which enabled Luff to make much-needed improvements. A new layout was installed at Bispham including a by-pass line for north-bound trams to avoid short-working reversals. The track to Cleveleys was relayed with check rail, so that a new service of open-top double-deckers could operate from Clifton Drive (Starr Gate) to Cleveleys. The delivery of the new double-deck cars, Boat cars and 24 more Railcoaches which had been ordered in December 1934 to replace the remaining old Fleetwood cars, presented a completely new image of Blackpool tramways for the 1935 season. Passengers were quite prepared to let old cars pass, in order to travel on one of the new ones: as one said, "All reet lad, we'll wait for the next. We don't want to ride on th' old uns when there's them there posh uns about."

Luff's theory that a more frequent service of modern cars would generate traffic, seems to be substantiated by record levels of service on the Fleetwood route. Traffic dia-ries record that in July, no less than 60 cars were running to Fleetwood, while on the opening night of the Lights on September 14th, a record 224 trams were operated, including 25 hired from Lytham St. Annes! The operation of railcoaches on the Fleetwood route, coupled with a tremendous building boom between Broadwater and Ash Street leading to the construction of a parallel Radcliffe Road, fundamentally changed the character of the route from an inter-urban tramroad to a tramway with frequent stops. In contrast the Douglas-Ramsey line in the Isle of Man which shared similar origins, was preserved like a time-warp in its original form.

The idea of a Fylde Coast tramway, all the way from Lytham to Fleetwood was an ideal which had long been espoused, but clearly the antiquated blue cars made a stark contrast with Blackpool's new streamlined trams. Blackpool turned its eyes southwards in 1936 as negotiations proceeded for the acquisition of the blue car track as far as St. Annes Square. This would be re-sited on a new track to the west of Clifton Drive, providing a reserved track tramway all the way from St. Annes to Fleetwood. Tragically the proposal was lost by the casting vote of the Lytham Mayor, and the blue cars were to be replaced by buses, making their final journey on 27th April 1937. Only the track in Squires Gate Lane was to be purchased to provide a link between Starr Gate and Squires Gate for the Circular Tour cars. A sample of what might have been was railcoach 200's epic journey from St. Annes Square to Fleetwood in 45 minutes on 13th October 1933, carrying a party of Yorkshire transport managers. A photograph must have been taken, and one day it might come to light!

With the prospect of losing a valuable reserve fleet of trams for hiring during the Illuminations, Walter Luff proposed buying a further twenty railcoaches in 1936. In that year the Squires Gate route had been relaid despite strong opposition, and a new service along Lytham Road to Fleetwood in 1937 would require new cars. Originally it had been planned to relay Lytham Road with central loading islands, and the new cars were planned to have driver-operated power doors to facilitate this. For the first time in years, Blackpool turned away from English Electric and had the new cars built by Brush of Loughborough, with bogies by EMB and equipment by Crompton Parkinson. The Brush cars were a continued development of the railcoach, designed by Mac Marshall who had by this time left English Electric. Numbered 284–303 the new cars were the very latest in streamlining, with chrome flares on the sides and ends, starting a new livery style. Although they operated to Fleetwood before the war, it was not until 1940 that they became the backbone of the service for the next thirty years.

Meanwhile in 1936, elsewhere on the system, the Layton & Central Drive routes closed at the end of the season, and a new bus service developed as replacement. While this is not part of our story, it represented a different aspect of Luff's policy towards the town routes where tramway operation was not ideal. Only the semi-circular Marton route was left operating as a self-contained entity, still using the traditional Standard cars. On the seafront routes everything had to be thoroughly modern, at least in appearance, and the Pantograph cars did not fit this image. They were now used in the season only on the back-road route, and in 1936-7 were throughly renovated with new air brakes, windscreens, platform doors, a restyled indicator box and a new livery. The new livery was a copy of the railcoaches: so detailed that the first cars even had twin badges on the sides, and all had the fleet number placed above the centre saloon window instead of on the dashes. At the same time the Pantograph tower was reduced in height by 15 inches to conform to the railcoaches, and in the depot it was hard to tell them apart! However the passengers were not easily fooled by cosmetic changes, and could easily identify them by the high platform steps, not to mention their raucous sound.

During the period of the Five Year Plan of modernisation, traffic on the Fleetwood route had increased by 34%, proving the success of Luff's policy. Further improvements to speed operation, included turning circles at the Pleasure Beach in 1937 and at Starr Gate and Little Bispham in 1938. A bypass siding was built at Thornton Gate in 1937 and a new sub-station at Copse Road in the same year. This extra capacity was much-needed when no less than 83 trams were operating on the Fleetwood route in August. In the same year, the crowning glory came in the form of new transport offices at the corner of Rigby Road and Blundell Street in the new art-deco style.

The final chapter was reached in 1939 with the delivery of the twelve Sun-Saloons 10–21 from English Electric, which would finally replace the remaining 13 old Fleetwood cars still stored in Bispham Depot. With the outbreak of war in September, events took a different turn for the new Sun-Saloons, but marked the end of the road of the old Company cars which were broken up at Copse Road Depot. So the extended Five Year Plan was complete, by this time there were 212 trams and 160 buses in stock and the mileage had doubled from 4 million in 1933 to 8½ million by 1938. The revolution was complete!

Starr Gate in 1938, with the new loop terminus, showing open-topper 237 bound for Cleveleys together with a new Brush car with a jaunty flare. **W.A. Camwell, NTM**

A busy scene at Cleveleys South in 1939, with a large queue and two railcoaches departing, one for the Promenade and one for North Station. Cleveleys Hydro can be seen at the seafront, where the track curves. **H.B. Priestley, NTM**

North Station terminus with Pantographs in the modern livery, just outside the store under demolition in April 1938, ready for the construction of the Odeon. **H.B. Priestley, NTM**

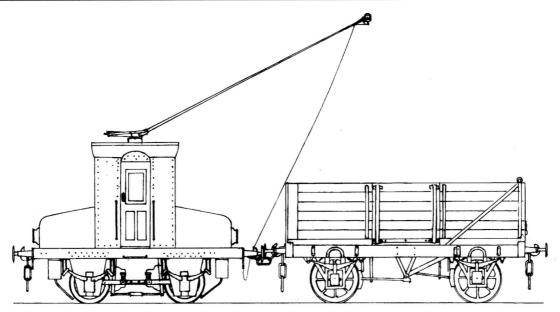

Electric Locomotive and Wagon

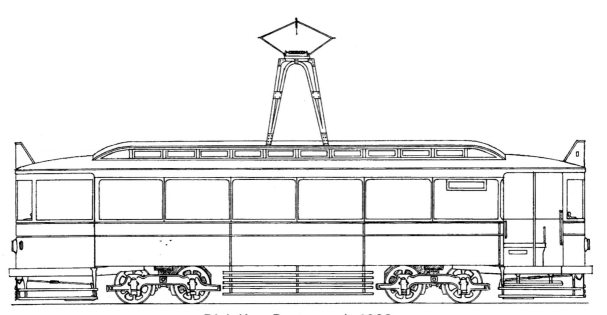

Dick Kerr Pantograph 1928

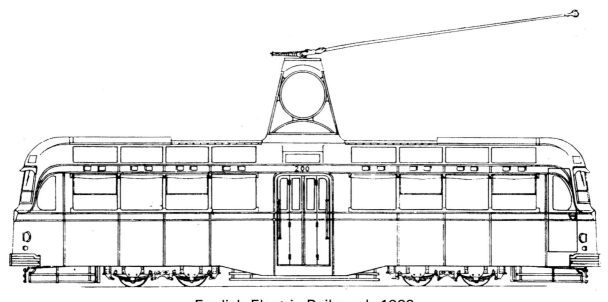

English Electric Railcoach 1933

NEW CARS ACQUIRED 1920–1939

PULLMAN or PANTOGRAPH CARS
167–176   Built: 1928   Total: 10
Builder: Dick Kerr, Preston.
Seats: 48.
Bogies: Preston McGuire type.
Motors: GEC WT 28 L (2 x 50 h.p.).
Controllers: BTH B510.
Notes: Delivered in red and white livery with pantograph collector 1932: full destination boxes fitted 1933–5: Green & cream livery 1937: Modernised and repainted in railcoach-style livery.

ENGLISH ELECTRIC RAILCOACHES
Series 1 200–224   Built: 1933–4   Total: 25
Series 2 264–283   Built: 1935   Total: 20
Builders: English Electric, Dick Kerr Works Preston.
Seats: 48.
Bogies: E.E. 4 ft wheelbase.
Motors: E.E. 305 (2 x 57 h.p.).
Controllers: Series 1: E.E. Z-4; Series 2 : E.E. Z-6 (with weak-field).
Notes: 200 was 2 feet shorter than the standard 42 ft 3 ins length of all streamliners in this period. All cars were 7 ft 6 ins in width.

ENGLISH ELECTRIC OPEN BOAT CARS
225–236   Built: 1934   Total: 12
Builder: English Electric, Dick Kerr Works Preston.
Seats: 56.
Bogies: E.E. 4 ft wheelbase.
Motors: E.E. 327 (2 x 40 h.p.).
Controllers: E.E. DB-1: 225, 226, 236; BTH B-18: remainder of cars.
Notes: Second-hand controllers were used from scrapped Blackpool cars. 225 was different in having low sides; same dimensions as railcoaches.

ENGLISH ELECTRIC DOUBLE DECKERS
237–249 Open-topped   Built: 1934   Total: 13
250–263 Double-deck Saloons   Built: 1935   Total: 14
Builder: English Electric.
Seats: Open-top: 94, Saloons: 84.
Bogies: English Electric 4 ft 9 in wheelbase.
Motors: E.E. 305 (2 x 57 h.p.).
Controllers: E.E. Z-6 (with weak-field and field-shunt notches)
Notes: 237 originally numbered 226, has a steeper-raked front end; Open-toppers were enclosed in 1941/2, the first car being 249, Aug. 1941.

BRUSH RAILCOACHES
284–303   Built: 1937   Total: 20
Builder: Brush of Loughborough.
Seats: 50 (including 2 on platforms).
Bogies: EMB hornless 4 ft 3 in wheelbase.
Motors: Crompton Parkinson C162 (2 x 57 h.p.).
Controllers: Crompton West CTJ.
Notes: Delivered in two batches of ten, the second having a green-end flare. ALL cars had side chrome sweeps on side panels, and sliding doors.

SUN SALOONS (CATTLE TRUCKS)
10–21   Built: 1939   Total: 12
Builder: English Electric.
semi-open with folding soft roof in centre.
Bogies: E.E. 4 ft wheelbase.
Motors: BTH 265C (2 x 35 h.p.) second-hand.
Controllers: E.E. DB-1 (From scrapped cars).
Notes: Fully-enclosed in 1942, but retaining wooden seats till post-war, second rebuilding 1948–1951 with new VAMBAC equipment for Marton route. Known as MARTON VAMBACS:
Bogies: Maley & Taunton HS44 6 ft wheelbase.
Motors: Cp C-92 (4 x 45 h.p.).
Controller: VAMBAC – Crompton Parkinson.

TRAMS WITHDRAWN

Ex-Company Cars   Totals
1926: Saloon 101   1
1931: 117, 118   2
1933: 103, 105, 107, 116, 119   5
1934: 102, 104, 106, 108, 109, 110, 111, 120, 121, 122   10
1936: 139 (works car since 1924)   1
1937: 113, 115, 141 became Illuminated Bandwagon (Progress)   3
1938: 138   1
1939: 112, 123, 124, 125, 130, 131, 134, 136, 139, 140   10
Total Scrapped: 32

Ex-Company Cars Used as Works Cars Scrapped In:-
1941: 135 (withdrawn 1937)   1
1942: 137 (withdrawn 1937)   1
1943: 129, 133 (kept as snowploughs)   2
1951: 126 - Works car 1939, renumbered 3 in 1942   1

1952: 128 - Works car 1939, snowplough based at Blundell St.   1
1955: 132 - Works car 1939, renumbered 6 in 1942   1
Total Scrapped: 7
1960: 127 - Works car 1939, Fleetwood snowplough; restored at No. 2
1960: 114 - Works car 1936, P.W. gang car, renumbered 5 in 1942, restored as No. 40. Both cars presented to NTM Crich in 1963.

Other Cars Withdrawn
19 Dreadnoughts (59 saved at Fleetwood until restored in 1960)   1934
6 Ex-L.U.T. open-toppers (93–98)   1934
7 De-Luxe double-deckers (62–68)   1934/9
24 Toastracks 69–92   1939
3 Standards 33, 46, 50   1940

CHAPTER 3

CHANGING TIMES 1940–1963

Second World War Times 1939–1945

With the outbreak of the Second World War on 3rd September 1939, the tramway was found to be in good condition, with no less than 116 new cars and a revamped system, with the exception of the Marton route. On the previous day, twenty-nine special trains had arrived in Blackpool bringing 23 000 boys and girls, and by the following day the total number of evacuees arriving that weekend totalled 53 000. Fleets of Corporation buses carried the children to schools in the Fylde, where they were dispersed to their foster homes. Any thoughts that Blackpool would become a quiet backwater during the War was soon dispelled when the population was swelled by 100 000 refugees, and 40 000 airmen in training. As a 'safe' area, the resort was an ideal home for London Government Departments displaced by the Blitz, who took over large hotels like the Norbreck Hydro, bringing new business to the tramway. The RAF, with HQ at Squires Gate, used buildings all over Blackpool for its activities, which included a Wireless School in Rigby Road works, a wet-weather parade-ground in the bus garage and the requisition of Marton depot as the home of Technical Training Command. This presented the Transport Department with something of a crisis, and an urgent need to dispose of a large number of obsolete trams stored in Bispham depot.

The first day of blackout was Friday 1st September when Blackpool was plunged into unaccustomed gloom, however a reporter wrote: "The tramcar indicators blazed, otherwise with interior lamps screened, head and rear lamps masked, the trams were scarcely visible. The buses had no interior lamps lit and were even darker." The Transport Department had taken emergency action, the first day after the outbreak of the War, one of the Transport staff was stationed at Starr Gate terminus with a brush and a pot of black paint, and as each service tram arrived, he would paint 90% of the head and rear lights. This was taking place at each terminus in the town, so that all cars could be dealt-with in one day. Inside the cars, coloured bulbs were fitted instead of white, and the curved-glass lighting panels in the modern cars were painted black. Each saloon of the railcoaches was fitted with a small metal box mounted centrally and containing a mere 15 Watt bulb, with the tip of the lamp painted blue. Conductors trying to make-up their waybills in the dark, could not be blamed for scratching off a bit of black paint! To counteract this subversion, one man spent the whole of the War repainting scratched bulbs black! As for the head and rear lights, these were fitted with masks and long hoods over the headlamps, just in case! The curved roof-glass on the Railcoaches and Balloons was painted green on the outside and cream on the inside, to harmonize with the colour scheme. To make the cars more visible in the blackout, the bumpers and lifeguards of all cars were painted white. Thus the Transport Department concealed itself effectively, and no-one could say that Blackpool trams had betrayed the town's position to an enemy aircraft above!

In November 1939 the Marton cars were transferred to Blundell Street depot, Bispham depot was cleared of 24 old toastracks and the 13 ex-Company cars, which were broken-up at Copse Road depot. Bispham depot re-opened as a running shed once more on 11th May 1940 and naturally it resumed operation of its traditional 'back road' routes from North Station to Fleetwood. A fleet of twenty Brush cars was allocated to Bispham, together with the ten Pantograph cars and some of the new Sun Saloons 10–21. No doubt the maintenance staff at Rigby Road were glad to off-load the Brush cars with their troublesome controllers. The Sun Saloons found a new use as troop-transporters from the RAF camp at South Shore to the Rossall rifle range each day. The re-opening of Bispham Depot had the additional benefit of dispersing the trams away from the central Rigby Road site, a reversal of Walter Luff's pre-War policy. For the same reason, four tracks in Squires Gate depot were wired and thus available for use should the need arise. There were various proposals for the enlargement of Copse Road depot, or the building of a twelve-car concrete shed at Rossall with additional storage track alongside.

Of course the trams played their part in transporting troops around town, most notably from the barracks at Squires Gate – later Pontins Holiday Camp – to the Rossall rifle ranges. A convoy of trams would set-off in the morning between 8.25 and 9.30 a.m., loaded with troops and with

Above: The memorable sight of Copse Road depot for the Permanent Way gang, complete with the locomotive towing the track-spraying trailer and 167 used as the gangers car, pulling the rail-carrying bogies. **Roy Brook**

Facing page: The Bandwagon dressed in the first of many Wartime designs to promote essential causes, and its crew are wearing gas-masks as a warning form air-raids to come. Of course it was still illuminated prior to the Blackout in 1939. **Fox Photos**

Below: The scene at North Pier in 1941, with the Promenade carriageway restricted by barricades – including the former Layton link-line – and the trams have few passengers. This season will be a finale for the open-toppers. **The Gazette, Blackpool**

The great snows of January 1940, which left the crews of these railcoaches stranded for 24 hours within these Lord Street snowdrifts. **Commercial**

On 5th December 1940, Standard 50 caught a gust of wind as it rounded the curve behind the Metropole Hotel and turned over. Workers are seen rolling the bogie away, the tram being returned to Rigby Road in several parts. **Author's Collection**

AIR RAID SHELTER FOR 50 PERSONS' at Bispham Top in 1940, with Pantograph 176 in the pre-war livery with headlamp hoods. **M.J. O'Connor, NTM**

ammunition boxes on their platforms. At Rossall the Fleetwood service cars would be held-up while the spartan Sun Saloons unloaded, and the officer-in-charge would give a time when the days shooting was due to finish, between 4.30 and 5 p.m. The trams would thus return at that time to await the armed forces, but frequently the troops were late at the appointed time and there would follow a long delay for the service cars. By July 1940 the situation had become critical and Walter Luff reported to the Transport Committee that since a loop was urgently needed at Rossall, work had begun on the site. Consequently, when the work to the east of the running track was completed in September, it comprised of a short siding which could take six cars. Gates were provided into Rossall Lane, so that troops could march-in from the range near Rossall School and fall-out to board the waiting trams. Thus the service trams were not delayed, and the military convoy could leave for South Shore when they were ready. Today the location of the former siding can be seen and the crossover is still in place, but disused.

The Unexpected Situation in 1940

A stick of bombs which fell in the North Station area in September 1940, gave rise to the fear of losing most of the tram fleet in one bombing raid. However, it was the weather that caused most disruption to the tramway in 1940. A heavy snowfall on 27th January meant that ten trams and a bus failed to reach the depots that night. It is remembered as the worst night in living memory, an Inspector and the crews of two railcoaches were marooned at Fleetwood, not getting home until 5 p.m. the next day! Seven Standards were stuck in Church Street, although their crews were able to abandon their cars and trudge home through the drifts. No trams were operated on the 28th or 29th January, although the snow ploughs were working north from Manchester Square on the second day. On the 30th January four Standards operated from the depot to Talbot Square, while by the 31st Gynn Square was reached at 10.20 a.m. and Cleveleys by 4 p.m. The snow ploughs were ex-Company cars 127 and 128, which were coupled to Box car 114 and Pantograph 176 respectively, for extra power in charging the snow drifts. By 1st February, there was a single-line service to Rossall and the Fleetwood service was finally resumed at 6.30 a.m. on 2nd February. This was the longest disruption that the tram route ever suffered and snow like this was not seen again until February 1996!

The summer service in 1940 featured 13 cars on the Fleetwood and 7 on Cleveleys services from North Station, while 6 cars operated a Cleveleys & Fleetwood local service between 11.45 a.m. and 3 p.m. In June the Promenade service was extended to Fleetwood using 14 cars, 11 from Rigby Road and 3 from Bispham. The total output was 51 cars, with an additional 19 cars for service personnel. A local Fleetwood town service, using two Pantograph cars operating between the Ferry and Broadwater, commenced in August 1940 from 10 a.m. to 6 p.m. providing relief for local residents in the season when the through-cars were full. In July 1940 thirty-eight female conductors had started work on the trams and the buses, and when signed-on they were given white dust coats and the hats that the men left behind. Certainly in the blackout they had to clip their tickets by torchlight, and renew the batteries with an allowance!

What of the tram fleet in wartime? By 1941 it became necessary to repaint the cars in a more subdued green livery relieved by a cream flare at each end. The quality of cream paint was poor and thus the darker livery was easier to maintain a clean appearance. Paradoxically the Pantograph cars remained in the pre-war cream livery throughout, although they looked rather shabby as time went by. Five additional Standards were enclosed during 1940, suiting the greater requirement for winter service cars. Sadly Standard 50 was broken-up, following its overturning at the Metropole in a December gale. A shortage of raw materials meant that cars due to be re-tyred were shunted to the back of the depot, until sheer necessity brought them out again! The Pantograph cars were increasingly used in year-round service as the War progressed. The Sun Saloons, which were regularly used in convoys for the troops, had become known as the 'Cattle trucks' by them. Since these cars had been built in 1939 to replace the old Tramroad cars, they were fitted with wooden seats, half-open windows

Cattle Truck 15 as refitted for the troops with full-windows, full-length platform doors and driver's cab partition, while the roof windows are painted and the nearest lights. Of course 15 is showing RESERVED to keep it exclusive!   **M.J. O'Connor, NTM**

In Bispham Depot during the War, showing crossbench car 128 fitted with brushes on its bogies and 127 fitted with the snowplough.   **E. Fielding**

The coal train is seen at the Thornton Gate tram stop, about to be shunted onto the siding to unload the wagons.   **J. Joyce**

Above left: Claude Lane and his conductress standing in front of 213 on his first day in 1941. Notice the uniforms, the badge and TIM for the conductress, and the hoods on the lights together with the white lifeguard and fender of the tram.

Above right: A revival of the pre-war poster updated for the new Coastal Tour by the new Twin-cars in 1958 – very attractive in appearance!

Below: Looking towards the Engine Sheds along the Tramroad, 168 approaches the stop at Southfleet Place – a post-war Council estate. The Pantograph cars were usually seen in the summer season and this year of 1960 was the last for these cars.   **Author**

Above: Fleetwood Ferry with the Coronation in-service to South Promenade and 304 can just be seen showing RESERVED for an LRTL tour. The Brush car is on service 1, and in the foreground is F. K. Pearson, author of a book about the Isle Of Man.

Right: Coronation 318 is seen in the rural location – passing Rossall School and Rossall Farm on each side of the Tramroad. By 1964 the style of Coronations was simplified with only one green band and no streamlining. **Author**

Below right: Cleveleys Station in 1955, with the leading railcoach about to turn for Fleetwood and the other bound for North Station. This is the post-war fifties livery with green flares, seen under Walter Luff and subsequently removed. To this day Balloon trams turn here in-service for Pleasure Beach. **Roy Brook**

and a centre roof of opening canvas. Thus in 1941, having obtained permits for rebuilding, work started on making them more acceptable for the troops, including a bulkhead to separate the driver's cab and an enclosed saloon. The pressure upon the tram fleet – especially large capacity double deckers – was created by the busy situation at Squires Gate with the huge Vickers factory and RAF camp. Thus the open-top cars 237–249 were enclosed like the other Balloons, and certainly they resembled them without the sliding roofs and with the moquette-covered wooden seats! Thus the fleet now included 27 Balloons and

Three generations of trams at the Ferry in 1953, with Pantograph 168 and the railcoach on service 1 and the Coronation going to South Promenade.

The scene in Lord Street during 1950 when the track is being relayed, with Works car 5 – now 40 again – and the railcoach.   **The Gazette, Blackpool**

At Stanley Road stop the passengers board the Brush car on service 1, still in wartime livery by 1952.   **Alan A. Jackson**

39 Standards albeit reducing the seaside appearance by a functional service.

Fleetwood was a place of some importance at this time, with repairs to naval vessels taking place in the docks, and the main service to the Isle of Man sailing from the port. The Manx boats had been diverted from Liverpool, since that port had become too dangerous and congested with mines and Atlantic convoys, and it was locally hoped that this service would continue after the War. However, the Fleetwood Council were again concerned with the transport of its residents along the Tramroad as during the summer season packed trams sailed past waiting workers along Hadcliffe Road. Relations with Blackpool Transport reached a low-ebb at this time, and Fleetwood Council threatened to ask another operator –the Ribble Bus Company – to operate along the route. In response, Mr Walter Luff suggested that a shuttle service should be run between Broadwater and the Ferry, in view of the many workers engaged on essential War-working. Two cars were required and of course the oldest available cars – namely the Pantographs – were sent to work on the local service, showing 'BROADWATER & FLEETWOOD' on their indicators, and did not need changing all day! The crews found that it was a very monotonous day, travelling up and down the short stretch of track, but at Broadwater the crossover was paved so that the guards had something to walk upon while turning the trolley. After first having appeared in August 1940 this service was introduced on a regular basis during the season when Blackpool first cars were busy with holidaymakers. Thus the tramway service improved for the local residents during the War. Incidentally, Fleetwood's option to purchase its part of the Tramroad had expired in 1940 and thus, given the difficult war situation, they asked Blackpool for an extension of the time into the post-war years. While they objected, Fleetwood's rights were extended until 1947, after which its powers would lapse.

Blackpool Transport was almost a woman's world by April 1941, with 350 girls on the platforms of the trams and buses, and only 150 men conductors left. The manager said that the remaining men were being trained as drivers, and that it would not be long before they began to train women for tram driving. Whitsuntide 1941 saw the first women at the controls, the first ten having been trained during the preceding weeks. The conditions for being accepted were to be 5 ft 7 ins tall and 26 years of age or more. Experiences were quite memorable, one of the trainees remembered being narrowly missed by a falling trolleyhead from a Standard in Talbot Square, having just turned it. Another remembers guarding a fully-loaded Standard with 216 passengers, on its last journey from Talbot Square one night. The passengers were packed like sardines throughout the tram and some were hanging over the balconies, while the conductress had to stand on the platform step passing back tickets upon receipt of the fares! One of the male volunteers – Claud Lane – recalled: "I started there in August 1941, actually the first tram for me to drive in Blackpool was Railcoach 213 on the Fleetwood service. All cars had the usual wartime headlamp masks, and no useful lighting inside, making me wonder how a conductor could get a waybill right – although they did carry a torch! For all the wartime difficulties, the staff discipline was of a high standard, loads carried were tremendous and when the doors would not shut, the cars were full. Aircraft workers to Squires Gate, munition workers to Marton, dock workers to Ash Street and drill squads on the Promenade, kept the drivers busy and alert! Night driving was particularly trying, with barely a rear light one had to keep a careful lookout for the car in front, though I am glad I was a tram driver as my war effort!" In May 1942 five women were made inspectors, but were obliged to resign soon after, following protests from the Union. They did continue tram driving in post-war years, the final wartime colleague, Margaret O'Farrell, retiring in 1965.

By 1943, passengers carried on the trams had risen to 76 million a year, double that of 1939. This resulted from a revival of the holiday trade while all the wartime pressures still persisted. This conflict of interests led to the famous Civil Service demonstration at Norbreck on 9th July, when the tram track was blocked for an hour at 5 p.m. by a sit-down. This was a demand for priority travel over the holiday makers: "Is your journey really necessary?" they chanted. "Have you ever been on

Engineering car No. 4 seen in 1957 outside its home, Bispham Depot. It was always kept at the front of Pit 1 for easy departure in an emergency. **John Price, NTM**

A once familiar scene outside North Station. The conductor turns the trolley of Pantograph 173, in July 1954.

Talbot Square in 1949, with a contrasting scene of the traditional Standard 150 and the Sun Saloon 12, just before its conversion to its status as a Marton Vambac. By 1952 this class had taken over the service from the Standards. **R.R. Clarke**

55

hours, a demurrage charge was payable to the L.M.S. Railway who owned them. In 1943 a dispute arose between Blackpool Corporation and the coal merchants about the payment of this charge. Blackpool had paid the L.M.S. their demurrage charge, but the merchants stubbornly refused to pay the Corporation. When legal action was threatened, the merchants paid-up, but the mineral traffic was an activity which Blackpool Transport would willingly have given-up!

holiday yourself?" replied the holiday-makers. "We want Luff to give priority travel for workers, not visitors," they chanted. The police arrived to disperse the crowd, and everybody boarded the waiting 30–40 trams to get home. Mr Luff's response was that there were twice as many passengers as in peacetime, with half of the transport facilities.

Another trouble-spot was Thornton Gate sidings, where coal deliveries had been taking place throughout the War. Here a number of coal merchants had their offices, and on most days the electric loco pulled a train of wagons from the railway sidings behind Copse Road Depot to Thornton Gate. Here the wagons were shunted on to a spur line and unloaded into bunkers at the track side. The loco would then return to Copse Road with empty wagons, and many passengers on the Fleetwood cars were delayed by the slow-moving trains. When the wagons were left in the sidings for more than 24

By 1944, the relaxation of wartime restrictions was evidenced on Good Friday, when Walter Luff contacted the Regional Traffic Commission and asked for permission to revert to normal running on the tramway. During the War, services had finished at 10.30 in the evening to save fuel. Immediately new routes came into operation: the Cleveleys services were extended to Thornton Gate, the Squires Gate service was extended to Little Bispham loop, and the through-service from Starr Gate to Fleetwood was resumed once again. A loop line was constructed at Cabin for through-cars, and it was announced that Marton Depot was to be de-requisitioned by the end of the year. When V.E. Day came on 8th May 1945, all the staff got an extra days pay, there were parties everywhere, bunting flew from the trolley arms, garlands from the balconies of the Standards. Happy days were here again!

Right: The scene in Pharos Street, Fleetwood on 9th July 1960, during a tour by the TMS using 1898 Crossbench car 2 and 1902 Dreadnought 59. In 1998 No 2 is expected here again for the Tramroad Centenary. **Roy Brook**

Left: On 18th April 1963 B&F cars 2 and 40 were driven to the empty Copse Road Depot, which may have become a transport museum, but soon after they went to Crich. **Author**

Right: No 2 crosses Copse Road towards the gate of the depot in a rare scene, photographed for posterity. **Author**

The Post-War Years – a Personal View

The immediate post-war years were characterised by austerity, and the fleet continued in its dowdy green livery which I can remember as a child living on Radcliffe Road in Fleetwood, facing the tramway. From an early age I became conscious of the differences between the trams which passed our house; the Railcoaches on the Promenade route which had a broad cream flare at each end and the Brush cars on the North Station route with their sliding doors and brown upholstery. Most distinctive were the large cream Pantograph cars with their trolley ropes billowing out behind them and their raucous howl, known to the passengers as high steppers. I remember them operating the Broadwater and Fleetwood service, which caused some resentment in the town: that the oldest trams were good enough for us. Certainly at that time when the fish trade was at its height, lumpers and filleters from the fish dock would get on the car reeking of their trade, and would be expected to stand on the platforms to avoid spoiling the seat cushions. However by that time, the railcoaches had been in service for more than ten years and the moquette was getting decidedly shabby. From our house, opposite the engine sheds to Ash Street it was ½d half and 1d full on the tram, and we would sometimes walk down and tram-it back, just to save the fare!

Just down the road was Copse Road Depot, a source of fascination for a child interested in the tramway. I was never allowed to go there, sited as it was in a rough area near to the Jolly Sailor pub, but I was able to watch all the comings and goings from our front lawn. The arrival of the coal trains to Thornton Gate was announced by the clanking of the buffers, and I would run to the gate to wave at the driver of the little green electric loco as it slowly passed with its procession of wagons. Often the pieces of coal would fall on to the trackside, to be eagerly gathered up by children with baskets. I was never allowed to do this as it was classed in our house as stealing! In the afternoon, the clanking buffers would signal its return, this time pushing the wagons with a flagman perched on the front, signalling to the driver with a green or red flag. Usually coal trains would be followed by a procession of service cars running late, their passengers looking fed-up with the delay. One day there

were no more coal trains and the little loco found a new role, that of towing the weedkilling car. This was in 1949, for – unknown to me – The House Coal Distribution (Emergency) Scheme Committee had notified manager Luff that after 1st May, coal deliveries would be diverted to Thornton and Layton railway goods yards.

Equally fascinating for me were the other inhabitants of Copse Road, including Crossbench car 127, still in its passenger livery and No. 6, a similar car in green (ex 132) and Saloon car 5 (ex 114) with cream painted windows. The open cars were usually used for towing rails, while the Saloon Box-car made a daily run to Blackpool to transport the track-gang to and from work. I fantasised about the sinister appearance of this car with covered windows, but nobody was able to tell me its true purpose. My favourite amongst the works trams had always been the weed-spraying car 7 (ex 161), with its two tanks mounted fore and aft of the trolley mast. Its progress past our house, spraying weed killer in all directions including a cascade from tubes at each end, filled me with childish delight. On hot summer days we would stand at Heathfield Road tram stop in our bathing costumes to take this unique shower. At other times we sat on the railings shouting, 'Any rolls?' to the conductors of passing trams. Some would fling us a partly used TIM roll from which we made streamers for our bikes.

Gradually the scene changed: the Railcoaches changed their colour to cream in a reversal of their wartime livery, while conversely the Pantographs went into the wartime green style, which they kept to the end of their days! In 1950 the track was relaid in Lord Street, and I remember the novelty of travelling on the wrong side of the road in a tram whose driver had received a red 'square rolling pin' or single line staff. However, the most exciting event for me was the revival of the Blackpool Illuminations in 1949. The first indication of this event was when the railcoaches appeared with coloured pictures of Disneyland characters in their trolley towers, which at night were lit from inside. Our visit to the Lights was a revelation to me: there were trams of all shapes and sizes, including the big green double-deckers which never came to Fleetwood. The rival merits of the tableaux on the cliffs, brought out of wartime storage since 1939, were lost on me when the beautiful Gondola illuminated tram appeared followed by the swaying

Lifeboat with its sails ablaze with white lights. Better was yet to come! In a halo of light along the tramway floated the new illuminated car Progress, playing music and 'Wishing Health and Happiness to our Visitors.' Everyone – including me – was transfixed as it passed with a warm glow from the heat of its bulbs. Its double deck profile and the silhouettes of passengers in its

Left: Contrasting types of tram at Fleetwood Ferry in 1954, with Coronation 315 on the Promenade service and the green railcoach on No. 1 to North Station. Notice the decorated trolley towers for the Illuminations.

opaque windows deceived me into thinking that it was really one of the double-deckers specially dressed-up. However it was in reality ex-Company car 141 which had formed the basis of Progress, reconstructed from the short-lived 1937 Bandwagon. The crowds were enormous, the occasion magical, so much so that I went on my own one night to ride all the way to Starr Gate and only just succeeded in catching the last Fleetwood tram.

One of life's little joys in those post-war days was a trip to Stanley Park; this involved taking a North Station car to the terminus and walking through to Church Street, where we would board a majestic Standard car. If it was lucky enough to have an open balcony, then "joy would be unconfined" as the leviathan swayed its way up Church Street and down to Devonshire Square. At each stop there would be a ting of the bell a winding-on of the hand brake, as the driver applied Armstrong's patent. At Hornby Road we would make our way along the duck-boards, clinging to the handrails down the steep and winding stair to the back platform, where the conductor would tug on the bell-rope and we would dismount into the road. I have few memories of those days at the park, apart from the time that I fell into the lilly pond and had to endure the journey back with water running from my clothes, down the wooden slatted floor and on to the platform. Everybody seemed to be staring at me! On happier occasions we waited at the stop on Whitegate Drive with baited breath to see whether the tram would be one of my favourites or one of the commonplace railcoaches, which resembled the ones on our route. Unknown to me, a battle had been raging in those years over the future of the Marton route, which Walter Luff had finally won when he got the track relaid. Then he wanted new trams, but had to be contented with the modernisation of Sun-Saloons 10–21, by the fitting of new bogies and equipment. These became known generally as the silent trams or to enthusiasts as Marton Vambacs. By 1952 it was possible to run the winter Marton service with these railcars, but it was not until 1954 that the old Standards finally disappeared.

Above: In June 1952 when the Mayor, Coun. Peter Fairhurst instructed by Walter Luff, drove the first Coronation 304 across the crossover at North Pier. Watched by a crowd, it was the start of the first journey along the Promenade for a Coronation. What a sensation! **The Gazette, Blackpool**

Below: The famous scene on the Central Prom in March 1960 – by tram to the Tower - with Coronation 326 dominating the passing railcoach on the Squires Gate service.

The Gazette, Blackpool

CROMPTON PARKINSON LTD
CHELMSFORD
ENGLAND

MALEY & TAUNTON LTD
WOLVERHAMPTON
ENGLAND

CHARLES ROBERTS & CO. LTD
HORBURY JUNCTION, NR. WAKEFIELD
YORKSHIRE, ENGLAND

CMR. 11   ISC. 9.52

Above: Front cover of brochure produced for the new Coronation cars.

Below: The scene outside the Odeon, as the new terminus of service 1 since 1961, with the trolley reverser facilitating the conductor's work. The Brush car is about to reverse and the railcoach has set-off along Dickson Road.   **Author**

Luff's Crowning Glory?

All this was a curtain-raiser for a fleet of new trams on the Promenade and Fleetwood route, which Luff was determined to introduce before he retired in 1952. His Marton cars with their PCC-type equipment had proved themselves on this town route with its frequent stops. However he had a vision of an 8-feet wide type, for which he had been preparing since 1933 by increasing the clearances of the track during relaying. In a Presidential message to the Light Railway Transport League, at its 1952 AGM in Birmingham, he explained his philosophy which justified his purchase of the new cars.

"Here in Blackpool there is no talk at all about abandoning tramways, but on the other hand our progressive modernisation programme continues. We have now got into use 6 of the 25 resilient-wheeled railcoaches, and others are coming along at the rate of 2 per month. We have named these `Coronation Rail Coaches' and in all probability these cars will be running and giving good service very many years after buses now put into use have ceased to operate. The life of a railcoach, if properly maintained, exceeds the working life of most people, and even if railcoaches cost more initially... the effective life of a tramcar or railcoach is four times longer than a petrol or diesel bus. In future probably all the cars and railcoaches we operate will be single deck, because we find that people do not like to go up and down stairs for short journeys, and the conductors prefer single-deckers because they can get their fares much easier." Significantly the pre-war double-deckers still remained in their green livery, and it is assumed that Luff intended the Coronations to be their replacements, since there was no other requirement for new cars.

The first new coronation tram was delivered on June 2nd by Pickfords, from the Horbury Works of

Charles Roberts. The bogies were delivered from Maley & Taunton, of a type similar to those fitted on the Marton cars, with the addition of track-brake shoes. By 7th June, 304 was on test with the engineers; on June 11th it passed its Board of Trade test, and on 3rd July made its first passenger-carrying journey on the Promenade. Later that month it was joined by 305, which on Wednesday 6th August became the first and last Coronation on the Marton route. In response to press criticism that the expensive new cars (£12 000 each) could not manage the curves of the newly-relaid route, Walter Luff laid-on a test after the normal service had finished. Collecting a party of Councillors in Talbot Square, 305 traversed the route as far as Marton Depot, with frequent press stops on the way. Fortunately – and probably intentionally – the car was not taken down Waterloo Road or Lytham Road, where the steep gradients of the railway bridges would probably have left 305 well and truly stuck!

Up at Fleetwood the news of a new super tram was exciting for me. I sat in my bedroom window one Sunday morning in 1952, all agog for a sight of the new tram. Eventually, after what seemed like an age, the cream apparition appeared round the corner from Broadwater, and to my amazement proved to be rectangular in shape like a modernised Pantograph car, rather than a curvaceous railcoach. On October 11th that year, four Coronations entered service on the Fleetwood route, but it was Tuesday 10th March 1953 before there was a full Coronation service of ten cars, 304–314. Much to my disappointment, the new cars soon proved defective, and often passed our house ignominiously towed by a loudly-protesting Pantograph car. The problem arose from the lengthy trolley

arms and swivel heads, which created a 'whipping action' leading to some spectacular dewirements. Soon the arms were shortened and fixed heads fitted, which seemed to solve the problem, and the Coronations became a regular part of the passing scene.

In 1954, the unbelievable happened: the twenty-one year reign of Walter Luff, a name that was synonymous with Blackpool Transport, ended. On the trams and buses a new name appeared: J.C. Franklin M.Inst.T, which meant that a new era was dawning. Walter Luff had stayed-on for an extra two years beyond his retirement age in order to see his fleet of Coronations in service. 328 went into service on

Above: Engineering car 3 turning from Red Bank Road into Bispham Depot yard in 1963, returning from a job on the overhead. **Author**

Below: Bispham Depot in 1963, with a bus terminating on route 15A, while the Railcoach and Pantograph are to be seen in the doorways. The office building can be seen on the left and the original power station – then a substation – behind. Notice the headstone over the doors – now at the National Tramway Museum.

2nd June, and Walter Luff retired on the 19th. Among many generous tributes. The Transport Chairman, Ald. Rhodes Marshall said of him: "Mr. Luff can go into retirement proud of his many and considerable achievements. We who remain will always remember him with pride and affection." In his final report to the Committee, Walter Luff was able to report a thirty seven thousand pound profit, which over his twenty-one years had totalled nearly four million pounds. Of this, half a million was contributed to rate relief: he warned that so much had been taken in this way that it was now necessary to borrow money for new trams and buses. However, because a new fleet of 100 buses and 25 trams had just been introduced, there would be no need for new vehicles for 'some years.'

New Management

Reflecting on his career after his retirement, Joe Franklin recalled how he had always wanted the Blackpool job, and that Luff's extra two years in post had given him the opportunity. He had been manager at Rochdale, but prior to that had been at Salford just after the war, when the sad remains of the tramway was still operating. He had been the Chief Engineer of a tram fleet of 57 trams, of which only 15 could operate at any one time. Fortunately this experience did not dim his enthusiasm for operating trams at Blackpool, where the circumstances were somewhat different. He did have one or two surprises in store however, as he subsequently recalled.

"My first weeks in Blackpool were an eye-opener, and I was soon wondering what sort of job I'd come to. I knew Walter Luff, of course, but I only had one official meeting with him before I took over. I asked him two questions: "You've bought 100 buses from Burlinghams and you still owe them a lot of money. I can't see from the accounts where you're going to get this money from." "There's nothing to worry about," said Walter, and that was all I could get out of him. The second question was about the new trams. "I know you're having alot of trouble with your new trams." "No, no, there's no trouble." He took me into the Works, where the Works Superintendent came up and said, "Mr Luff I've got 14 Coronations off the road." Walter whipped me out of there like lightning."

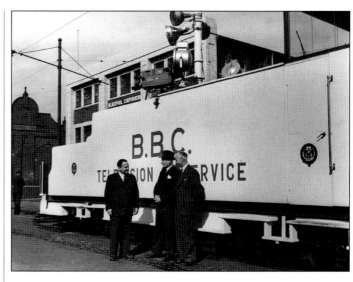

"The main trouble with the new cars were the bearings which were not strong enough: eventually new ones were fitted by Maley's, which solved the problems of the breaking axles. The Coronations were the world's worst buy; they cost £300 000 (£500 000 if you count the loan charges) and just before buying them £300 000 had been taken out of the reserves for rate relief. The Coronations had been bought with the idea of replacing the double-deckers, which hadn't had a penny spent on them for years. I started putting them back in order and increasing the seats from 84 to 94. I was a bit worried about how the extra ten passengers might affect the tilting of the car, but fortunately there was no compulsory tilt test for trams. I was astounded that double-decker never ran to Fleetwood, and on enquiring from the Ministry of Transport I was told that the rails would have to be fitted with a check rail to stop them overturning. So we bolted-on miles of angle-iron, which wouldn't have stopped a tram turning over, but satisfied the MOT. There was a sequel to this many years later, when Lt. Col. McNaughton inspected the first one-man tram in 1972. The inspector was most enthusiastic and drove the tram all the way to Fleetwood. On the way he noticed this angle iron and asked why it was there. When we explained, he said it was unnecessary, and we later received official confirmation that a check rail was not needed!"

"Right from square-one, I knew that the street routes would eventually have to go. The track on Lytham Road was unsafe, and Dickson Road had foundation troubles. Marton should never have been relaid in 1948, and there were heavy maintenance costs on the Marton Vambacs. The cost of spare parts for the Coronations was becoming astronomic, especially the rubber sandwiches for the resilient wheels. Once the loan charges were repaid in 1968, we started to get rid of them, having already converted some to conventional controllers. In the late Fifties, many people suggested that we

Left: The scene in Dickson Road on 1st July 1958, as the first Balloon on No. 1 service starts its journey to Fleetwood, and makes a good sight in this handsome green livery. **The Gazette, Blackpool**

Left: Joe Franklin, the new manager in 1954, was something of a showman. Here he is seen (left) with tramway engineers Frank Hirst & Stanley Holmes infront of 166, one of the two toastracks rebuilt for live transmission on the Illuminations in 1956. **Author's Collection**

Right: The construction of 276 as a towing Twin Car during April 1957, in the body shop at Rigby Road. **R.P. Fergusson**

Below: The first Twin Car unit, 276 and 275, with the Mayor at the controls and J.C. Franklin in the cab, on its first Coastal Tour for a Fylde Civic Party on 9th April 1958, watched by a small crowd. **The Gazette, Blackpool**

buy second-hand trams from systems that were closing-down, and I paid an official visit to Aberdeen to inspect their centre-entrance cars. They were short and narrow-gutted and not fast enough for us, and the inside was very cramped. I also went unofficially to Leeds and Sheffield and went out with Mr. Findlay (The Manager) on the all-electric railcar 602. It was too powerful for Blackpool, and would have blown our substations, especially Shannon Street."

"The old illuminated cars, Lifeboat, Gondola and Progress, were practically live, and they were a nightmare to us whenever it rained. Its a miracle that someone wasn't electrocuted! People asked why they couldn't ride on them, and eventually we carried passengers on the Lifeboat and Gondola. To increase this useful revenue, I put lights on two of the Standard cars in 1959, and we built a completely

new car called The Blackpool Belle. Publicity Director Harry Porter and I decided that it would be a nice idea if Jayne Mansfield could travel on the front of the car after she had performed the switch-on ceremony in 1959. Two chairs were placed on the front of the car, but the Mayor lost two buttons off his dinner jacket while squeezing through the gangway. There were similar problems for Miss Mansfield! A new generation of illuminated trams followed; the idea for the Western Train coming from Mrs. Franklin after watching a wild-west movie."

Mr. Franklin was essentially a dynamic character: a man of action who wanted to get things done. He took a new look at the tramway in changing times and made some far-reaching decisions, as we have already seen from his reminiscences. He was a great publicist and never lost an opportunity to hit the headlines, which began when he

Left: Illuminated Standard 159 seen here at North Station on the final Saturday of the route, 26th October 1963 on a tour for enthusiasts. **Author**

Below left: An historic scene as the last service 1 tram – Brush car 290 – turns into Bispham depot filled with enthusiasts and driven by Battling Bill Bracewell, on 27th October 1963. **Author**

Below left: Behind-the-scenes inside Bispham depot with the new engineering car No. 3, rebuilt from Standard 143 in 1958 and fitted with TD4 bus engine and a generator. **J.H. Price, NTM**

Below right: Copse Road depot interior in 1955 with the steeple-cab locomotive in attendence. **J.H. Price, NTM**

Facing page: The oldest Tramroad car, Crossbench 2, restored in 1960 and displayed infront of the depot with Twin Car 276–275 and Standard 160, after a tour in June. **Author**

shocked the Council by telling them in 1954, that the Transport Department was going to lose money. Immediately he set about reducing costs by cutting the number of trams in winter service, closing Marton Depot for the winter and cutting some previously-generous concessions. A total of 52 cars operated the service that winter, 35 from Rigby Road and 17 from Bispham. During the summer season there had been a maximum of 134. Mr. Franklin's stewardship coincided with far-reaching national trends over which he had no control. Firstly, the growth of television viewing was cutting evening travelling and closing cinemas; there was a steady growth in car ownership, rising wages costs resulting from national agreements, and finally the increased costs of loan charges.

Looking on the positive side, Mr. Franklin sought to exploit the novelty value of the Promenade tramway as much as possible: in 1956 he introduced Illumination Tours by tram, while in 1957 the pre-war circular tram tour was re-introduced which involved the re-opening of disused track in Squires Gate Lane. The innovation which made the most lasting impact was the introduction of double-deckers to the Fleetwood route, for the first time in the tramway's history. At Easter 1958 the first cars ran into the town, making an impressive sight along Lord Street, although they seemed slightly out of place on the open tramroad. Their 94 seats certainly made an impact on Market Day crowds!

It was at this time that a delegation from Blackpool went to Zürich to study trailer car operation there. It was a pity in retrospect that they did not go to Germany instead to look at new articulated trams. The visit resulted in a decision to operate trailers which had an early and unsuccessful beginning on the tramroad in 1898. In great secrecy during 1957, a prototype twin-set was constructed in the works using railcoaches 276 and 275, which was revealed in a blaze of publicity on 9th April 1958. All the Fylde Coast Mayors,

with the exception of Lytham, were invited for a ride to Fleetwood where they posed with a proud Joe Franklin in front of the cars. The original intention was to run a limited-stop service along the tramroad, where certain loading platforms were lengthened and special stop signs erected. This caused endless confusion when regular passengers were carried beyond their normal stop. Any financial advantage given by the 114 seats, was partly eroded by the need to have two conductors and pay the driver an enhanced rate of 17% above normal. However, the experiment was deemed a success and ten trailers were ordered from Metropolitan Cammel, while the works rebuilt eight more towing cars and 275, the prototype trailer. Unfortunately no consideration seems to have been given to flexible operation, dropping the trailer at off-peak times and operating the motor-car independently. An articulated car would have been at once more flexible and cheaper to operate with one driver and a seated guard, as was the European practice at that time.

The 75th Anniversary 1960

It had long been Mr. Luff's policy to keep one tramcar of each main type, and so there were lingering in outlying depots a number of historic tramcars. Up at Copse Road, there was 127 (the original No. 2 in the Company fleet) which had been a snowplough, alongside Dreadnought 59 which had been saved at the 11th hour in 1935. At Bispham was a diminutive open-topper which had been the overhead line car until 1934, and which was actually one of the original 1885 cars. In my youth, during visits to the depot, we endlessly examined it for traces of the original number, and once were given a short ride along the depot track. The fourth of the historic quartet was the former gangers' car 114, which was Company Box-car 40, and now served as a rest room in Rigby Road Depot. Now they were dislodged from their resting places and moved to the Works for

restoration. Fortunately there were body-builders who had the old skills, and it was possible to restore them relatively inexpensively. When they emerged, the two Company cars were in chocolate and cream, and the two Blackpool cars in red and white. Commercialism intervened to proclaim 'This Is It!' on the 1885 car, while 59 became 'Ye Olde Dreadnought,' and 2 was 'The First Tramride from Blackpool to Fleetwood,' 40 more accurately being described as 'A Saloon Tramride 1914.' The purists cringed, but as Joe Franklin explained, running them during the season was a way of

Above Left: Rossall Square with Crossbench car 2, halted for photgraphs during the TMS tour. Today this is a busy crossroad with a STOP sign for motorists. No. 2 should appear here again in 1998!
Author

Centre Left: A vintage line-up at Fleetwood Ferry in July 1960 with three generations of trams: B&F Box 40 of 1914, Brush car of 1937 and Coronation of 1953.

Below: A very nostalgic scene of the 75th Anniversary Procession at Little Bispham loop on 29th September 1960, with the vintage trams in order of age: Conduit 1 of 1885, Crossbench 2 of 1898, Dreadnought 59 of 1902 and Box 40 of 1914. They are crowded with free passengers enjoying themselves.
The Gazette, Blackpool

recouping the money which had been spent on their restoration. While the 1885 car only ventured forth on special occasions, the others provided a considerable attraction along the Promenade, and the Box car returned to Fleetwood on Market Day specials. I once had the unusual experience of conducting No. 2 mostly on Circular Tours, but also on a hectic lunchtime special from Bispham to Pleasure Beach. Collecting money and issuing tickets from a TIM machine, while clinging on the woodwork was not an experience I would have missed, but I would not care to repeat!

The great day was 29th September, which being a mid-week, I was at school and many other people were at work. A grand procession of ten cars representing each type in service, formed-up at the Pleasure Beach in time for a 10.45 a.m. start. This included restored cars 1, 2, 59 and 40, plus Standard 40, Pantograph 170, Railcoach 217, Boat 236, double-deck 249, Coronation 321 and trailer 76-T3. Free rides were given to those who wanted them, but many of the cars ran empty and it was a pity they could not have been filled with school children. The celebration had a hollow ring about it, but it was an attempt to focus media attention on the historical and tourist value of the line at a time when the storm clouds were gathering round the tramway.

The arrival of the new trailer cars in 1960 neatly counterpointed the 75th anniversary of the tramway, which Joe Franklin saw as an opportunity for much needed publicity. The climate was getting decidedly chilly for trams, with the closure of all the remaining British systems in Leeds, Sheffield and Glasgow, and an attack on the North Station route in Blackpool itself. This came in 1959, and centred on the traffic flow at Gynn Square and North Station terminus, where congestion was heavy. Franklin put up a stout defence of the route, which deflected the attack temporarily. His report to the Committee read:

"DICKSON ROAD TRAMWAY SERVICE"

"The tramway route between North Station, Blackpool and Gynn Square, is part of the original Blackpool and Fleetwood tram route opened on the 13th July, 1898 under the Act of Parliament 1896, and the Blackpool Corporation purchased the Blackpool and Fleetwood tram route in 1919, under the Blackpool Improvement Act of that year, the Corporation having operated this tram route from 1st January 1920. In addition to passenger conveyance we provide a service for parcels weighing up to 56 lbs, between the Dickson Road terminus, Bispham, Cleveleys and Fleetwood terminus, and newspapers are carried daily for newsagents, wholesalers and suppliers in Blackpool and Fleetwood."

"The North Station to Fleetwood service operates throughout the year, and during the summer months is augmented considerably, in fact there are times during the Summer months when it is necessary to put double-deck 94-seater tramcars on the Blackpool end of this route between North Station and Bispham or Cleveleys. For over 60 years residents and visitors alike have had a service of tramcars between North Station and Fleetwood, and this service would appear to be very necessary to the Hotels on the Promenade between Gynn Square and Norbreck, and if the hoteliers and their visitors ceased to enjoy a direct service by either tramcar or bus between the Hotels and North Station, it could possibly adversely affect their businesses."

"If the tram service was not available between North Station and the Gynn, it would not be possible, because of the weight of motor traffic and the congestion which occurs on the Blackpool Promenade between Gynn Square and Bispham, and again from Bispham to Cleveleys, to operate a bus service between North Station and Fleetwood. Density of traffic on the Promenade during the Illuminations period must also be considered, and at the Illumination weekends, a bus service would have to be diverted when one-way traffic was in operation. It may be suggested that a bus service could operate between North Station and Fleetwood by diverting at the Gynn, then proceed via Warbreck Drive or Holmfield Road, probably joining the Promenade at Bispham, but this would not serve the Hotels on Queens Drive between Bispham, Cleveleys and Gynn Square."

"A bus service between North Station and Fleetwood would not serve the whole of the route now covered by tramcars, because we should not be able to contact stopping places such as Rossall Square, Broadwaters, Lindel Road, Heathfield Road etc., which are main local stations on the private track, and any bus service we operate into Fleetwood would immediately involve the Ribble Bus Company, who would ask for co-ordinated services, which could mean a substantial loss of revenue to us. It has always been considered that the Dickson Road service, like the Lytham Road route, is part of our tramway system, because of the link-up they make with the Promenade for the benefit of the general public, and when the weight of our Promenade tram traffic is with us in the height of the season, the Dickson Road tram service caters for the workers, particularly those wishing to travel to Bispham, Norbreck and Cleveleys."

"If trams were taken-off Dickson Road it could mean that during the winter months when only a minimum number of tramcars are operated, that there would be a redundancy of tram drivers, too old or otherwise unsuitable to learn bus driving, and there must also be taken into consideration the cost of operating Bispham Main Sub-Station and Depot, both of which would still be necessary. If it was considered that a link-up could take the place with our present North Shore bus service, and that these bus services should be partly or wholly extended to Fleetwood, then we should most probably experience difficulty and receive complaints from the local service-users of North Shore, who would not have the full-use of the local services as at present."

"Regarding the proposed traffic layout at Gynn Square, it should be remembered that a number of years ago the Thornton-Cleveleys Council were faced with similar difficulties at Victoria Square, Cleveleys, and as a result of discussion which took place, a traffic roundabout was put there, which allowed our tramcars to proceed through the centre, and apparently this arrangement works very satisfactorily. With regard to financial commitments, the track on Dickson Road was last renewed in 1948 and certainly will last until 1973 the unused capital value being approximately £20,000. Similarly the overhead wiring was last renewed in 1958 and will last until 1972, the unused capital value being approximately £1000 i.e. approximately £21,000 in total."

"The total cost of additional omnibuses at approximately £5,200 each would depend on the extent of any new services which were substituted for the existing Dickson Road tramway service."

"Transport Offices,   " J.C. FRANKLIN
February 1960"   General Manager"

Elsewhere on the system, the Lytham Road track was in dire need of relaying. Last renewed in 1936, it was now 24 years old and the breaking-up of the foundations meant that the cars pitched and rolled to an alarming degree. Although the junction at Royal Oak had been completely renewed during the winter of 1957 by the Highways Department, the Transport Committee at its meeting on 7th October 1960 took the decision to convert the route to buses. Mr. Franklin reported that the renewal of the track would cost a minimum of £140 000, while the cost of ten new buses would be £52 000. Elsewhere on the system, it was recommended that the Dickson Road terminus be cut back to the Odeon, where a trolley reverser would contribute to quicker reversals, and the Marton route be cut back to St. Johns Church. Work started at North Station during the winter and was completed by Easter 1961, when three of the Pantograph cars (170, 172 and 175) deprived of their trolley ropes, ran for the last time. The new terminus of the Marton route was opposed by the Church authorities, who quoted an agreement of 1927 banning crossing places there. The culmination was the decision to abandon the Marton route at the end of the 1962 season, which would only leave street track in Dickson Road.

Until this time, the Blackpool and Fleetwood tramway had operated in its time-honoured way. When I first went to work at Bispham Depot in 1960, we were operating a 10-minute service to Fleetwood requiring 9 cars, alternating with a 10-minute service to Cleveleys using 4 cars; additionally we had 7 cars on the ten-minute service from Bispham to Squires Gate. Rigby Road operated 13 cars on a ten-minute Starr Gate & Fleetwood service, alternating with 9 cars on Starr Gate & Thornton Gate, all operated by Coronations. Additionally, the same depot had six double-deckers on Squires Gate & Cabin, while Marton operated a twelve cars on a four-minute headway with every third car going to South Pier. This made a total of 60 service duties between the three depots, while all of them doubled that number at busy times by operating 'specials' without time-cards. In truth, things weren't what they used to be: on the back-road route we would be busy going to the station in the morning and to Fleetwood on Market Days, but at off-peak times we often ran empty, especially between Gynn and Cleveleys, where there was a 2½ minute service of cars! Tuesdays and Fridays were the Fleetwood Market days, when a long queue would form at North Station, and sometimes a double-decker would be sent up there to clear the crowd.

By 1963 there was no longer the need for two tram services to Fleetwood and a separate depot at Bispham, which in winter was only operating about ten cars. There was a move towards centralising all tramcar operations at Rigby Road, just as Walter Luff had intended in 1935, except this time it would be permanent. The old tramroad back-road route was killed-off by economics, and the axe fell at the end of the 1963 season, just as it had on the tramways of Leeds in 1959, Sheffield in 1960 and Glasgow in 1962. Blackpool was the only conventional tramway left in Britain, and the future was very uncertain for the coastal line. In that last season at Bispham Depot, I savoured every detail of operation on the No. 1 service. Each time I cycled

to Bispham Depot, collected my TIM machine from the little office, and walked across to the depot with my driver, I was conscious that soon it was to end. There was a certain timelessness about it all, with the old power station buildings, the bowling green and Mr. Cameron's house – now the Bispham Conservative Club. Amazingly there was still a driver at the depot who had worked for Mr. Cameron: 632 Tommy Leeming had joined the Company in 1917 and had never left 'The Other Firm.' Now the family atmosphere was threatened and the cold winds of change were blowing: several familiar faces had disappeared to bus driving and our break times were dominated by one topic: what would happen at the end of the Lights?

The devastating blow finally fell: there would be no Promenade tram service that winter, it would be operated by buses and the only trams would run between Cleveleys and Fleetwood on a shuttle service requiring seven trams. So the last act on Sunday 27th October 1963 had a special poignancy: it was the end of a Fleetwood tram service which had operated since 1898 from North Station. The last car, newly-repainted Brush 290 left the station for Fleetwood driven by 'battling' Bill Bracewell, followed inappropriately by two double-deckers as far as Cabin, the last car being 256. Someone had attached a placard to 290, showing a black Tower and reading 'Dickson Road's Last Tram'; Joe Franklin was not amused, sensitive by this time at the growing criticism from the pro-tram fraternity. It was small and sad crowd that watched the last car run into Bispham Depot: a few flashguns popped, pennies were put on the line and the last driver raised his hat. The depot was silent as the large green doors rolled to: no night cleaner, no fitters, no shed man; the last money was paid-in at the office, and an era had ended. The last link with the Company had gone.

Railcoach 221 unloading on a quiet Sunday morning in October 1963 outside the Odeon. **Author**

The last night at Bispham depot as Brush car 294 swings into the depot yard, driven by Jimmy Booth. **Author**

A rather sad scene at Gynn Square in December 1963 as the junction with Dickson Road is finally removed. **Author**

Left: The fine trolley reverser in action as Railcoach 211 reverses and thus creates no delay for the traffic. The wide-angle of the overhead allows trolleys with fixed-heads to be used here, unlike the Marton cars with swivel-heads for the Royal Oak reverser. **Anthony Stevenson**

FLEET CHANGES 1940–1965

NEW CARS

CORONATIONS
304-328   Built: 1952–1954   Total: 25
Builder: Charles Roberts of Horbury.
Seats: 56.
Dimensions: 50 ft x 8 ft.
Bogies: Maley & Taunton HS44 (+ track brakes) 6 ft
wheelbase.
Controllers: Crompton Parkinson 'Vambac'(Variable
Automatic Multinotch Braking & Acceleration Control).
*Notes: 304 delivered June 1952: 328 delivered January 1954.
Sliding standee windows replaced and steel trim removed
1955–7.*

TRAILERS
T1-T10   Built: 1960-1961   Total: 10
Builder: Metropolitan Cammell. Birmingham.
Seats: 66.
Dimensions: 43 ft 10 ins x 7 ft 6 ins.
Bogies: Maley & Taunton, 5 ft 6 ins wheelbase, rubber
suspension.
*Notes: T1–T7 coupled to motor cars, 1962–1970,
T8–T10 withdrawn 1971.*

RAILCOACHES CONVERTED TO TOWING CARS
272–281
1958: Prototype twin-car 276–275.
1960: 272, 277, 280, 281.

1961: 273, 278, 279. (275 converted to motor-car).
1962: 274.

FLEET SUMMARY 1961

	Totals
Standards: 40, 41, 48, 49, 147, 158, 159, 160	8
Pantographs: 168–175	8
EE Railcoaches Series 1: 200–224	25
EE Open Boat Cars: 225–236	12
EE Double-deckers: 237–263	27
EE Railcoaches Series 2: 264–271 & 282–283	10
Brush Railcoaches: 284–303	20
Marton Vambacs: 10–21	12
Coronations: 304–328	25
Towing Cars: 272–281	10
Trailer Cars: T1–T10	10
1961 FLEET TOTAL:	167

FLEET REDUCTIONS 1961–5
Standards: 40, 48, 49, Preserved; 41, 160 scrapped;
158–60 survived.
Pantographs: All withdrawn from passenger service; 168,
170, 174 formed the basis of illuminated Rocket, Frigate
& Train trailer.
EE Railcoaches: All withdrawn, except 220, 221, & 224.
Brush Railcoaches: 303, Vambac-equipped was scrapped
with Marton cars.
Marton Vambacs: All withdrawn & scrapped, apart from
11 preserved.
1965 FLEET TOTAL: 117

Left: A busy body shop scene in May 1960, as railcoaches 281 and 272 are restored as trailer-towing cars, thus transforming their appearance.　**Author**

Right: The new Maley & Taunton bogies for the trailer cars, with the rubber-insert suspension, to be compared with the EMB bogies nearby – for the elevated Brush car.　**Author**

Below: The first trailer arrived in July 1960, and the Maley & Taunton bogie is rolled underneath. Notice the surprise destination: SOUTH PIER via MARTON, on the indicator!　**The Gazette, Blackpool**

Below Right: Central Promenade with the Twin-car 278 + T6 looking very handsome with the Tower, in November 1960.　**The Gazette, Blackpool**

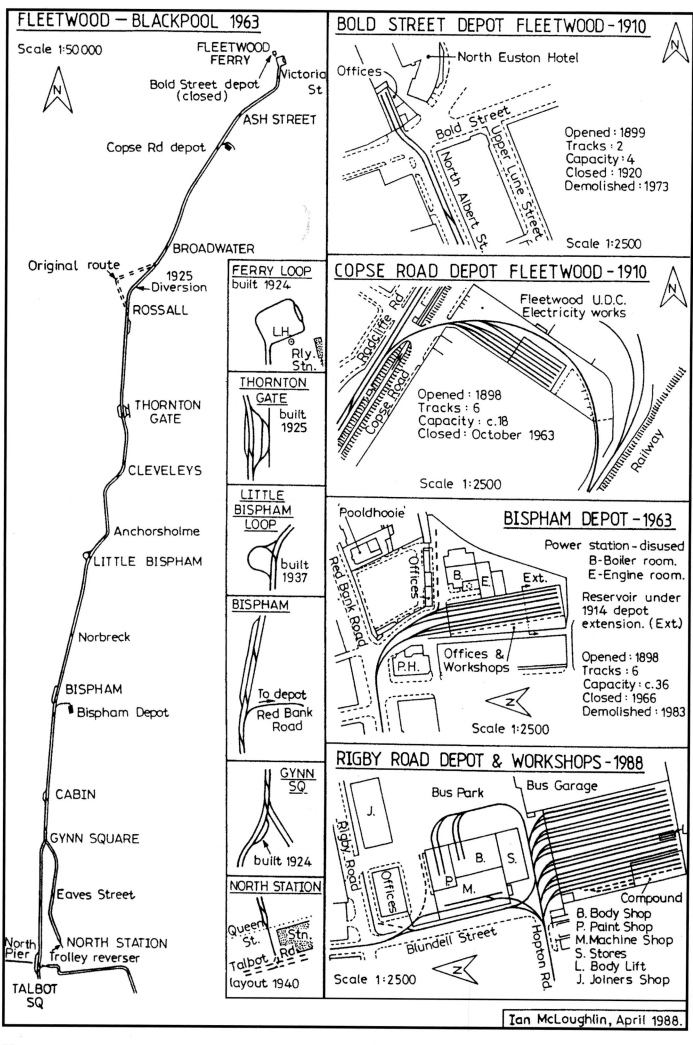

FLEETWOOD – BLACKPOOL 1963

Scale 1:50 000

N

FLEETWOOD FERRY
Bold Street depot (closed)
Victoria St
ASH STREET
Copse Rd depot

BROADWATER

Original route
1925 Diversion
ROSSALL

THORNTON GATE

CLEVELEYS

Anchorsholme
LITTLE BISPHAM

Norbreck

BISPHAM
Bispham Depot

CABIN

GYNN SQUARE

Eaves Street

North Pier
NORTH STATION
trolley reverser

TALBOT SQ

FERRY LOOP built 1924
L.H.
Rly. Stn.

THORNTON GATE built 1925

LITTLE BISPHAM LOOP built 1937

BISPHAM
To depot Red Bank Road

GYNN SQ. built 1924

NORTH STATION
Queen St.
Stn.
Talbot Rd
layout 1940

BOLD STREET DEPOT FLEETWOOD – 1910

N

Offices
North Euston Hotel
Bold Street
Upper Lune Street
North Albert St.

Opened : 1899
Tracks : 2
Capacity : 4
Closed : 1920
Demolished : 1973

Scale 1:2500

COPSE ROAD DEPOT FLEETWOOD – 1910

N

Radcliffe Rd.
Fleetwood U.D.C. Electricity works
Copse Road
Railway

Opened : 1898
Tracks : 6
Capacity : c.18
Closed : October 1963

Scale 1:2500

BISPHAM DEPOT – 1963

'Pooldhooie'
Red Bank Road
Offices
B. E. Ext.
P.H.
Offices & Workshops

Power station - disused
B - Boiler room.
E - Engine room.

Reservoir under 1914 depot extension. (Ext)

Opened : 1898
Tracks : 6
Capacity : c.36
Closed : 1966
Demolished : 1983

N

Scale 1:2500

RIGBY ROAD DEPOT & WORKSHOPS – 1988

Bus Park
Bus Garage
J.
Rigby Road
Offices
B. S.
P.
M.
Compound
Blundell Street
Hopton Rd.

N

B. Body Shop
P. Paint Shop
M. Machine Shop
S. Stores
L. Body Lift
J. Joiners Shop

Scale 1:2500

Ian McLoughlin, April 1988.

CHAPTER 4

A NEW ERA 1964–1985

Following the upheavals of the early Sixties, it took some time for the dust to settle. The winter of 1963/4 marked an all-time low in the fortunes of the tramway: no tram was seen in Blackpool Borough, apart from the daily special at 4.00 p.m. from the depot to Fleetwood. The all-change policy at Cleveleys was severely attacked by Fleetwood Council, which quite rightly demanded that the through tram service be restored. A poll of passengers was taken which came out heavily in favour of the trams, probably because they repre-sented the traditional through service. The economies achieved by this exercise were minimal, since the substations had to be operated and maintenance facilities provided at Rigby Road. The bus service along the route of the tramway was numbered 25, while a 25A provided the Dickson Road replacement and operated to Cleveleys bus station. This latter route survived the return to tramway operation between Starr Gate and Fleetwood on Good Friday 1964, but the 25 bus route was abandoned. A new pattern was now established with a 12 minute service over the whole route and an intermediate service between Tower and Fleetwood. Blackpool's famous landmark featured on tram destinations for the first time, following the demise of Central Station. Fleetwood was again provided with a six minute service in the season, but the cars now did not go to North Station.

The tram fleet had by this time been reduced to 117 cars, although some railcoaches were stored at Bispham Depot awaiting disposal. The fleet was accommodated at Rigby Road and Blundell Street Depots, the latter having been reopened to trams in March 1963 to house seasonal cars from Marton Depot. In the Spring of 1963 Marton had become the graveyard of the Pantograph cars, Marton Vambacs and many of the 1934 railcoaches; the last car – (Standard 48) – leaving on 11th March. The tramcar rationalisation policy seemed to centre round getting rid of the Vambac equipped cars and the oldest cars first, but any claims that equipment was being salvaged was dispelled by the loads on the scrapman's lorry leaving the depot. A scene of total devastation greeted the visitor to Marton at that time, with heaps of twisted metal filling the inspection pits while forlorn trams at the back of the depot waited for their turn. A little boy standing at the depot door asked his father: "Why are they scrapping them daddy?" "Because they don't want them any more," came the reply, and by way of confirmation a route 26 bus roared by. Surprisingly the Brush-cars with their non-standard equipment survived and were gradually transferred to Rigby Road Depot for refurbishing ready for the 1964 season. These were to become the backbone of the Fleetwood service, following the subsequent demise of the Coronations.

Altogether, 38 cars were scrapped during the period 1961-65, while no less then 11 found their way to Museums in Britain and the USA. By a happy chance, the National Tramway Museum at Crich in Derbyshire had been established in 1959, and was able to receive a fleet of cars from Leeds, Sheffield, Glasgow and Blackpool! It came as something of a blow when Blackpool offered its four historic cars, two Standards, a Pantograph, prototype railcoach 200, a Marton Vambac and subsequently, the electric loco and a grinder car. The museum was overwhelmed by the generoslty of the offer and the additional burden on resources. A desperate appeal was launched, and groups were organised to raise money for the transport costs and depot accommodation at Crich. For Blackpool it was a sad day brought about by the harsh reality of economics and a lack of space. All the outlying depots were for disposal: Marton had been sold for a garage, and the ex-company depots at Fleetwood and Bispham were to go. Copse Road had been used as the permanent-way yard, which was transferred to Thornton Gate siding in January 1963, and the building sold following the collapse of a Museum project there. On 18th March a procession of cars, comprising of Company cars 2 and 40 together with Standards 40 and 147, had been driven there and stored to this end. Today it is the only one of the ex-company sheds in existence, confirmed by its headstone still proudly reading: 'Blackpool and Fleetwood Tramroad 1898'. Bispham depot had a twilight existence as a store and a breaker's yard until 5th January 1966, when the last tram left. Ironically this happened to be Coronation 313 which remained here on trestles in order to provide a float pair of Maley & Taunton bogies for the other Coronations. On this day, green works car 5 (ex-221) made a last trip down Red Bank Road to pull 313

At Fleetwood Ferry in December 1963, railcoach 270 on the winter shuttle represented the only tram service left in Britain. Note the dredger.   **Author**

out into the daylight once more. I travelled on this bizarre procession up Red Bank Road: the first and last time for a Coronation, and Bispham' depot's last tram!

The start of the 1964 season saw a reduced but smartened fleet of trams: the livery was now simplified to a half-cream half-green style on the single-deckers with the trolley gantry was painted in a hideous orange. One of the first victims of this style was Coronation 323, which had been stripped of its Vambac equipment and fitted with a conventional controller. During the Sixties, 13 cars were re-equipped in this way, with the idea of providing enough cars for the basic winter service. However this was not to be: scrapping of the class started in 1968 with 313 and continued through to 1975 when the last four were withdrawn from service. 324 – now 660 following the 1968 renumbering – was retained as a last memory of a failed experiment. One could debate the rights and wrongs of the policy to scrap the Coronations, with the benefit of hindsight. Possibly the cars could have been stored in Blun-dell Street depot and later re-equipped with bogies and thyristor chopper equipment now used on the Centenary-class cars. However, this was all in the future, and the Coronation saga remains one of the biggest and costliest tragedies in the history of the tramway.

Economics dominated the Department in Mr. Franklin's latter years. The changes in holiday patterns arising from cheap package holidays abroad affected Blackpool in the sixties and seventies. This was seen most dramatically in the decline of the railways and the closure of Central Station in 1964. As an illustration, tram miles had dropped from 3.3 million in 1959 to 1.2 million in 1970; during this same period, passengers declined from 34 million to 11.9 million. These kind of facts were the background to a crisis which broke around the tramway in 1969, over a projected loss of £60 000. The Transport Committee debated the future of the system: views being polarised between trams as a luxury or as a valuable asset. The Chairman said that apart from the special cost of the permanent way and the overhead line, the running costs of trams and buses were almost identical. Alderman Ward: "All the factors I have mentioned are apart from the sentimental aspect of the tram undertaking. The fact is that it was the first and is now the last in the British Isles and is the oldest in the world (sic). The fact is that the tramway draws people to Blackpool, that its publicity value cannot be calculated: all-in-all it is just unthinkable that we should consider scrapping the trams at this stage." This provided a much needed vote of confidence in the future of the Blackpool tramway, at a difficult time.

One Man Operation

With the demise of the Coronation cars, the brunt of the service was borne by the pre-war railcoaches, but there was a need to reduce the costs of operations, especially in the winter. In 1968 an enlarged railcoach 618 – seating 56 passengers – was reconstructed, but the costs involved did not seem to justify the modest improvement in capacity. One possibility which did offer reduced costs was one-man operation, as the General manager J.C. Franklin said: "If I had tried to build a one-man tram in 1958 it wouldn't have stood an earthly, but after one-man buses had been introduced the climate was different." In 1969, following the order for single-deck one-man buses, the concept of a one-man tramcar was mooted for the first time. Accordingly a 1937 Brush railcar was adapted to have a front entrance, using the centre doors and platform as an exit. Unlike the 618 experiment, the rebuilding was fairly minimal, with the removal of internal partitions and the installation of the resistances inside the trolley gantry. Painted all-cream, in keeping with the new one-man buses, this tram was doomed to failure. The modest rebuilding had given the car a narrow front entrance, situated behind the driver and thus making the fares difficult to collect, and was therefore condemned by the transport union at the outset. Mr Franklin subsequently described this car as a 'false start': "We rebuilt Brush car 638, but that was no good from the start". 638 spent most of its time in the depot, or operated as a two-man car, to which it was subsequently reconverted. Despite this set-back, the General Manager clearly saw this one-man tram as the answer to their lightly-trafficked winter tram service, and was determined to try again.

Following the favourable vote on the future of the tramway operation in Blackpool at the beginning of 1969, an all-Party Committee was set-up in 1970 to study the financial future of the undertaking, with the express purpose of examining the operation of the tramway system. Mr Franklin remained convinced that tramways were still the best means of transport along Blackpool Promenade to Fleetwood, and sought to present a reasoned case for a more economical operation in the future, based one one-man trams for the winter service. The thought of curtailing the tramway at Thornton Gate or Little Bispham and relegating its role to a purely seasonal attraction, was considered by the Committee. It became apparent that if a tramway system was to be continued at all, there was a lower limit of operations receipts below which the capital expenses could not be justified. The Fleetwood route provided a 'raison d'etre' for the tramway: not only as a link between the two towns, but as a popular ride in the season, without which there would be a serious loss of revenue. The expenditure saved by restricting the mileage would be far-outweighed by the loss of revenue, and thus the remaining few trams would still need the supporting services of a Depot, Works, Track and Electrical Supply. The Transport Department argued that for a modest investment, taking into account a possible grant from the Ministry of Transport for conversion of trams to one-man operation, the tramway system could be run more economically in the off-season. This would maintain the unique Promenade transport facility for the heavy seasonal traffic.

The Department won the day, and by 1972 Mr Franklin was quoted as saying: "Tramcars are part of the Blackpool scene: as a means of unhindered transport along the Promenade, they cannot be equalled. During extensive investigations which have taken place over a lengthy period, no obvious alternative form of passenger transport has become apparent for the Blackpool Promenade in particular and the Fleetwood route in general." The General Manager fought hard and continuously for a grant towards operating costs from the rates fund, and even though a large proportion of the Council agreed, a grant was never made. The battle to maintain the tramway in operation had been a long and hard one, it remained for the Transport Department to prove that continued tramcar operation would be no more expensive than the alternative. Owing to the unhappy experience with the prototype OMO ('One Man Only' tram) 638 in 1969, Mr Franklin fully discussed the position with the Trade Union and decided that a Consultative Committee should be formed. This would meet regularly under the Chief Engineer, Alan Williams, and include members of the Works to ensure that the outcome would be a first-class 'team' result.

A complete new design, incorporating a wide front entrance with the driver sitting adjacent, was completed after several designs had been considered. It was based on the underframe and running gear of the pre-war English Electric railcoaches, thirteen of which were still in-service with reliable equipment. The new design lengthened the 43 foot body to 49 feet, to enable the new entrance to be fitted on the extended platform. This raised various technical problems, including clearances of the over-hanging ends at curves. One alternative was cutting the body in the centre and splicing a new section in, thus increasing the wheelbase. This would have still necessitated redesigning the front ends to accommodate the wider entrance. However, this would have been a more expensive lengthy process than adding a platform to each end, and thus the latter course was adopted. For political and financial reasons it was more important that the new cars should not be delayed in entering service, and expediency was the order of the day.

Tests for clearance were carried out during 1971, using an open Boat car rigged with a wooden frame at the end, to simulate the length of the one-man-operated (OMO) cars. It became obvious that a tapered-end would have to be incorporated in the new design, more typical of the Continental practice than at Blackpool. The tapered ends restricted the space in the driver's cab, creating a problem of including the large E.E. Z-type controller. It had been hoped to include a modern lightweight remote-controller, but the additional expense involved precluded this and the traditional controller had to be fitted on the right-hand side of the cab. This meant that the motorman had to drive with his right hand, breaking with a long-held tramway tradition. The detailed cab layout was agreed with the driver's union before the design left the drawing-board, so that no practical problems existed.

Once general acceptance of the design was gained, no time was lost in starting work. At least nine cars would be needed to operate the basic winter service, and the first into the Works was car 616 (269), closely followed by 620 (283). The ends of the cars were completely removed and the bodies stripped down to the basic frame, allowing re-

Below: A dramatic scene in Fleetwood's Lord Street from Standard 159, as 147 passes 299 during the last tour and prior to its departure to Ohio, USA, in September 1967. **Author**

wiring to take place as well as a complete overhaul of the bogies. Platform extensions were fitted to the ends of each car, and the side framework strengthened to carry the extra loads created by the overhang of the new ends. The body design featured flush sides and roof, swept at each end to a single windscreen width and surmounted by an indicator. The entrance door and two-step platform into the saloon, occupied the full length of the tapered ends, and the existing centre doors became exits. To facilitate movement along the saloon, the centre gangway was made level throughout, with two steps down to the centre exit doors. The seating layout created a problem and special back-to-back seat frames were fabricated and arranged in pairs, apart from near the exit where bench side-seats were used. With the 7 ft 6 in body, this arrangement left a rather narrow gangway for a passenger-flow car, whose capacity was 64 including 16 standing! Thus a continuous grab-rail was fitted over the centre gangway, and the seats provided with grab-handles, while a bell-signalling strip was installed over the windows. All this would facilitate the passengers! The whole car was panelled in aluminium, and presented a very sleek Continental appearance – apart from the traditional Blackpool trolley gantry, which unfortunately revealed its origin!

Above: In 1966 railcoach 264 has been styled like a towing car and panelled in Darvic ICI vinyl sheet. It later became 611 then OMO 12. **Stewart Bale**

Left: A redesigned and lengthened railcoach 618 on a trial journey, at Fleetwood Ferry. With the tapered end it pioneered the design of the OMOs – and became OMO 13. **Author**

Below left: The first and unsuccessful OMO was Brush car 638 converted in 1968 to this rather smart appearance, with front entrance behind the driver's cab making it impossible to function as PAYE. **The Gazette, Blackpool**

By December 1971 the conversion programme was in process, with two more cars – 610 (224) and 608 (220) – were fully stripped in the Depot, waiting for a space in the Works body-shop. The impending use of the permanent-way gang car No 5 (221) reflected the shortage of cars suitable for conversion. In the early sixties, it had been the policy to break-up the oldest of the thirties streamliners first, hence the few cars deemed suitable for this programme included the permanent-way car and the derelict 220. These two non-passenger fleet trams were used early in the programme, enabling other railcoaches to be retained in service as long as possible. Consideration was given to eventually convert a total of thirty cars to OMO state, which would have involved the 1937 Brush cars, seventeen of which remained in

service. However upon closer examination, it was found that the Brush cars had underframes which would not easily lend themselves to be extended. This factor – together with the lightweight design of the EMB bogies –precluded their inclusion in the programme. The benefit of hindsight shows that the Brush cars would have been better candidates for scrapping than the 1934 EE railcoaches, twenty-one of which had disappeared in the early sixties. However this is purely a retrospective opinion – by the author!

The 'Plum & Custard' OMO

By April 1972, the first OMO car 616 was rolled out of the Works for inspection by the press, in a striking new livery of sunshine-yellow with a crimson roof and doors. This was the first change in livery since the arrival of railcoach 200 in 1933, but the aim was to make the OMOs more easily distinguishable to the travelling public, especially during the period of mixed operation with the conventional centre-entrance cars. With such a break in tradition, it was felt appropriate to start a completely new numbering scheme, hence the transfers of 616 were hardly dry before it was renumbered '1'. Thus OMOs became 1–13, giving most of these cars their third fleet number, and providing some identity problems! The new tram was inspected by Lt.Col. McNaughton of the Ministry of Transport, who is reported to have said: "By jove, plum and custard, I like that." He drove it all the way to Fleetwood and stated that he was impressed by the standard of workmanship throughout the tram. Hence the design and planning of the OMOs was officially approved, which ensured their introduction into service.

One-man tramcar services on the Fleetwood route were due to start after the 1972 illuminations, and by August cars 1–4 were present in Rigby Road Depot ready to enter service. Preparations along the route included the modification of the shelters and queue barriers, changing the direction of loading so that passengers would face the front entrance of the new cars. The traditional circular tram-stop signs 'Cars Stop By Request' and 'All Cars Stop Here' began to disappear in favour of the new 'Tram Stop' showing the OMO. In the street section of Fleetwood, the number of stops were reduced to minimise traffic congestion while passengers were boarding and paying. The public was prepared for the innovation by an attractive leaflet, showing one of the new trams in a series of cartoons, demonstrating: 'How they cannot work efficiently without your help.' The new service was due to operate with a 12 minute headway and simplified fare structure printed on the leaflet. Since there would only be four cars ready in time, conventional cars would be alternated in service, thus training the passengers' observation!

The introduction of 'OMO' trams – as they became known – presented a greater staffing problem to that experienced on the 'OMO' buses in 1969, where volunteers had been sought. With the trams, it was necessary to train the older drivers first – learning to deal with fares and tickets with their left hand and operate the controller with the right hand. In order to give them this new experience, several of the new cars were given trial operational journeys along the Promenade during the summer season. There were teething troubles at first, since the public was unaccustomed to having money ready, and the drivers were unfamiliar with handling coinage.

Left: Only five Coronations remained and emerged as 'specials' in 1973, which was their final year as fleet cars. Note the twin-indicator Balloon. **Author**

Frequently the traditional cars followed the one-man trams in convoy, and it became necessary for them to miss stops to avoid congestion. After the illuminations, when the OMOs entered the Fleetwood service, it was necessary to increase the running time. Despite the initial difficulties, and the 20% bonus paid to the drivers of one-man trams and buses, the new mode of operation did save money by dispensing with 170 conductors from 1969, when OMO operation was introduced.

During the winter, rebuilding work was resumed with the fifth OMO (railcoach 221 + Engineering car 5), the Works in the season having been busy with accident repairs. Two more cars – 6 and 7 (617 & 619) – had been stripped in the Depot during the summer months and had their frames extended in the fitting shop. Thus they went back into the body shop during the winter months for conversion, and the progress of the programme was resumed. Some of the railcoaches selected for conversion were due for major overhaul, and others had been involved in accidents, thus necessitating rebuilding – appropriately as an OMO! An exception to the rule was 618 – the lengthened car – which was repaired in the Body Shop during the summer of 1972 after a crash, and continued in that form until the end of 1975. Finally it became OMO 13, the last OMO conversion in this scheme.

1973 proved to be a vintage year on the Tramroad, with seven OMO cars in service, along with the final railcoach 615 and two hybrids: the plastic tram 611 and the extensively rebuilt 618. Additionally three of the trailer towing-cars 678–680 were running as single railcoaches. Thus the ubiquity of the English Electric railcoach could be seen running in five different guises during that season. The remaining five Coronation cars made occasional appearances on the Promenade as 'specials', while the Balloons had taken-over the Fleetwood service from July 1st. At that time the OMOs were restricted from running in Fleetwood during the busy season, and were used on a Little Bispham and Starr Gate service. The conversion programme subsequently produced OMO cars 8 and 9 in 1974 and 10, 11 and 12 in 1975, thus allowing the Works to service other cars at the same time. The slowing-down of the OMO programme took account of the 'human factor' in the Transport Department. There were a number of tram conductors who had never done bus work, and for whose benefit traditional trams continued to operate during the winter months. Thus gradual retirement and retraining reduced their numbers to one all-man crew by 1975. That winter season, Driver Lascelles and Conductor Hollingsworth staffed the one conventional service tram until December, after which they retired and the trams became fully one-man operated for the first time.

Changes at the top were to have a far-reaching effect on the tramway. The creators of the OMO programme – the General Manager J.C. Franklin and the Chief Engineer B.H. Williams – had both left the Department by Easter 1974. Mr Franklin had retired after twenty years at Blackpool, and he could look back with satisfaction at the metamorphosis of the tramway to a slimmed-down, but

more cost-effective operation. Local Government reorganisation now gave Lancashire County Council a role to play in regional transport policy, which was to benefit the tramway financially. The new County Transportation Committee voiced its support for the tramway as an amenity, and the future looked much brighter. The same reorganisation which had created P.T.E.s, brought Mr Derek Hyde – the former Coventry Manager – to Blackpool as Mr Franklin's successor. His contact with tramways was more of a family-one, since his brother – Geoff Hyde – was an official of the National Tramway Museum at Crich. This seemed to bode well for future co-operation between two tramway operators! The new Chief Engineer, Mr Stuart Pillar, had been the Deputy Manager and Engineer at Preston, and the new team was able to take a fresh look at the situation, now that some experience had been gained of one-man operation on the tramway. Most apparent was the deterioration of the new 'plum and custard' livery, which looked somewhat drab after their exposure to the salt and sand of the Promenade.

New Technology for the Tramway

Under the leadership of the new Manager and Chief Engineer, new ideas were sought to improve the efficiency of the trams. With the number of OMO cars in service, some very high mileages were gained by the new cars: one operated 44 000 miles in 7½ months, while the average was 35 000 miles – far exceeding that of the conventional cars. Some technical difficulties were becoming apparent with the running-gear and car-bodies, due to the increased length and heavy loadings on the Promenade. The extended bodies and front entrance platforms had begun to droop at the ends, while loads and car movements were affecting bogie life. An investigation was undertaken and the conventional primary suspension was redesigned and replaced by 'Metalastik' rubber suspension, similar to that used on London Transport and many Continental trams. OMO 10 was the first to be modified and made its initial test run on 17th January 1975, and was soon named 'Bouncing Bessie' by the crews, because of its jogging motion. Modifications followed to the bogies, and by 1976 six OMOs were equipped with the new suspension, resulting in improved riding qualities.

It has to be said that the new OMOs were not very popular with the travelling public. Their upright seats, cramped aisles and the oscillations caused by the unsupported weight at the ends, made for an uncomfortable ride. In 1975 the 'plum-and-custard' livery gave way to red-and-cream, so that passengers could still identify the PAYE trams from those with conductors. The appearance of a green-and-cream conventional car was usually greeted with relief by the regular passengers on the Fleetwood route. The best that could be said of the OMOs was that they were functional and probably saved the tramway at a critical time. Hence the debacle over the Coronations had made the Transport Department fight-shy of technical innovation, choosing to rely instead on the well-tried and tested pre-war English Electric equipment. Consequently the Brush cars had received the motors and controllers from the scrapped EE railcoaches in the early Sixties, thus standardising the fleet equipment. Now an extensive track-renewal programme was started on the Promenade, with the aim of renewing all the rail between Cabin and Starr Gate over a period of years. The cost of this operation was supported by grants annually from the County Council. The technique of ribbon-welding by Electro-Thermit of Essen was introduced to

the newest pantograph! Subsequently – 3rd July – 678 went into service between Little Bispham and Starr Gate, fitted with a Brecknell pantograph, which could be raised and lowered from the driver's cab. It ran though the season without undue incident, a buzzer in the cab warning the driver of any snag which made the pantograph lose contact with the overhead line. This was only a preliminary trial and the real test came when OMO 5 was fitted with the pantograph in February 1976, followed by cars 4 and 13 later in the year. The fact that 5 and 13 were refitted with trolleys by the year-end indicated that there had been some problems which needed to be eliminated. However, since the modern collector eased problems for the driver of an OMO, eventually all of them became familiar with a pantograph in the future. In 1976 came the Centenary of the Borough of Blackpool. Since the Civic Trust had made a special project of securing the return and restoration of Dreadnought 59, it contributed a memorable tramway sight. It was ironic that the red-and-white Dreadnought with twin staircases and an open top, contrasted strikingly with the OMOs!

To the travelling public, the most obvious change to the OMO trams was the new red and cream livery, introduced to 10 and all subsequent cars in the series. With their red roof, doors and 'dash' panel, the OMOs looked brighter and more distinctive than their 'plum and custard' predecessors, the last of which was repainted in August 1976. When 13 had emerged in spring 1976 with the added sophistication of fluorescent lighting, this had completed the planned programme. The lack of further EE railcoaches for conversion could only have strayed into sacrificing the trailer towing car 678–680 or the Boats, and thus indicated a new direction for the fleet modernisation programme. Following the demise of the twenty-five Coronation cars, only one of which remained in Blackpool by the end of 1976, the twenty-seven Balloons remained the largest single class of trams left in the fleet. Two of their numbers – 714 and 725 – had been derelict in Blundell Street Depot for a number of years, awaiting rebuilding, and this indicated possible development.

Towards A New Tram – with 761

The thirteen new OMO cars were no more than a short-term measure: a means of achieving economic operation at a relatively-cheap cost. Some of the Ministry grant remained after the completion of car 13 in June 1976, and attention turned to future development of the fleet. A retrospective look at the words of Mr Franklin was interesting: "The Brush cars had been ruled out for conversion because of the design of the frames and partly because they bounce and roll too much to allow them to be extended. I suggested in a report that the Boats should be

extend the life of the rails and reduce the effect of corrugations upon the track surface. It was notably used upon road crossings and in the street sections of Fleetwood and at the Metropole, quieting the noisy effect of the corrugations.

Meanwhile, preparations were under way during 1974 for a limited experiment with a modern pantograph collector, which at that time was being developed by Brecknell Willis for the American Boeing Corporation light rail vehicle. In April 1974 overhead-line car 754 was fitted with a wooden frame to investigate what work would be necessary to reposition the overhead in order to accommodate a pantograph, especially round curves and turning circles. Then 754 was fitted with the pantograph for trials, and in June 1975 made a test run to Fleetwood, somewhat incongruously the oldest tram in the fleet with

---

Blackpool Corporation Transport

NOTICE TO PASSENGERS

INTRODUCTION OF ONE–MAN OPERATED VEHICLES

LOOK FOR THE
GOLDEN YELLOW AND
CRIMSON SINGLE DECK
PAY AS YOU ENTER
ONE-MAN OPERATED TRAMS

PASSENGERS ARE REQUESTED TO NOTE THAT WHEN ONE– MAN OPERATED VEHICLES ARE OPERATING ON THIS SERVICE, ATTENTION IS DRAWN TO THE FIVE POINTS LISTED BELOW, AND YOUR CO–OPERATION IS REQUESTED.

1. PLEASE SIGNAL THE DRIVER TO STOP IN GOOD TIME.

2. PAY THE DRIVER AS YOU ENTER.

3. HAVE THE EXACT FARE READY IF YOU CAN.

4. SIGNAL IN GOOD TIME WHEN YOU WISH TO ALIGHT.

5. ENTER BY THE FRONT DOOR, ALIGHT FROM THE CENTRE DOOR.

SEE FARE LIST OVERLEAF:-

TRANSPORT OFFICES,
BLUNDELL STREET,
BLACKPOOL.
MAY 1973

J. C. FRANKLIN,
GENERAL MANAGER.

Above: In July 1963 Dreadnought 59 had survived in Blackpool following the departure of the other historic cars, in its new role as Daily Mirror tram – for charity. Seen here near Waterloo Road, 59 is filled with passengers on a sunny day.   **Author**

Right: The most amazing sight on 7th January 1966, as Works railcoach 5 pulls Coronation 313, the last tram out of Bispham depot.   **Author**

Below: OMO 1 reserved for driver training and very striking in the new plum and custard livery at Bispham. Its tapering shape features the compact dash panel, complete with coat-of-arms, lights and PAY AS YOU ENTER panel.
Roy Brook

used and possibly the two derelict double-deckers 714 & 725 which were stored in Blundell Street shed." It was the latter cars which were chosen for one-man operation as double-deckers, since the Department needed a new all-purpose tram for summer and winter operation, with enhanced capacity. Experience with the thirteen one-man cars showed that more advanced design techniques were needed to give rebuilt cars a longer life. The one-man cars had proved highly successful in operation, but were not structurally withstanding the heavy loadings experienced on the Promenade. When 725 was stripped of its panels for inspection, the pre-war teak frame was found to be sound and it was decided to use it, with the addition of new ends. Since the OMO programme had taken its toll of routine maintenance, it was decided that the new metal-framed end-sections would be made by Metal Sections Ltd of Birmingham.

The concept of the new car – as revealed in drawings produced in 1975 – was a front-loading tram, capable of one-man operation in winter while offering a high seating capacity. The traditional Blackpool Balloon had, by union agreement, two conductors owing to the centre entrance and twin staircases. This expensive crewing would be reduced on the new car, using only one conductor at peak times. Work commenced on 26th October 1976, when the shell of 725 entered the Body-shop. The complete ends of the car were removed, and the floor was lifted to allow extensive alterations to the main frame. Experience with the single-deck OMO cars had shown the mistake of leaving the bogies in the same position, when the length of the cars had been extended to 49 feet. The length of the new car would be extended to 46 feet, and the bogie centres increased from 19 ft 6 in to 22 ft 4 in. The frame extension

allowed a full-width body at each end, with a 4 ft 8 in entrance and a more spacious platform than had been possible on OMOs 1–13. The teak framework of the existing body was altered by the removal of the central entrance and stairways, and the enlargement of the windows to take load-bearing metal window-frames.

While the car body was taking shape during 1977, the bogies were undergoing an equally-thorough rebuilding in the fitting-shop. Primary Metalastik rubber suspension, which had increased the tyre life on the OMO cars to 100,000 miles, was incorporated to give a softer ride and reduce maintenance costs. The braking system was changed to railway-type disc brake units supplied by SAB, while still retaining the traditional steel brake shoes. These would be self-adjusting, saving a considerable amount of maintenance time. An emergency braking system was provided by a spring brake, which was held-off the wheels by pressure in the air system. The Railway Inspectorate agreed that the rheostatic and hand-brake linkages could be dispensed with. By the end of 1977, work on the body of the car had stopped – owing to financial restrictions – and priority was given to the bogies. In early 1978 the bogies were completed, and it was decided to test them under Balloon 708, which went out on trial in February with test-equipment mounted in the saloon. Loading tests were carried out using brake shoes piled inside to simulate full loads in the upper and lower saloons. It was found that the new bogies gave a fairly 'soft' ride, and this was attributed to the new suspension. Shortly after Easter the bogies were rolled under 761 in the Body-shop.

Meanwhile, problems in the supply of new control equipment led the Transport Department to reluctantly consider using one of the old Z6 controllers in their new tram. There had been some consideration of an electro-pneumatic system operated by a lightweight controller in each cab, but finally it was decided to use more modern sold-state equipment. Fortunately the Westinghouse Brake and Signal Company expressed an interest in developing sold-state control systems for 761, having seen the car under construction. An order was placed with Westinghouse for a prototype sold-state chopper control system. This would operate by rapidly switching on-and-off the 550 Volt supply for short periods, reducing the voltage supplied to the motors and ensuring smooth acceleration. The driver would operate a joystick control lever, forward for power and back for braking, and the control-unit would be housed under the front stairs and behind the cab. It was not considered necessary to provide rheostatic braking traditionally, and the Railway Inspectorate gave a dispensation for 761 to be exempt from the legal requirement. Discussion took place with them on many facets of the tram, in the early design stages.

Since the new car was a prototype, discussion on the interior layout took place with the representatives of the platform staff. Originally it had been planned to seat 110 passengers, but this was reduced to 100 by the use of single seats at the stairhead and the centre of the upper saloon, to improve passenger movement. Fixed bus-type seating was adopted because of the one-man operation, with each side of the gangway facing in opposite directions, apart from

Left: The interior of Blundell Street Depot in July 1971, with the stored Balloons 725 and 714 which became 761 and 762, and also 706 on the left – which later became an open-topper. **Author**

the end seats upstairs which face outwards. This would give the passengers a simple choice, but subsequently it was found unsuitable and would have been better facing forward and backwards in each half of the saloon. Following the fitting of the electrical equipment by Westinghouse during autumn 1978, there was testing in the fitting shop. Work continued on the lower saloon and the driver-cabs were completed, with good visibility of the driving position, and its adjustable pedestal seat. An impressive row of instruments, including a speedometer, faced the driver on a single console with the control lever mounted on the right. Added refinements on this tram included designing an air-operated reset mechanism for the lifeguard and for lowering the pantograph collector, together with air-sanding equipment. Before painting, 761 looked very tall and slender from the front and massive from the side, but the new Atlantean livery improved its proportions and gave it a distinguished appearance. Although 2½ years seemed a long time for reconstruction, Chief Engineer Stuart Pillar was anxious to 'get it right' the first time. 761 had to be a success with everybody from the start!

On 19th April 1979 at 8.20 a.m., your author witnessed the emergence of the new car from the paint-shop at Rigby Road Works. 761 made an impressive sight with its new Atlantean livery accentuating its length. The similarity with a modern bus was so great that one of the platform staff was heard to say: "When that gets to Talbot Square, the time-keeper will probably send it on route 5 to Layton!" The complete transformation from a pre-war Balloon 725, left no clue as to its antecedents, in effect it was a completely new tram numbered 761. The similarity to a bus was not accidental, since 761 had been created from components copied from bus practice, including windows, seats, handrails, windscreens, wipers and lights. The impact of the new car was reminiscent of that of the first Coronation car which, in 1952, was named after a royal event, and thus 761 was christened 'Jubilee Car'.

With the painting completed and the mini-pantograph mounted, 761 went on trials during May and June 1979, attracting public attention whenever it appeared. Some of the trials were undertaken at night – after the normal service had finished – and on one occasion an anxious moment occurred when 761 went 'dead' at the foot of the Gynn Hill. After a few minutes silence, the car started moving forward again as another tram passed on it on its way back to the depot. An explanation was later realised, the solid-state control equipment had been programmed for a voltage between 450 and 600, while at night the Gynn substation was supplying 604 V to its section. When another car passed 761, the voltage was reduced below 600, enabling the new car to move again. This problem was soon solved by altering the voltage range in the solid-state equipment. The critical test came on 7th June, when the Railway Inspector came to examine 761. He passed it for driver-training which commenced on 25th June, and finally on 2nd July 761 went into service on the Fleetwood route, driven by Jim Ingham and assisted by a conductor. During the following winter, after negotiations with the Trade Union, one-man operation commenced achieving a crew-passenger ratio of 1:98! Incidentally the circulation at the foot of the stairs had been helped by the removal of one seat at each end, hence the capacity of 98 passengers!

The general public liked the new car, as did the crews who operated it. Acceleration and braking were smooth,

controlled by the 'chopper' system, which eliminated the possibility of bad driving. Riding was extremely steady on the newly re-laid Promenade track, but could be lively when running on the poorer sleeper track and it pitched and rolled. Loading and unloading on the busy Promenade through the single doorway, tended to be slower than the Balloons or the OMO cars with their separate entrance and exit. Therefore it seemed that future Jubilee cars should follow the effective practice on the OMOs with passenger-flow. Undoubtedly the large car provided useful extra capacity to the service, without the crush-loading of the single-deckers including the OMOs. 761 had been a success, and the experienced gained stimulated a desire to develop the Jubilee class in future. Clearly the stored Balloon 714 was the next candidate!

In 1980 a second car was started, using 714 as the basis for the construction of 762. After loading and unloading trials with students from the local Technical College, it was decided that 762 would have a front-entrance and centre-entrance with a central stairway. This would reduce the seating to 90, but would improve the passenger flow through the car. While there would be much in common with 761, the second car would have redesigned bogies, incorporating primary and secondary rubber suspension, while using the original wheels and EE 305 motors. The new bogie frames were manufactured locally and their large dimensions were designed to protect the brake cylinders and integrated slack-adjusters on the wheels. The handsome 762 was rolled-out in April 1982, just in time for the retirement of Chief Engineer Stuart Pillar, whose award of the M.B.E. was commemorated on the indicator blind which read: 'Congratulations Mr. Pillar M.B.E.' as a tribute to his achievements.

The two Jubilee-class cars 761 & 762 which remained in all-year service on the Fleetwood route proved to be highly successful at moving crowds – indeed, they became known as 'vacuum cleaners' by the crews! The time taken to rebuild the two cars made it apparent that the Transport Department did not have the resources necessary for such a major exercise, coupled with the routine maintenance of the tram fleet – especially the OMOs! In 1982 the Transport Committee authorised the construction of a prototype single-decker, which would use the technology incorporated in 762. This would provide a new generation of trams to replace the OMOs, which had proved troublesome with their sagging body-frame, needing constant uplifting and adjustment by the body-shop. The tender of East Lancashire Coachbuilders at Blackburn was accepted for the prototype car, which would ensure common parts with Blackpool's fleet of Atlantean buses by the same manufacturer. By this time the Brush Company had taken over Westinghouse, and thus provided the control equipment as used on the Jubilee cars. Incidentally, responsibility for the project lay with Mr Bernard Browne, the new chief Engineer, whose experience had been with the Bradford trolleybuses.

Contrasting Events With Bolton 66

Neatly counterpointing the modern development was the arrival of the restored Bolton 66 in June 1981, following its restoration by a team led by Derek Shepherd. Following the absence of vintage trams from the Blackpool tramway since the departure of its Standards in 1966, came a contrast with the return of Dreadnought 59 in 1976. Now with the

Above: 1973 was a vintage year in which the final railcoach 615 was still in service, seen here near Manchester Square with the new track being laid towards the Pleasure Beach. **Author**

Left: OMO 10 in the new red-and-cream livery in 1975, known as 'Bouncing Bessie'. The pedestrians are warned 'Look Out Trams About' along the Promenade. **Author**

Below left: OMO 5 was fitted with the Brecknell Willis pantograph in February 1976, and is seen here in June having lost part of it and being towed away. **Author**

On the Centenary of the Borough – 12th June 1976 – the Dreadnought was displayed as restored, and provided the Civic Trust with a grandstand to watch the procession. Subsequently they had a ride to the Pleasure Beach. **Author**

761 in January 1980 seen in front of the Transport Office, as the largest double-decker tram in the fleet with a pleasing livery. **Author**

A contrast between 761 and Bolton 66 as they pass at North Pier in August 1981. **Author**

Centenary of the Tramway in 1985 impending, Blackpool Transport Chairman – Stanley Parkinson – suggested operating vintage trams again. The presence of the Bolton tram, restored by enthusiasts, marked the achievement of people from their native town, where trams closed on 29th March 1947. The lower saloon of the tram body was found, used as a chicken coop on a farm, and was bought in 1963. Regular weekly working parties were held and the lower saloon was stripped down and new wood fitted where necessary, being completed by 1973. In the following year, the Bolton group offered to buy a pair of Brill 21E bogies from the Belgian Vicinal tramway museum at Schepdaal. One of the first jobs was to re-gauge these bogies from metre to standard gauge, using a suitable lathe to make the wheels operate on grooved rail. An entirely new enclosed top deck – as fitted in 1930 to the 1901 open-topper – had to be built by Shaws Wood-Working specialists of Bolton, using timber from a former local Methodist Church In 1979 both halves of the car were moved to the Back-o'the-Bank Power Station at Astley Bridge, so that the complete 66 could be assembled. Seating for 74 was fitted, with 44 wooden seats upstairs and two facing longitudinal seats for 30 in the lower saloon. By autumn 1980, 66 was ready for painting, and in January 1981 the press reported Councillor Parkinson's statement that Blackpool should borrow trams fron elsewhere for the Centenary. The Bolton group offered to loan 66 to Blackpool – and they accepted, subject to an inspection and an agreement. Councillor Parkinson viewed the handsome 66, in its primrose and maroon livery, and decided that it would be a vintage attraction to the tramway. Thus on Saturday 20th June the tram was winched out of the workshop on temporary track and transported to Blackpool on Tuesday 23rd June thus making a striking addition to the conventional fleet. This boded well for the future of museum car operation at Blackpool, as thoughts turned towards the Centenary in 1985.

A negative development took place in November 1982, when the historic Blundell Street depot was demolished following gale damage to the roof. This had been caused by the movement of the central roof-bearer, to which was attached a dividing partition between the ambulance garage and the tramway store. A survey of the whole building, which had been enlarged in 1898, indicated that the three-floor former office over the original entrance to the depot was unsafe. Also the Blundell Street depot wall had elements of leaning, together with the damage to the roof-member. Since a new ambulance depot was to be built in Waterloo Road, the Council decided that the whole depot could be demolished, even though it was useful to the Transport Department, as they used this

building for housing the works car unit and equipment for the track work, while the side stores housed fittings and equipment for work on tbe overhead. Based upon its historic status as the depot for the first tramway in 1885, an appeal was made to the Ministry to have the building listed and thus prevent its demolition. Sadly this was not successful because it was felt that the building was not the original structure. Thus the demolition proceeded, resulting in Blackpool Transport having to house all the working equipment in the tram depot, thus reducing the capacity for as many service trams. Thus Blackpool Transport had lost four tram depots during the post-sixties period, and it was merely fortunate that a larger new depot had been opened in 1935 as part of Walter Luff's five-year plan. Subsequently it was realised –especially when many historic trams were visiting for the Centenary – that Blundell Street Depot would have provided an excellent location for an historic museum. Unfortunately today the former depot is represented by the stone plaque 'Corporation Tramways' in front of the Transport Office, and the mundane car park site upon which can be seen the depot track and fan. Thoughts may be given to the creation of an historic transport museum on this site as an appropriate celebration of the Millenium.

At this time, the Lord Street track in Fleetwood was at the end of its useful life, having been laid some thirty years before. Wyre Borough Council complained about the state of the road surface, and a combined effort between Blackpool Transport and Lancashire County Council ensured that the track and the road surface were renewed in concert. Work proceeded during the winter of 1982–3 and was completed in the winter of 1983–4, a bus service between Ash Street and the Ferry giving uninterrupted access to the site. Each track was relaid in turn, allowing rail delivery alongside by the works car unit 259 & 260 – complete with a useful crane! New concrete foundations and drains were laid and the continuously-welded track spiked-down to the concrete, and set in bitumastic pitch. It was estimated that this track would have a further thirty-year life, thus providing a vote of confidence in the future of tramway operation in Fleetwood.

Right: During the rebuilding of 59 in the workshop of the Technical College in Palatine Road, showing the structure of the side-frame with the panels removed, and resting on lowered jacks for clearance.   **The Gazette, Blackpool**

Towards The Century

Events now gathered momentum for the celebration of the Centenary of the Promenade tramway in 1985: plans were made for the operation of vintage cars from museum lines. In 1983, with the Bolton car in seasonal use and the Dreadnought also available for private hire, the last remaining Coronation 660 was restored to its former glory in June 1983. In the November of the same year Edinburgh 35 arrived from the Scottish capital, sponsored by the National Savings in a deal which paid for its transport in return for advertising rights. This was to be the pattern for future arrivals, and in April 1984 Glasgow 1297 arrived, sponsored by Sealink. This enabled a Great Tram Race to take place between trams of the rival Scottish cities on 6th April: the Edinburgh car won and the driver was presented with a haggis! In exchange for the Glasgow car, Blackpool had loaned Balloon 710 to the National Tramway Museum at Crich for a period of two years. The 17th April was a significant date in the history of the tramway, when new car 641 arrived from Blackburn on a low-loader. The £138 000 tram was launched on 15th June by Councillor Stanley Parkinson at North Pier and named 'The Centenary Belle'. 641 went into service on 6th July on the Fleetwood route, and a new generation of Blackpool trams had arrived.

1985 was to be a year of celebration and enjoyment on the tramway, but it was also to be the year of the Government's new Transport Bill which would have widespread implications for the future of the tramway. The Deputy General Manager, Mr. Anthony Depledge, had to spend most of the year preparing for the future while the past was celebrated in style. He was designated as the Managing Director of the Company which would operate the trams in future. The White Paper which was published in July made no mention of trams, leading Blackpool Council Leader Tom Percival to observe that Whitehall had again apparently forgotten that Blackpool had a tramway. The Labour Party in the town pointed out that after privatisation, businessmen would be queuing-up to operate the profitable mile of track in the town centre, but the rest of the Blackpool & Fleetwood line would die. Things did not turn out this way, as we shall see.

The year began with extensive preparations for the Centenary events: attractive publicity leaflets and posters were produced, cars were prepared for exchange with Museums. Sheffield Roberts car 513 had arrived towards the end of 1984, enabling the Fylde Tramway Society to use it for the annual Christmas party tour in December. In the works, the conversion of double-deck car 706 to its pre-war open-top condition was proceeding in the first part of the year. It was ready for the FTS convention in May, when it made its debut. The Society had bought the advertising spaces on the sides of the car to congratulate the tramway on its Centenary, and its badge was proudly carried throughout the year. 26th April saw the arrival of Standard car 40 from Crich, beautifully restored in their workshops and painted in the red and white livery. The car was used as the Centenary logo, and was exchanged for repainted Boat car 607. Soon after, Boat car 600 was exchanged for Manchester car 765 at the Heaton Park Tramway, while on 7th May Pantograph 167 returned. This had been restored to its post-war green livery by an MSC workshop at Bolton, which had been created to restore old trams and buses under the guidance of Derek Shepherd, a well-known enthusiast. Sadly, after one trip to Fleetwood on May 11th, 167 was covered with adverts by its sponsor ICI, who added a hideous orange box round its trolley tower. Surely this was a case of over-kill by a sponsor, effectively diminishing a fine restoration job?

The Great Centenary Party

The official launching of the Centenary celebrations was held on Thursday 16th May at North Pier, when comedian Les Dawson flagged-off a parade of trams from Sheffield, Edinburgh, Glasgow and Blackpool. Dreadnought 59 was displayed on a new siding which had been built opposite North Pier especially for historic trams. A Royal occasion occurred on June 6th, when Princess Alice Duchess of Gloucester arrived at Squires Gate Airport and travelled by red-carpeted 40 along the Promenade to North Pier. Here a line-up of immaculate cars greeted the Princess, with 706 on the specially constructed siding as the star of the show. Red velvet curtains on the side panel next to the doors were unveiled to reveal the name Princess Alice, together with a stainless-steel plaque commemorating the event. Two souvenirs of the Centenary were presented by Stanley Parkinson: a handsome Wedgwood souvenir plate and a copy of the book Century of Trams by your author. Princess Alice then boarded a waiting 641, which took her to the Tower where she made the famous ascent to the top. This was the first Royal tram ride since 1937, when the Duke of Kent drove the Lifeboat illuminated tram along the Promenade and up to North Station.

For the first time in living memory, an open day was held at the Transport Depot on 16th June, when a special service of trams was operated from North Pier via Lytham Road. Thousands of people came for the occasion: you could try

LIST OF CARS IN THE CENTENARY PROCESSION 29th SEPTEMBER 1985

1.	Blackpool ex-conduit 4	(1885)
2.	Blackpool Dreadnought 59	(1902)
3.	Blackpool Standard 40	(1926)
4.	Blackpool Open-top 706	(1934)
5.	Blackpool Pantograph 167	(1928)
6.	Blackpool Centenary 641	(1984)
7.	Edinburgh Standard 35	(1948)
8.	Blackpool Twin-set 674-684	(1962)
9.	Hill of Howth (Dublin) 10	(1902)
10.	Manchester California 765	(1914)
11.	Blackpool Railcoach 679	(1935)
12.	Blackpool Jubilee 762	(1982)
13.	Blackpool Boat Car 606	(1934)
14.	Glasgow Cunarder 1297	(1948)
15.	Blackpool OMO 8	(1972)
16.	Sheffield Roberts 513	(1950)
17.	Blackpool Balloon 726	(1935)
18.	Bolton Car 66	(1901)
19.	Blackpool Coronation 660	(1953)
20.	Steam Tram John Bull	(1885)

Notes: Numbers given are the processional order of the cars. The order of the procession seems to have been fairly random, apart from the first six cars, but produced a colourful spectacle!

Above: Bolton 66 enhances the tramway scene on the Golden Mile in August 1981, when it poses for this view during the first tour. **Author**

Left: The renewal of the rail in Fleetwood's Lord Street is helped by the hydraulic crane on 751, seen here taking up the old rail in December 1982, prior to bringing the new rail from Thornton Gate. **Blackpool Transport**

Below: Overhead line car 754 crossing-over at Norbreck in April 1983, in the last season before its transfer to Beamish for restoration as Marton Box 31. **Author**

Above: The first Fleetwood Tram Sunday on 14th July 1985 provided this perfect scene of the two Scottish trams, Edinburgh 35 and Glasgow Cunarder 1297 operating together on a traditional urban street.   **Author**

Below: An historic scene at Fleetwood Ferry on 11th May 1985, as Pantograph 167 arrived newly restored in the post-war livery, followed by Manchester 765.   **Author**

Above: Bolton 66 in Back O'The Bank power station in 1980, newly fitted with its top-deck which was being panelled.

J.H. Price

Right: Having arrived in Rigby Road Depot on 23rd June 1981 is Bolton 66, seen here with its team of workers: John Markham, David Shepherd, Graham Mather and Alan Ralphs.

The Gazette, Blackpool

your skill at wiring a trolley or driving a bus, the band played in the bus garage, and there were displays of all the maintenance skills including track welding. Equally exciting was the Fleetwood Transport Festival on 14th July, when for the first time, Lord Street was closed to vehicular traffic and lined with a display of vintage buses and commercials. Bands played, street organs blared and some people paraded in vintage costume, including the police dressed as Peelers. The only moving vehicles in the street were the vintage trams which gave rides at 20p between Ash Street and Fleetwood Ferry. The tram crews were dressed in vintage costume, and there were trams in service from six towns or cities. It was certainly a day to remember, and the event has now become annual, which in 1988 will commemorate the 90th year of the Blackpool & Fleetwood Tramroad.

Everything in Blackpool featured the trams in 1985, as the holiday guide said, it was tram-endous. There was a fine floral tramcar by the Parks Department outside St. John's church, a tramcar pub-trail by Bass Brewers, displays in shop windows and an illuminated tableau featuring a moving model of Standard 40 in the Lights. On July 13th, the 1885 car No. 4 travelled down the Promenade to be handed over by the Tramway Museum Society to Councillor Parkinson at North Pier. It was painted in what purported to be the original Blackpool Electric Tramways Company livery and was powered by batteries to give the impression of a conduit car. Operation was by a control baton, which projected through a stair-riser: sensationally the original had been discovered in the possession of a descendent of Alderman Harwood, Mayor of Manchester, who had started the first tram on 29th September 1885. Alongside the diminutive No. 4 was 651, a new Centenary tram especially built for GEC to demonstrate their switched-

reluctance motor, and loaned to Blackpool for two years. In August there was a television programme in two parts entitled "A Toast to the Trams", which gave an impressionistic view of the line and its history partly related by your author!

The final car arrived in time for the switch-on of the Illuminations by Joanna Lumley on 30th August: it was Hill of Howth 10 which had also been restored by the Bolton Manpower Services Commision workshop and was sponsored by the new Sandcastle. The scene was now set for the grand cavalcade of trams on 29th September, but there was one more surprise in store! 1985 also happened to be the Centenary of the steam tram engine John Bull at the National Tramway Museum. It was suggested that it would make a fine spectacle to have a steam tram – a mode which Blackpool rejected in favour of electric traction – in the Centenary Parade. The great day dawned fine and sunny, like all the other important days in the Centenary year, and work went ahead frantically at the depot to steam John Bull. Crowds gathered there to board their allocated car in the Cavalcade and officers of the Department were in vintage costume appropriate to their positions. Thus General Manager Hyde wore a top hat, whereas Chief Engineer Browne wore a bowler! It had been planned to give John Bull a run to Harrowside early in the morning, but this had to be abandoned when a fault developed and the fire had to be dropped. Happily all was well by 10.30 when the procession cars were due to start leaving: Nos. 15–19 to Little Bispham; at 10.40 Nos. 10–14 for Bispham, at 10.50 8 and 9 for Cabin, and at 11.00, Nos. 1–7 to North

Pier. From these destinations the cars would form-up for the procession, due to leave North Pier at 11.45. By this time your author was mounted on top of a tower wagon in Lytham Road and so got a grandstand view of the cars' departures and a large crowd had gathered at the end of Hopton Road and gave a cheer to each car as it turned into Lytham Road. The diminutive 1885 car, humming along on its batteries, looked toy-like and evinced a sumpathetic 'Ah', from the crowd.

Up at Talbot Square a crowd of thousands surrounded the barriers where the ceremony of unveiling the commemorative plaque was to take place. All the cars were in position when the unmistakable sound of a steam whistle indicated the approach of John Bull. All heads turned as the plume of steam drifted distainfully across the shiny electric cars: now John Bull was the centre of attention. The civic party arrived in period costume by landaus, and included the Mayor of Halifax, home of the inventor Holroyd Smith, represented here by his grandson. In truth, the ceremony was rather lost in the mêlée, especially when service cars were allowed to unload passengers there. The grand cavalcade started at 11.45 with the Mayor using the original starting handle to drive No. 4, and a band played on the top deck of Princess Alice to provide the atmosphere. This twenty-car cavalcade was the largest tram procession in living memory, and the sight of it as far as the eye could see along the Golden Mile, will be one of my lasting memories. The rest of the day was a whirlwind of activity: the procession cars were lined up on both Pleasure Beach loops, while John Bull turned at Harrowside and retired back to the depot. There was an official lunch for the guests at the Pleasure Beach, hosted by Managing Director Geoffrey Thompson, who said in his speech that the tramway and the Pleasure Beach mutually depended on each other. During the afternoon a tram-pull was organised

in Princess Street, when teams had to pull Sheffield 513 (sponsored by Bass) along a measured distance. The transport drivers won. A vintage tram service was operated to Fleetwood, and there was a bus rally on the Middle Walk. It was estimated afterwards that a million visitors had come to Blackpool on that day; which was certainly a day to remember!

Yet the celebrations were not quite over: late in the day, the officers of the Transport Department decided to organise one last fling: The Last Night on the Prom. This was a grand tramway party, using all the vintage cars, which assembled at North Pier on Sunday 27th October for a final tour of the Lights. When the procession arrived at the Pleasure Beach loop, the passengers dismounted and enjoyed a buffet dispensed from Coronation 660. The finale took place at Talbot Square with community singing accompanied by a band on the top of Princess Alice and a grand firework display from North Pier. It was an emotional occasion for Councillor Stan Parkinson, who had so ably led the Centenary celebrations that year. When the cars returned to the depot, some at breakneck speed, the Centenary year was effectively over.

A New Company Tramway

The Centenary was effectively the swan-song of the municipal era: in 1986 at the end of the season, Blackpool Transport Services Ltd became the operator of the trams and buses. The Borough of Blackpool retained the ownership of the track, overhead line, electrical distribution system and the depots, but the trams became the property of the new Company. The maintenance of the infrastructure would be the responsibility of the Council, supported financially by Lancashire County. The Company would pay the Borough a percentage of the tramway profits, which must not be less than £25 000 per annum. A new logo displaced the historic

Above: A close encounter for Balloons 705 and 706 at the Pleasure Beach loop in 1980, which was the first head-on collision in the history of the tramway. 705 was subsequently scrapped and 706 became an open-topper again.   **The Gazette, Blackpool**

Left: Conduit car 4 seen here in the historic location of Princess Street. It is powered by batteries to simulate conduit operation.
Blackpool Transport

Below: On Centenary Day – 29th September 1985 – the procession of twenty trams was to be led by Conduit 4, seen here with Dreadnought 59, surrounded by a crowd surprised by the arrival of a steam engine. **Author**

Right: The royal naming of 706 by Princess Alice, Duchess of Gloucester, on 6th June at North Pier. Notice the historic plaque, its name and the vertical pantograph, showing that 706 was standing on the special display siding. **Author**

Below: Princess Alice 706 – with FTS members and a band – is followed by Pantograph 176, Centenary 641, Edinburgh 35 and many others! **Author**

Above: For comparison, a pre-war picture of 247 with the gantry-arch for the trolley, twin-indicators and half-drop windows. **R. Wilson**

Above: 706 in its traditional pre-war form, restored for the celebration of the Centenary in 1985. Of course it should have had a trolley rather than the pantograph and mini-roof, but in 1997 the trolley was restored. **Blackpool Transport**

Below: A busy scene of the Open Day at the transport works and depot on 16th June, with great crowds. Transport there was provided by Sheffield 513 & Pantograph 167. **Anthony Stevenson**

Corporation badge, and Mr. Depledge became the Managing Director. Chairman of the Board was Councillor Robert Battersby, who had been Mayor in the Centenary year. The new situation presented some strange anomalies: the track gang was now employed by the Borough, whose Transport Manager was Derek Hyde; the overhead line men were employed by the Company, but charged their renewal work costs to the Borough.

By this time three more Centenary cars 642–644 were in service on the tramway, and competition had appeared in the form of Baby Blue buses which were operated by the former Fylde Transport. Three more of the new cars were delivered in 1987–88, 645–647, but a halt was put on more purchases pending a full review of future requirements. The seven Centenary cars and 651, enabled seven of the original OMO cars to be withdrawn. The winter 20-minute service required eight cars, and so 761 and 762 made regular

FLEET CHANGES 1964–1988

WITHDRAWALS

CORONATION CARS

Converted to conventional EE Z-6 controllers, 1964–70 in order: 323, 328, 310, 306, 324, 327, 318, 326, 322, 325, 321, 320, 319. Total: 13

Years Scrapped:	Totals
1968: 313 (Vambac)	1
1963: 310 (Z-car) 312, 316 (Vambac)	3
1970: 308, 303, 311, 314, 315, 317 (Vambac)	6
1971: 305, 306, 307, 322, 323 (Z-cars)	5
1972: 315, 320, 321, 328 (Z-cars)	4
1976: 319, 325, 326 (Z-cars)	3
Total:	22

Preserved: 304 (Vambac), 327 (Z-car)
Retained in Blackpool: 324(Z-car) 641, 663, 660

BRUSH CARS

1966: 301
1969: 291 (628) Railcrane 751
1971: 287 (624) P.W. car 259
1972: 292 (629) scrapped 1980
1974: 298 (635) preserved
1980: 302 (638) scrapped
Total: 7

1968 RENUMBERING SCHEME

Boat Cars:
600–607: 225–237 (except 229, 231, 232, 234 scrapped)
Railcoaches:
608–620: 220, 221, 224, & 264–271, & 282–283
Brush Cars:
621–638: 284–302 (except 301 and 303 scrapped)
Coronations:
641–664: 304–328 (except 313 scrapped)
Towing Cars:
671–680: 281 & 272–280
Trailers:
681–690: T1-T10
Double-decks:
700–726: 237–263

1972–6 CONVERSION TO OMO CARS

1972: 1 (616), 2 (620), 3 (610), 4 (608), 5 (609).
1973: 6 (617), 7 (619).

1974: 8 (612), 9 (613). 1975: 10 (614), 11 (615), 12 (611).
1976: 13 (618).
Notes: Liveries – cars 1–9 in plum & custard, 10–13 in red & cream. 615 was the last traditional railcoach body. 611 was a rebuild to towing-car style ends and plastic panels. 618 was lengthened and the body tapered and seated 56 passengers.

NEW CARS 1979–1988

JUBILEE DOUBLE DECKERS 761–762

1979: 761 (rebuilt from 725).
1982: 762 (rebuilt from 714).
Body: English Electric (1934/5), lengthened to 46 ft 3 in with new platform ends by 'Metsec'. Front exit/entrance on 761 and separate front entrance and centre exit on 762.
Seats: 761: 98, 762: 90.
Bogies: 761 E.E. modified by Metalastic suspension and SAB brake units. 762 BCT bogies 5 ft 4 in wheelbase, Metalastic suspension + SAB brakes.
Controllers: Westinghouse/Brush chopper-control solid state system.
Motors: EE 305 (2 x 57 h.p.).

CENTENARY CLASS 641–648

Body: East Lancashire Coachbuilders, with front entrance and centre exit.
Seats: 53.
Dimensions: 50 ft x 8 ft.
Bogies: BCT 5 ft 6 in wheelbase, with Metalistik suspension and SAB brakes.
Controllers: Brush chopper control.
Motors: EE 305 (2 x 57 h.p.).
Notes: 641 delivered 1984, has roof-mounted display advertising boxes 648 (then 651) delivered April 1985, and was on loan from GEC Traction, and fitted with Maley & Taunton bogies with experimental switched reluctance motors. Purchase of the body effected in 1988, and re-equipped as car 641–647 and renumbered 648 in January 1990.
642–644 delivered in 1986 and entered service in 1987
645–646 delivered in 1987 and entered service 1987/8
647 delivered in 1988 and entered service May 1988
648 entered service on 3rd January 1990

---

appearances throughout the year. A new development in 1987 was the commissioning of a replica crossbench car from Bolton Trams Ltd, an organisation dedicated to restoring and building vintage tramcars. The frame of OMO 7 was used as the basis and the resulting Vanguard numbered 619 looked entirely different. It was delivered in July, and after some minor difficulties went into service during the Illuminations. The concept of creating replica vintage trams is an option which Blackpool Transport are considering as part of their future operating policy. The development of light rail transit in Britain which is having a resurgence in some of the major cities, may well affect the future for the Blackpool & Fleetwood Tramway, which has for so long kept the concept of railed electric traction alive in this country.

There will always be a sense of history on the line, and it is with a personal sense of pleasure that tramroad car 40 is returning in 1988 for the 90th Anniversary of trams between the two towns. It left Blackpool in 1963 for the National Tramway Museum, and has since been operated at Heaton Park in Manchester, where it has been restored. Through the generosity of Lofthouses, makers of Fisherman's Friend cough lozenges, 40 is being thoroughly overhauled and returned to running order for Blackpool. Members of the Fylde Tramway Society have also given their time and money to make its return possible, while much work has been done in Manchester by members of the MTMS. The sight of the old car speeding through the fields at Rossall with its trolley rope billowing in the wind, will recall the pride and spirit of Cameron's Kingdom, where it all started in 1898.

Above: The 100th birthday of steam tram "John Bull" with Dr Robert Tebb as driver, just after the procession, having returned from Harrowside.
Author

Left: GEC car 651 of 1985 and conduit car 4 of 1885 outside Blundell Street depot in Centenary year.
Anthony Stevenson

CHAPTER 5

A NEW COMPANY TRAMWAY 1986–1998

A New Organisation

The Centenary was effectively the swansong of the Municipal era: at the end of the 1986 season, on 26th October, Blackpool Transport Services (BTS) became the operator of the trams and buses. The Borough of Blackpool retained the ownership of the track, overhead line, electrical distribution system and the depots, but the trams became the property of BTS. The maintenance of the infrastructure would be the responsibility of the borough council, supported financially by Lancashire County Council. The company would pay the Borough 50% of the tramway profits, which must not be less than £25 000 per annum. A new logo displaced the historic Corporation badge, and Mr. Tony Depledge became the Managing Director. The Chairman of the Board was Councillor Robert Battersby, who had been Mayor in the Centenary year. The new situation presented some strange anomalies: the track gang was now employed by the borough, but the overhead line men were employed by the company, whose renewal work costs were charged to the borough.

Centenary cars 642–644 were delivered in November and December and all the new bogies were waiting at the depot in front of the compound. A further three cars were ordered for delivery in April 1987, financed by shares in the new Blackpool Transport Services, but a further three were reconsidered in the light of costs and the necessity for winter service. While the original borough plan had been to acquire ten Centenary cars to replace the OMOs, BTS thought that if the GEC car 651 was re-equipped, there would be eight Centenary cars, and two Jubilee double-deckers in the same category. Thus there would be ten OPOs (one person operated) for the winter service, requiring eight in service. Subsequently from experience, it had been felt that there should have been a further two Centenary cars, which would have completed the programme to eliminate the OMOs, and yet not deprive the fleet of the necessary trams. The eight Centenary trams thus replaced thirteen OMOs, resulting in the loss of five trams from the fleet. Incidentally the original Centenary car 641 was fitted with illuminated advertising roof panels, which added to its appearance and effective stature. The other cars of the same type were designed to be fitted with the same roof panels by Blackpool Transport,

but sadly remained without, leaving 642–648 of a diminutive appearance dominated by a tall tower for a diamond pantograph. Clearly there could always be an improvement by enhancing their appearance and increasing their number by two Centenaries, thus creating a distinctive class – as planned!

The OMOs were withdrawn as the mileage of 160 000 was reached. 3, 6 and 7 were withdrawn in 1986, leaving six in service. Significantly 11 had the Corporation badge in the green livery, along with 1, 5 & 8 in this colour, 12 in red and 10 in advertising livery for Bispham Kitchen. Under BTS, advertising liveries became more common, e.g. Brush car 623 was showing the Viking Hotel and railcoach 679 depicted the Isle of Man boat sailings. Following the example of the Hong Kong fleet, all-over advertising provides a revenue for Blackpool Transport Services, but the fleet livery continues to exist in the fine tradition of transport history! The majority of Balloons are in the standard livery with advertisements on the upper panels but Coronation 660, Boat 605 and Balloons 700 & 703 today show the original handsome livery appropriate to each type.

The events of 1987 continued with the popular historic trams, and on 4th July Keith Terry organised the 'Topless Tour', using Howth 10, Dreadnought 59 and open–top Balloon 706. This created a fine sight along the Promenade to Starr Gate and then Fleetwood, in perfect sunshine with the open-top seats well filled by enthusiasts enjoying the tradition. Centenary 651 – still equipped with GEC equipment and ex-Coronation Maley & Taunton bogies – was occasionally seen, but its running proved noisy from the trucks and brakes. A new development in this year was the commissioning of a replica crossbench car from Bolton Trams Ltd, an organisation dedicated to restoring and building vintage tramcars. The frame of OMO 7 was used

Right: North Albert Street with Howth 10 playing the role as a Liverpool tram during the filming of 'A Man from the Pru'. Vintage vehicles and 66 showing PIER HEAD on it's blind complete the scene.
R.P. Fergusson

as the basis and the resulting Vanguard, numbered 619, looked entirely different. It was delivered on 29th July from Mode Wheel in Salford, and thus it was the same length as an OMO but with an open platform, while the crossbench saloon was enclosed by a waist rail and perspex screen. While it was intended to capture the traditional appearance of the Tramroad Company Vanguard, unfortunately a trolley tower was surmounted by a pantograph, and the tapered-end made it clearly a rebuilt OMO. The concept of creating replica vintage trams was an option which BTS were considering as part of their future operating policy. Consequently the underframes of OMOs 3 & 4 were retained at Thornton Gate sidings, and are still there ten years later! During that season the Fleetwood service was crew operated by OMOs and Centenaries, alternating with the Balloons and increasing capacity on the route. By the end of the year 646 was in service, while the track in Gynn Square was re-laid improving the double curve from North Shore to Queens Drive.

Below: Fleetwood Tram Sunday in 1988 made a welcome return to the traditional Tramroad Box 40, seen here in North Albert Street together with vintage buses from many towns. **Author**

Top Left: A striking view of Centenary 647 in Lord Street on a Sunday in 1987, with the traditional buildings and the Rowntree clock tower in Albert Square – the location for many tram scenes over a Century! **Author**

Centre left: The launching of restored Marton Box car 31 at Beamish on 17th August 1988, which is being enjoyed by the public – in the sunny weather! **Ian McLoughlin**

Right: Track-laying in North Albert Street in January 1990, showing the foundations and the rail newly-welded, with wooden blocks temporarily keeping them level. The men are well wrapped up for warmth. **Author**

Left: Two vintage trams together in May 1990 – B&F Box 40 and Dreadnought 59 - on tour in the final season before 59 returns to the National Tramway Museum at Crich. **Author**

Below left: 701 restored with the new mounted-windows and without the upper deck curved ones, but very attractive in the red-and-white livery like the Routemasters here. **Author**

Below right: OMO 5 acquired a smarter appearance in the new fleet livery, seen here at Cabin in September 1991 during its final season. **Author**

Epic Festivities

1988 was very notable for tramway events in Beamish, Glasgow and Blackpool. In January work upon Marton Box Car 31 was progressing well at the North East Open Air Museum, restoring it to 1919–1928 open–top condition. It was launched in September, looking very spectacular in its red and white livery fully lined-out in gold and red, with bevelled glass in the saloon windows. While the Museum had committed a considerable amount of money towards restoration from its Works car 4 condition, Blackpool had retained ownership with rights for its return upon special occasions. Consequently it is now possible to look forward to 31's return to Blackpool, in keeping with the 1998 Centenary of the Blackpool & Fleetwood Tramroad. Further north, the Glasgow Garden Festival was created on the banks of the Clyde, with a delightful tramway through the site using a vintage fleet of trams from the National Tramway Museum (NTM) and Blackpool. In the month of March, Boat 606 departed in the blue and yellow livery advertising beer, along with Edinburgh 35 which had been smartened up by the body and paint shops. While in Blackpool, 35 had operated for the first time since in its native city of Edinburgh in 1956. The NTM provided Paisley 68, Glasgow Standard 22 and Cunarder 1297, and we enthusiasts made a preliminary visit to enjoy the first tramride in that city since the last Glasgow tram ran in 1962.

However, in Blackpool there will always be a sense of history on the tramway, and it was with a personal sense of pleasure that Blackpool & Fleetwood Tramroad car 40 was to return in 1988 for the 90th Anniversary of trams between the two towns. It had left Blackpool in 1963 for the National Tramway Museum, and had been operated at Heaton Park in Manchester since 1979, where it had been restored. In January that year, BTS Managing Director Tony Depledge commented that Box 40 was to return to Blackpool in time for the Fleetwood Tram Sunday on 17th July: "At this stage it is a question of finding out what needs to be done and what sort of money involved." While the car body had been restored with external repanelling, repainting, lettering and lining in gold leaf, very little engineering work had been done. Thus the wheels needed re-tyring, the electrical circuits rewiring and the motors servicing. At this stage there was an appeal to enthusiasts towards the costs, but since this would not be adequate sponsorship by a famous local firm Lofthouses 'Fisherman's Friend' was sought. In return for the payment of £7000. Lofthouses would advertise discretely upon 40 and the essential work could commence, organised by 'Friends of 40'.

It was pleasing to find that the re-tyring of the wheels was completed by BR Derby in April, and 40 was reunited with its bogies at Heaton Park. The rewiring was then complete and a working-party from Blackpool was busy repainting the display boards and the saloon floor. 40 ran for the last time in Heaton Park on Sunday 12th June together with Boat 600, and arrived in Blackpool on Tuesday 14th June. For its first trip in Blackpool since 1963, 40 was driven to North Pier with the working party from Heaton Park. Unfortunately on the return journey one of the motors failed, and on the following day was sent to a specialist firm for rewiring. It was repaired by 16th July, when it went on a tour for the 'Friends of 40' and was able to lead the procession of trams to Fleetwood Tram Sunday on the following day. By this time 40 was carrying the advertisements for 'Fisherman's Friend' on its panels above the saloon windows and also large panels fitted between the bogies, concealing the fenders. While this was one disadvantage to the car's appearance, two very neat metallic plaques were fitted on each internal bulkhead giving a brief history of the car.

> **"BLACKPOOL FLEETWOOD TRAMROAD COMPANY No. 40"**
> **BUILT IN 1914**
> **BY THE UNITED ELECTRIC CAR COMPANY, PRESTON**
> **PRESENTED TO THE NATIONAL TRAMWAY MUSEUM, CRICH, DERBYSHIRE**
> **IN 1963 BY BLACKPOOL BOROUGH COUNCIL**
> **RESTORED BY MEMBERS OF THE FYLDE TRAMWAY SOCIETY AND MANCHESTER TRAMWAY MUSEUM SOCIETY:– 1981–1988**
> **RETURNED TO BLACKPOOL FOR THE 90TH ANNIVERSARY OF THE BLACKPOOL & FLEETWOOD TRAMROAD 1898–1998**
> **SPONSORED BY LOFTHOUSES 'FISHERMAN'S FRIEND' PRODUCTS**

A further development took place in early August, with the refitting of the indicator boxes, which had been removed from 40 during restoration. Blackpool wanted these to be in-keeping with current operational requirements, although 40 is in the Company livery and thus carried the Corporation indicator boxes in the post-1920 era. Early in 1989 'Friends of Forty' arranged the removal of the seat cushions for re–upholstering at the workshop of Mode Wheel. When they returned and were fitted, 40's saloon was graced by attractive ruby–coloured seats in a Scotch–plaid pattern. It so happens that this was obtained from Blackpool Transport and was originally used in the AEC Swift buses. Following

Left: Brush car 298 at Mode Wheel workshop in Salford in 1996, showing its original saloon end and lights, alhambrinal-type ceiling and the missing sliding roof. **Author**

all this attention to 40 since its arrival, it became a useful asset to the tramway fleet – in a long tradition!

The sight of the vintage car speeding through the fields at Rossall with its trolley rope billowing in the wind, will recall the pride and spirit of Cameron's Kingdom, where it all started in 1898.

Incidentally restoration work had been proceeding on Brush car 298 (635) at MSC workshops at Smithills, Bolton, with the body suspended above the underframe. In this position the frame could be grit–blasted and new corner plates fitted to strengthen it. The cabs had been taken off and replaced by new frames and flooring, while new domes had been made by British Aerospace at Warton from galvanised steel sheets. A considerable amount of work was carried out on every feature of 298, including overhaul of the controller, new air pipes and grit–blasting of seat frames, before the body was re–assembled in February 1988. Certainly this looked very encouraging and subsequently it was transferred to Mode Wheel in Salford. In 1997 however, 298 was still not complete, though there was some hope of its return to Blackpool for the Tramroad Centenary. Now it seems that the detailed restoration by Keith Terry and his team – with the sliding sunshine roofs, winding down saloon windows and stainless steel mouldings shaped on the panels – will prevent its return for commercial operation with the other Brush cars in the Centenary year.

Contrasting Fleet Events

Events continued to provide interest for the tramway enthusiasts in 1989, with the evolution of the tramway fleet – and its respective departure. Four of the OMO Cars – 5, 8, 10 and 11 – were in use during the year, while 1 and 12 were scrapped in December.

In April there was a fascinating scene in Fleetwood when the BBC filmed their drama 'A Man from the Pru', set in Liverpool during 1931. Of course the authentic street scene – using North Albert Street and Pharos Street – required period cars, lorries and trams. Bolton 66 and Howth 10 were used. The two trams carried the Liverpool Corporation Transport fleet name and showed the famous destination of 'PIER HEAD' on their indicators, together with period adverts. They were given a cosmetic overhaul, so as to appear well–used and battered, concealing their smart restoration livery. The filming took place on Sunday 9th April, and the local tram service had to be terminated at Ash Street with a shuttle bus service to the ferry. Subsequently the removal of the transfers used was found to have damaged the paintwork, and the two trams had to be repainted. When they appeared on Fleetwood Tram Sunday in pristine appearance, Bolton 66 and Howth 10 were restored fully into their native liveries. Unfortunately on this occasion Howth 10 came to a halt outside the library in North Albert Street, with its motors 'grounded' on the raised tarmac between the rails. It had to be shunted clear by Boat 607 and was returned to Blackpool, safely from this track! The National Tramway Museum duly claimed Howth 10 to return there, and a final tour was held on 21st October when devotees enjoyed a memorable ride along the Tramroad. I always remember sitting on the longitudinal seats in the lower saloon and thus facing outwards as the view passed. The motion of the car was a gentle swaying, while there was an uneven rhythm of the Peckham maximum traction bogies, making a different sound. A large crowd at the North Albert Street tram stop looked hopeful as Howth 10 reversed on Kent Street crossover, but it grounded again and was pushed clear by the next service car. Certainly Howth 10 was very popular and ideal for a seaside resort, but since its return to NTM it has remained purely on display in the Exhibition Hall – a sad loss to Blackpool and the tourists.

During that year, Blackpool's compensation for the loss of the visiting vintage trams was the repainting of Brush car 636 in the wartime livery of an English Electric railcoach. In largely green livery, with cream lines and end flares, BTS used this eye–catching livery as a useful setting for adverts of Travelcards and Fylde Coast Rovers. This, along with the original curved roof windows which gave the passengers better upper–views, made the 636 distinctive from the other Brush cars. Further developments of the fleet proved interesting, as the Boats were fitted with new twin–windscreens. 602 was painted in the yellow and black Handybus livery and 604 was in the red and white Routemaster livery. By December of this year, 648 was ready for service and fitted with the Brush Chopper control equipment, but its first day of service was not until 3rd January 1990. In the same month, 701 became the first of the Balloons to be rebuilt substantially, with rubber–mounted windows in safety glass and an altered front appearance without the traditional upper-deck curved glass. In the saloons reversible seats were replaced by fixed Routemaster seats, facing outwards at each end, and new concealed panels of lights installed. When 701 appeared on 17th February 1991 for photographs, it undoubtedly looked very striking in its new form, especially enhanced by the red and white livery, fully lined in the style of the Routemaster. While the colours were of the pre-1933 fleet livery 701 remained unique, while establishing the Balloons with a rebuilding policy for the future!

Left: 754 making its trial run at Cleveleys early in 1993, showing its clear desigination, ventilators for the engine, lamps on its upper deck handrail and the inspection platform from 753. **Eric Berry**

Right: A scene in the Paint Shop on 13th July as 40 is being prepared for Tram Sunday once more, in the correct shade of the Company livery. The pictures on the dash are for the guidance of the artists doing the work. **Author**

Centre left: An unusual sight at Westbourne Road tram stop with 754 under its own power towing 260, taking new poles to Broadwater in May 1994. **Author**

Right: Friends of 40, who raised funds for its return and restoration, were allowed a free tour on 10th August, seen here at Fleetwood Ferry. **Author**

Bottom right: The appearance of Stockport 5 at Tram Sunday 1996 proved to be unique, since it carried a team of restorers at speed and had to rest at Fleetwood Ferry to cool down with its trolley off! **Author**

Below: A remarkable scene as the two native Hong Kong trams 69 & 70 in the Birkenhead fleet, are seen on Central Promenade near the Tower, en-route to Fleetwood. **R.P. Fergusson**

The New Decade of the Nineties

Commencing a new age, in which would occur the Centenary of the Blackpool & Fleetwood Tramroad, the year 1990 included a variety of events. In January work was under way on the relaying of the track in North Albert Street, Fleetwood, while service trams terminated at Ash Street. However, away from Blackpool, work had been on schedule for the construction of a tramway at the Gateshead Garden Festival and in Manchester work was about to begin on laying the Metrolink tramway from Victoria Station to Piccadilly. In April new-style tram stops had been fitted, complete with the Blackpool & Fleetwood Tramway logo, each stop was named, with the direction 'NORTHBOUND' or 'SOUTHBOUND' indicated. From the fleet, the year had commenced with Centenary 646 in a new-style livery, simplified with a green roof and skirt, rather than the zig-zag lines also seen on the OMOs. Following the aesthetics of new liveries for the Boat cars, 605 was described as 'Cinderella', neglected and dirty at the back of the depot, so that the Fylde Tramway Society offered to pay for the refurbishment in its original livery. When it appeared for the convention in May, it looked more striking and eye–catching than the other Boats.

In sad contrast was the dramatic fire of Engineering Car 753 at Gynn Square at 6.30 a.m. on Saturday 30th June which arose from being under power by its engine. Having been dealt with by the fire brigade, 753 was withdrawn from service, having been created from Standard 143 in 1958. At the end of the season Dreadnought 59 was also withdrawn from the Blackpool scene, having been a popular open-top tram since its restoration for Blackpool's Centenary in 1976 by Blackpool Technical College. A final tour was held on Sunday 11th November, which ironically included a photographic stop outside the historic Foxhall public house due for demolition, and a full ride from Starr Gate to Fleetwood. Since 59 returned to the National Tramway Museum on 14th November, it has never been operated and is stored out of view in the Clay Cross store. Since the original design was bought by Blackpool Council from Mr Shrewsbury of Camwell in 1897, it thus created the Dreadnoughts as unique and with

A splendid scene in Fleetwood with Coronation 660 and Boat 605 in May 1990, standing parallel at Kent Street as though they are in a race! 605 is newly restored in traditional livery with FTS badges on the side panels. **Author**

Boat 600 was located at Heaton Park in Manchester. It is seen here at the front gate with some visitors from Blackpool. It has since returned to the seaside for the Centenary in 1998, as pioneer Boat 225. **Author**

It is amazing what passes your bedroom window in Market Street, San Francisco – Blackpool Boat 228, very popular with the locals and tourists, is seen advertising Bay Bridge anniversary in 1986 on surface streetcar line F. **Author**

advantages! Consequently there is a local feeling that 59 should return to its native town where it would be welcomed and appreciated at the turn of the Century!

By the end of 1990, the creation of a new tramway in Manchester was evidenced by the track in High Street, Mosley Street and Aytoun Street. In January 1991 work on the Metrolink started in Piccadilly and on the ramp next to the G-Mex Centre, as a link with the Altrincham line. Good news also came from Sheffield, with the Government granting permission and funding for the creation of a Supertram system at a cost of £230 million. In contrast to the new track–laying scene in cities, Blackpool provided a maintenance scene since, in Fleetwood, the Ferry loop-line was being re-laid and the service trams were turning on the Kent Street crossover. By this time the number of Balloons fitted with pantographs had increased to nine, and trolleys were gradually disappearing. In the 1990 Company Report, published in March, it was stated that there had been considerable growth in the Travelcard business, with 160 agents selling them. During the winter it had been found that the Centenary cars were being frozen-up in Arctic conditions, while the four remaining OMO cars with conventional equipment continued in service! The old Foxhall Inn had been demolished at this time, while the track gang had been carrying out maintenance to the adjacent tram track before the resurfacing of Princess Street.

In June a pleasant surprise was the repainting of OMO 5 in the new style of livery, emphasising that it was still a valuable member of the fleet. The programme to increase the number of pantographs in the fleet at this time was established by the appearance of twin car 677 appropriately fitted in June, only seven Balloons then being left with trolleys. Box 40 had begun to look a sorry sight, as its gold leaf lining was partially missing and it numbers had faded. Blackpool Transport had offered to restore the appearance of the panelling, but the Tramway Museum Society decided that 40 should return to the museum as an historic exhibit at the end of the season. Unfortunately on 30th July 40 failed outside the Imperial Hotel by one of its motors and gears seizing up, causing a huge delay to the tram service. 40 was lifted and towed back to the depot by the Diamond-T vehicle, where the rewinding of the motor was carried out. Meanwhile, Manchester's first new tram 1001 was delivered to its Queens Road depot on 29th August, and here Boat 606 was driven to Foxhall for the opening of the new pub in Princess Street!

With the final day of the 1991 illuminations on 3rd November, Box 40 made a farewell trip along its native tramroad to Fleetwood for a party of enthusiasts. Waiting at the depot, the saloon of 40 was bright and welcoming, with its lights blazing in the gloom, the red tartan moquette of the seats and cheerful bunting decorating the windows. The journey to Fleetwood was brisk – especially around Rossall – demonstrating the smoothest ride in the fleet. When 40 left Fleetwood Ferry for the final time at 6.00 p.m., it was ironic that fate was to intervene to prevent its departure from Fleetwood. In North Albert Street the tram track was blocked by an Irish Sea trailer, bound for the docks. As the truck resisted all attempts to move it, there was a feeling that the ghost of John Cameron – the Tramroad Manager – was trying to keep 40 in its native town! However, a return visit to the Ferry and an exit on the northbound track, ensured its final return to the depot and certainly 40's days of glory here were over. It departed for Crich on 10th December, Blackpool Transport removing the indicator boxes and modern lights. While 40 went on display in the Exhibition Hall at the National Tramway Museum, it did not operate and was consigned to the store at Clay Cross with Dreadnought 59. However, locally thoughts were being given to 40 for the Tramroad Centenary in 1998!

An interesting review of 1991 was given by BTS Managing Director Tony Depledge to the Fylde Tramway Society. Certainly 1991 had not been an easy year; there were fewer visitors but there had been a growth in the sale of Travelcards. A new engineering car was under construction by East Lancashire Coachbuilders, and would be fitted with a diesel engine, while resembling the Centenaries in appearance. Regarding the visiting of vintage cars again, he mentioned the possible loan of Stockport 5 and a discussion with Beamish about the return of Sheffield 513. During the year, Blackpool Transport would receive two Hong Kong cars which were destined for the new Wirral Heritage Tramway. He hoped to have at least one example of an OMO tram for continued operation and eventual preservation. He said "I still believe in the future of the tramway here in Blackpool and the major role which it plays in the tourist industry of the town. Thus it is a major asset to the town, and we remain committed to its future."

Right: The poster announces that the trams will return shortly, and here is the first tram on 27th April 1992 carrying the Manchester coat-of-arms and the same number as the Last Tram in 1949!
Anthony Stevenson

'Trams Return To Manchester'

Undoubtedly the great tramway event of 1992 was seen in Manchester, when on Monday 6th April trams entered service from Bury to Victoria Station. The first tram to travel through the City Centre to G-Mex on 27th April was 1007 carrying a plaque 'It's great to be back – Trams Return to Manchester'. Significantly 1007 – carrying the City coat-of-arms on its front – held the same number as Manchester's last tram in 1949. Undoubtedly the sight of a modern tram gliding down Mosley Street attracted the attention of the Mancunians – in amazement – and added European modernity to the scene! Subsequently, on 17th July, there was a visit by HM the Queen, who formally inaugurated the system in St Peter's Square by boarding a tram for Bury. The success of Manchester's £133 million investment in Metrolink has proved that tram services along private right–of–way, and travelling along the City Centre streets, are ideal for the residents who need access from the suburbs to the heart of the city. Here the Blackpool & Fleetwood Tramroad had for nearly 100 years provided the evidence that unhindered travel on reservation with easy access for the public was desirable. Following the modern light rail development in Manchester, other cities were interested in planning new systems, while detailed design was under way in Sheffield.

The Blackpool scene was more mundane in that year. In January two trams were stranded at Rossall owing to freezing fog, with frost insulating the overhead from collection by the pantographs. Centenary 647 had failed to stop at Cocker Street and hit seven cars which were waiting for the traffic lights, and consequently it was concluded that the low temperature had frozen open the air-brake valve open. Sadly, buses replaced the trams in service showing route number 1, formerly used by trams until 1963,

THE THIRTEENTH FLEETWOOD TRAM SUNDAY

All facing page:

Top left: Bolton 66 dominates the scene and intimidates the modern buses from Reading and Manchester, however the public are watching a display by the clog dancers!   **Author**

Top right: The next of the special trams between the Ferry and Ash Street is 719, adding a most unusual and colourful attraction and tempting it's many passengers for ice cream!   **Author**

Bottom: However Tramroad Box 40 is in its correct location, as a native since 1914 and announcing the Centenary in 1998.
                                          Author

THE WALLS ICE-CREAM TRAM

Left: The walls Ice Cream tram No. 719 is very eye-catching with its colourful shapely features.   **Ian McLoughlin**

Below left: The Walls Ice Cream Parlour where ice cream can be purchased on a tram journey in 719.   **Ian McLoughlin**

Below right: The upper saloon with bright red seats, yellow hand rails, but a darkened end.   **Ian McLoughlin**

on the North Station & Fleetwood route. Elsewhere, at the East Lancashire Coachworks in Blackburn, work had started on the new Engineering car 754 during January, with EE Z4 controllers, engine and generator-set delivered by Blackpool Transport. At this time talks were taking place with NORWEB regarding replacement of feeder cables to the tramway and the illuminations. Alarmingly Blackpool Borough Council had become anxious to cut expenditure, and found that money could be saved by terminating the trams at Bispham. Fortunately consideration was given to grants from various sources, including the Government, EEC, Lancashire CC and Wyre Borough Council.

On the tramcar front, railcoach 680 was repainted in the handsome revised livery in spring and fitted with a pantograph. The four remaining OMOs were being used in service to compensate for the absent Centenaries under repair, although 644 was about to take over the advertising livery for Bispham Kitchens from OMO 10. There was concern about the repainted OMO 5, which was withdrawn when it needed extensive repairs to the underframe; however it did return by June. Boat 604 was the first to be fitted with a pantograph, but for safety a nylon rope was attached to the plate-skate to avoid it hitting exposed passengers if it fell off. From May work progressed on the refurbishment of Coronation 660 with repanelling, resealing of roof windows, new platform flooring, it was also to be fitted with streamlining in stainless steel and chrome–covered aluminium. This work was funded by the Fylde Tramway Society, whose members were pleased to play a part in the restoration of such a significant tram in the history of the Tramroad. When yellow and black Boat 602 was fitted with a pantograph in July and, with red and white

Above: The rather sad appearance of 753 in the depot after its fire in June 1990. Having now been replaced by 754, it is stored for future restoration as Standard 143. **Author**

Above right: Box 40 seen in the Fitting Shop over the pits for inspection after its breakdown on 30th July 1991 but looking as handsome as ever! **Author**

Below: Storm clouds gather as 40 makes its final nostalgic journey to Fleetwood on 3rd November 1991, with its saloon decorated. **Author**

604, attended Fleetwood Tram Sunday – the Author doubted the appropriateness of the situation, since the sliding pantograph would shower the passengers with dirt in the wet weather. This was proved correct, following claims from passengers for damaged clothing, and the trolleys were returned eventually, restoring their appearance and safety. During summer, Bolton 66 was fitted with air-brakes and Engineering car 754 was delivered on 28th August, with wiring still to be completed. Elsewhere – by coincidence – construction of the Sheffield infrastructure had now started on the Meadowhall line, which would result in a 32 km network on three lines, including Middlewood, Malin Bridge and Halfway. The two 'Hong Kong' type cars, 69 & 70 in the Birkenhead fleet, were delivered to Blackpool on Thursday 1st October, but the Railway Inspectors subsequently recommended modifications – including full-length platform doors. The year concluded with the return of OMO 5 to service in November and 754 commenced the 'Engineering' trials in December.

A Significant Tramway Report

A detailed report on the Tramways and illuminations electrical infrastructure by Merz & McLellan (Consulting Engineers) was presented to the Policy Committee of Blackpool Borough Council in January 1993. They found that the electrical infrastructure systems for the tramway, illuminations and street lighting were in poor condition and suffered from similar problems. The problems had been caused by under-investment, and by the systems being continuously modified over many years, resulting in the depreciation of the electrical performance, reliability and

safety. The report declared that much of the equipment was life-expired and no longer complied with current electrical safety legislation. Many of the problems were listed, including: inadequate earthing and bonding, safety hazards caused by unguarded switchgear, pillars and tableaux, potential switching errors caused by the complexity of feeder networks, hazards risked by overhead-line staff because of inadequate section insulators and earthing, and the absence of centralised control and supervisory facilities. The report continued by identifying traction and illumination poles as being of considerable but uncertain age, and weakened by saline corrosion and the over-straining of the illuminations catenary wires. During the refurbishment work, all the poles were to be replaced, loading limits restricted and a pole-numbering scheme devised. There were considerable concerns about the illuminations infrastructure, which suffered from poor fault-protection and earthing standards, especially on the Cliffs tableaux. Comments in the report attributed the good safety record to Blackpool's experienced technicians and craftsmen, but urged that formal safety rules and procedures be established. In the report Merz & McLellan evolved and recommended a new infrastructure scheme, fully costed and feasible from the engineering and operational view points, and strongly recommended its adoption. Before this was undertaken, there was a suggestion that the involved concerns – including Blackpool Transport Services – make decisions about the future: overhead line support design, new substation buildings integration, and agreement upon the metering of electrical supply. Finally the consultants recommended a swift resolution of the funding issues so that contracts could be let before the 1994 season. The local press indicated that £7 million would be the cost of such a scheme and that £4.5 million could be eligible for grant-aid by the Government. Apparently the report indicated a saving of £1.5 million would necessitate the pruning of the tramway system – and illuminations – to Pleasure Beach in the south, and the tramway to Thornton Gate in the north.

The Council adopted the report, but the time taken to secure funding delayed the letting of a contract until November 1994. The contract was won by James Scott Ltd of Preston, with AMEC Power and Brecknell Willis acting as their tramway overhead line sub-contractors. Project Management and Site Supervision services were provided to the Council by Merz & McLellan, acting as their engineers. The work had to be accurately dovetailed with the town's summer and illuminations seasons, so the bulk of the construction work was achieved over three winter periods 1995/1996/1997, working from Thornton Gate to Starr Gate. Completion of the authorised contract work was achieved in April 1997, with the overhead of the depot fan. At the time of going to press, the financial arrangements are not yet in place to renew the infrastructure north of Thornton Gate. This work would comprise of the replacement of the overhead-line poles and fittings, and the provision of two new sub-stations at Copse Road and Broadwater; its cost is estimated at around £1 million. There is certainly the will to complete this work, and it is hoped that a contract can be let to achieve completion before the end of 1999.

Above: When Blackpool Transport Services assumed control, its own insignia replaced the traditional coat-of-arms, as seen here on 678 at Starr Gate in May 1987.   **Ian McLoughlin**

Top right: Boat 602 is non-typical but attractive on the tramroad – seen here passing through the playing fields of Cardinal Allen High School.   **Author**

Above: Two Balloons passing at Broadwater – a new tradition since 1958 – but Fleetwood Road and the Post Office stay the same!   **Author**

Left: The striking appearance of newly-restored Boat 600 with open-topped double-decker 706 at Fleetwood Ferry for the Fylde Tramway Society convention on 3rd May 1998.   **Author**

Nostalgic and Positive Developments

On the fleet front, some subsequent nostalgic occasions took place when the OMOs operated in-service for the last time. OMO 5 had been used for the seasonal Tower & Cleveleys shuttle, and then replaced Centenary 647 on 30th December, but was last seen on 2nd January 1993. The finale came on 18th March, when OMO 11 replaced 647, but was withdrawn after a decision by the Traffic and Engineering Departments. Both of these events proved how useful a small reserve of OMOs would have been, since the eight Centenary cars are two–less than planned –and unreliable! However, consolation was given to OMO 11 when it gained a new role in testing the technical suitability

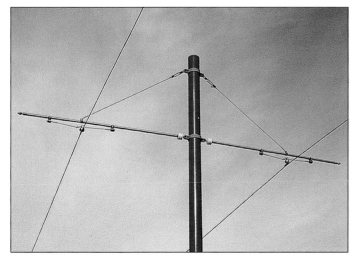

Above: The new standard overhead line equipment showing the slender stainless steel spacer arms and support wires. **Peter Fox**

Right: Blackpool & Fleetwood crossbench (toastrack) No. 2 after restoration at Crich. **Author**

Below: The new Roadliner, No. 611 on its gauging trial at Ash Street Fleetwood at 6.45 a.m. on 2nd June 1998. **Author**

Left: In 1993 the only OMO to be seen was 11, undertaking trials for the Tram Power bogie, hidden by a hinged flap. OMO 11 wore a plain livery and had shaded windows, but notice the bunny in the cab window – for safety! **Terry Daniel**

Centre left: The presentation of a plaque for Coronation 660 to Tony Depledge by the FTS, in the presence of Daphne Luff, daughter of Walter Luff, following the restoration of 660 with correct streamlining. **Eric Berry**

of a new type of bogie, and was sent to Carnforth Railway Works to be prepared. It duly returned on 18th November with the new bogie and equipment fitted, ready for trials on behalf of Tram Power's articulated car. At the 'Light Rail 94' exhibition in Birmingham, an interesting design of the new articulated car was shown by its front-section. OMOs 1 & 12 were broken-up in December to make room in the depot for the articulated car whilst on trial – possibly in the near future – or so it seemed at the time!

Fortunately there were positive developments in the existing fleet when Balloons 716 and 726 were fitted with new windscreens and lightweight folding doors on the platforms. In March, Balloon 723 appeared after a major overhaul with these features, and new–style bumpers rather than the traditional fenders. A major policy of overhauls for the Brush cars commenced with 632 appearing in the new–style livery with a green roof and short–skirt on the panels. While considerable work was completed on the structure of the ends, more obvious were the rubber–mounted windows surrounded by matt black paint. The Hong Kong trams, Birkenhead 69 & 70, were seen under test on the Promenade in June, and 70 appeared at Fleetwood Tram Sunday creating great interest in the traditional event, which had been deprived of the vintage trams since the departure of Box 40 in 1991. An interesting event occurred on 14th July with the presentation of a plaque for Coronation 660 to Tony Depledge, by the Fylde Tram Society, in the presence of Daphne Luff who is the daughter of the famous Walter Luff. The Evening Gazette reported

Left: The rebuilding of Brush car 626 in the body shop during 1994, showing the composition of the body lines and the new metal frame ends. Comparison with 1937 scenes of construction in Chapter 2, would be interesting. **Author**

Right: 626 in the new fleet livery, complete with matt black around the rubber-mounted windows. Notice the open windscreen and the sausage shaped lower glass and that there are no lifeguards.　　　**R.P. Fergusson**

Centre right: June 1992, a scene in the fitting shop showing 723 being stripped of its panelling prior to its rebuilding in the body shop. Behind it is Vanguard 619 – rebuilt from OMO 7.　　　**Philip Higgs**

that "the legendary Transport boss" was commemorated by the Coronation, "a green + cream memorial to the late Walter Luff".

Turning to other matters, it was stated that Manchester Metrolink had carried 9 million passengers during the first year of operation, and that there were prospects for the growth of the system – to Eccles, Wythenshawe, Ashton and Rochdale. There was now interchange in Piccadilly between Bury and Altrincham cars, and reduction in the price of peak fares, taking passengers from relevant bus services. In Sheffield the Supertrams were tested in the City Centre on 5th November. They were larger than those in Manchester with capacity for 250 passengers, but seats only for 88. A total of 25 were due to be delivered, and it was thought that the first route to Meadowhall would open in January 1994. Undoubtedly this situation was exciting for tramway enthusiasts, and commended the example of the surviving Blackpool & Fleetwood Tramroad!

Returning to the more mundane matters in Blackpool, the Lancashire County Council had agreed to continue its financial support towards maintaining the tramway at an annual cost of £956 300 – and thus gave half the total. As part of the agreement with the independent Blackpool Transport Services, they would give half of the tramway profits to the Borough, or £25 000 if it was greater. Regarding the future of the tramway, inevitably related to the costs of renewing the Promenade infrastructure, work was to start in November 1994. It was interesting when there was public discussion about a new tramway spur

Right: Autumn 1994, new track is in position and about to be moved into place by the two men with poles, meanwhile overhauled 723 passes bound for Fleetwood.　　　**Author**

Above: The scene in St Helens Transport Museum with Coronation 304 – 641 lifted for cleaning of the M&T bogies in the forefront and new floor fitted to the saloons in 1994.

Eric Berry

Below: Subsequently in July 1995, the Coronations met again when 663 (327) arrived as a refugee from Bradford Transport Museum. The future of 327 is questionable, since Blackpool retains 660 as an historic tram and 304 retains it's original Vambac equipment.

Eric Berry

along Burlington Road to make a terminus at Pleasure Beach station. However, it proved more relevant that Blackpool Borough Council did agree to fund the improvement of the tramway infrastructure as far as Thornton Gate – a mile into Wyre Borough.

As a finale in 1993, the 'Hong Kong' Birkenhead 69 & 70 cars were used on illumination tours from North Pier, but not using the loops at Little Bispham and Starr Gate, and providing a ride for only 48 people on each car. Engineering car 754 had been out on tests during the year, and settled–down to a useful role working on the overhead repairs and rewiring, like its predecessor 753. In its yellow livery, 754 carried the traditional inspection tower from 753 and had inspection spotlights, tool cupboards and useful fire extinguishers – for familiar emergencies. While generally seen in daytime for drastic situations and rewiring, inspection duties were carried-out at night. Fortunately 754 does include a toilet and washbasin facilities for the crew - a fine modern vehicle!

A Royal Occasion

Early in 1994 Beamish informed Blackpool Transport that they could not release Sheffield 513, in response to BTS's request for its return. While it was felt too modern for the museum line where the crews wore vintage clothes, Beamish, who would be happy to return it to Blackpool, were restrained because of the ownership of 513 by York Castle Museum. Originally this Roberts car was purchased from Sheffield in 1960, by John Rothera – a member of York Minster Choir – and he did present it to the Castle Museum with a view to them using it on a constructed local tramway. Following its storage in Fulford, when it got damaged and lost one of its B–510 controllers, 513 was willingly loaned to Beamish. In 1997, 513 was lifted from its four–wheel truck during the winter while repairs were being done to the wheels, motors and frame. This is the first time that work has been undertaken in its residence there, and certainly it is known that the 9 ft wheelbase of the Maley & Taunton truck wears the curves of the track, and thus it would be more desirable at Blackpool. Here in Blackpool we have another car by Roberts – Coronation 660.

Regarding another absent tram – Coronation 304 – which last operated here in October 1970, and is housed in St. Helens Transport Museum, this was lifted from its resilient-wheel bogies which were steam-cleaned and the saloon floor was replaced. Subsequently work has been progressing well with the rewiring of the traction system. It will be splendid if, in due course, it returns to its native route to celebrate the 50th anniversary in 2002! However the Birkenhead trams made a spectacular journey to Fleetwood in May for the Fylde Tramway Society, although their members felt somewhat cramped, compared with the native-passengers in Hong Kong! On the 27th June, 70 left Blackpool for the new Wirral Heritage Tramway at Birkenhead, especially to be on display for the 60th Anniversary of the Mersey Tunnel – 16th/17th July 1994.

In the same month HM the Queen and the Duke of Edinburgh arrived at Rossall School, and were then driven along the route of the tramway to Blackpool, where they ascended the Tower and visited the Grand Theatre on the occasion of their centenaries. However, I shall always remember the scene at Rossall when pristine Balloon 710 arrived from Fleetwood full of passengers, just as the Royal Rolls Royce turned into Broadway. The tram driver, very properly, slowly drove the tram parallel with the Royal family so that the passengers could wave – and were acknowledged by the Duke of Edinburgh, who was certainly looking amused by the unusual sight, unique in the United Kingdom. Later in their journey, many trams were halted outside the Tower, giving the passengers a useful grandstand. Of course there had been a precedent for such an occasion during the Prince of Wales visit in 1927, when he opened the Miners' Home.

Returning to the tramway developments in 1994, the emergence of restored Brush car 626 from the body shop with a restyled windscreen layout, caused some observations that it restricted the forward view of the driver and his passengers. While OMO 11 continued to run trials with the new bogie, in April it derailed at Rossall Square causing some concern. In contrast, it was delightful when open-top Balloon 706 was repainted in the fleet livery again, restoring its traditional name 'Princess Alice' to the panel adjacent to the doors on each side. Regarding the Balloons, they resumed service on the Fleetwood line for the first time since 1987, six being used on Cleveleys & Pleasure Beach and others on the Fleetwood route, alternating with the Centenary cars, and increasing the capacity of the service.

A Useful Scene on the Tramroad

In May there was action beyond Thornton Gate, with the service cars reversing there and being replaced by buses to Fleetwood, during the relaying of new track at Ash Street in preparation of the new Fisherman's Walk. Leaving the reservation clear, works-car 754 and towing rail-crane 260 delivered five new traction pole between Thornton Gate and Broadwater. It was interesting to see the railcrane lift each pole on the site, while the men set them in concrete. 754 was travelling using its own generator-engine, since the power was switched off to enable working with the overhead structure. It was joined by Unimog 441, so that the crew could work from the two parallel inspection platforms, to fit the bracket arms to the new poles. By the end of the first week on 6th May a useful task was completed of phase-one. In the second week the new poles were painted – along with the neighbouring older ones – by a painter on a ladder, equipped with a sprayer, helmet and goggles. Meanwhile at Ash Street, the street track was welded and laid upon new sleepers at each side of the concrete foundation for the road crossing. This would then divert road traffic from the end of Radcliffe Road across the tramroad to Copse Road, leaving Fisherman's Walk a pedestrian precinct. In the third week 754, now moving with it's trolley drawing power, was seen at various locations to the north of Thornton Gate. With 754 was a working team mounted on the platform, painting the tops of the poles and the bracket arms, these being out of reach to the ladder–mounted painter. Permanent-way cars 259 and 260 were seen collecting the old dismantled poles from their location. By the end of the week, the road crossing was prepared for the road–surface, together with the traffic lights and signals

for the trams, and the trams could return to Fleetwood again. This proved an efficient Tramroad exercise!

In the Managing Director's Report in April, Tony Depledge reported depot improvements consisting of new lighting and canteen facilities. There was also reference to Balloon 723 being refurbished at a cost of £50 000. Regarding the Promenade infrastructure, he said that the Borough Council recognised that the system needed renewal at a cost of £7 million, of which £3 million included new traction poles, feeders and substations for the tramway. BTS declared that it was committed to the retention of the whole system, which was confirmed by experience. In Sheffield came the early-morning official opening of the Meadowhall line on 21st March, with the Supertrams restoring the City's love of trams, the old system having been closed in 1960. On the home front, Blackpool Transport acquired a controlling interest in Fylde Transport – formerly Lytham St. Annes – based at the former tram depot in Squires Gate Lane. Ironically, this recalls Blackpool's erstwhile attempt to purchase it in 1937, with the intention of extending the South Promenade reservation to St Annes Square. Unfortunately the casting-vote of the Mayor declined Blackpool's offer, which would have enhanced the coastal tramway between towns rather than terminate at Starr Gate, as it sadly does today. In autumn 1994, it seemed that Blackpool Borough was preparing to keep the scheme within financial constraints and remove the illuminations from the South Promenade. At the end of 1994, one-third of credit approval had been given for the first phase of the programme.

Thinking about the celebrations of the Tramroad Centenary in 1998, Blackpool Heritage Trust suggested that the pioneer Balloon 700 should be restored to its 'original' 1942 condition, in the wartime livery. Since Blackpool Transport was sympathetic to the proposal, they said that 700 needed fundamental repairs to its underframe. In order to augment the celebration of V.E. Day in May 1995, it was decided that 703 was to be repainted in the wartime livery and refitted with the appropriate trolley. At the same time, it was hoped that work would start on 700, to complete the originally numbered 237 by 1997. Thus Blackpool Transport, while modernising its fleet in keeping with modern standards, recognised the historic nature of its fleet by having the first Balloon restored to its original style. This would achieve the interest and enjoyment of the public – and the enthusiasts – always creating a desire to ride upon something different.

Digging a Hole for Success

On the 21st January 1995 a ceremony took place near the North Pier, when the Mayor of Blackpool dug the first hole – in wind and rain – to formally inaugurate the Electrical Infrastructure scheme by the contractor James Scott Ltd. While their Chairman assisted him, his Company had established their base upon the car park at Little Bispham, where they stored poles, drums of cables and fittings. The Evening Gazette reported that the total cost of the work would be £8.88 million – financed by Blackpool Borough Council and Government approved borrowing – of which the Tramway would use £4.12 million, illuminations £3.44 million and street lighting £1.32 million. During the same month, the Operational Services Department had paid £45,000 for Speno of Switzerland to come and undertake rail grinding to eliminate corrugations, especially in Lord

Street, Fleetwood. In recent times the local people had found the trams deafening and they could be heard all over the town. The work was done in the evening, while the service cars turned at Ash Street, at a time when the traffic was quiet. Certainly when the grinding was completed, the trams were quiet once again – as they always should have been. Undoubtedly it seems that some of the corrugations had developed from the intense bonding of the concrete, without the European practice of insulating the base of the track with rubber pads. Incidentally regular grinding, using their own 752 grinder, could have kept the corrugations in check from when it was newly laid in 1983.

Top left: The SPENO rail grinder in action on the track at Pleasure Beach, showing the rail wheels of the towing vehicle on the track having raised its road wheels to tow the grinding unit.　　**Eric Berry**

Left: Good Friday of 1995 with 644 in trouble, mounted on blocks and with its broken bogie in the foreground before it was removed by a crane. 644 was mounted on an EE bogie for its return. The smartly restored Brush car 626 passes, looking more reliable!

Eric Berry

Below: Planting of one of the new poles is shown at Pleasure Beach loop in December 1995. This will replace the leaning pole behind.

The departure of Birkenhead 69 in March, followed driver-training for the future tram drivers of Woodside Heritage Tramway, and it joined 70 already there. However, it was interesting here when a mock-up design of a new-look appearance for Balloon 707 was seen at the depot. It conveyed the appearance of a twin–car, with a large single windscreen removing the centre division from the original appearance. This would give the driver a better forward view, but without a cab door for easy exit outside. It was a further two years before work was to begin on this project, depriving 707 from service, while the Works had been preoccupied with 700's restoration. At Easter, more pleasant was the appearance of repainted 733 in the wartime green livery with cream flares, and a warning for the driver that it had a trolley. However, on Good Friday there was a big catastrophe in the cutting from Anchorsholme to Little Bispham, when Centenary 644 was derailed and its front bogie became detached from its body. It took all day to lift the car, remove the damaged bogie and return it to the depot on the rail-trailer 260. 644 was fitted with an EE bogie from an OMO, and was towed to Bispham for storage until the end of the day, completing the journey subsequently. This created delays for the service trams, having to use single line between Norbreck and Cleveleys. This incident seemed to question the suspension of the Centenary cars, which created a bouncing motion, particularly on uneven track.

As the season progressed, there were encouraging signs as the new poles appeared on the tramway between Gynn Square and Cleveleys, in the traditional colour scheme of maroon and cream. Certainly it was interesting for the author to receive a conducted tour of the overhead and hear a report about the work carried out by James Scott Ltd in November 1995. Initially, when deciding upon the method of suspending the overhead, Brecknell Willis – experts in manufacturing overhead equipment – helped James Scott Ltd to design the overhead equipment to suit both the pantographs and trolleys, used by different trams. Clearly the Company's previous experience on new tramways – in both Manchester and Sheffield – was based upon the new systems using modern pantographs on the cars. When the Blackpool system was surveyed, it became clear that it was 'elderly and suspect', though being regularly maintained by the BTS staff efficiently. There had been non–compliant pieces like frogs on bracket–arms, and these were now to be suspended by span wires from above.

It was commented that the learning–curve was severe for the Company when they began the large renewal programme! A key factor of the scheme included the renewal of 1600 poles on the whole system, and the price had been lowered by the fitting technology. Thus poles were planned to be installed during a 3½ hour period at night, when the power was switched off. However the preparation was to be undertaken during the day, when the holes were excavated by a mobile digger and the tubular base was installed with a plastic sleeve. Gravel in its base stops the pole pivoting, and once installed during the day, it was covered until the poles were fitted at night.

The bracket arms on the new overhead are made of stainless steel which will result in less maintenance by removing the need for painting. They are fitted with plastic finials at their ends. The new poles are surmounted by larger plastic finials, thus preventing seagulls from perching on the top! The arms are suspended by stainless steel bow

Little Bispham. The first of these three also supply the illuminations, whilst the smaller one latterly is exclusive to the tramway and thus bridges the supply, between Bispham and Thornton Gate. Regarding the northern section, which has not yet been finished, Thornton Gate feeds as far as pole 589 at Broadwaters, where the electrical 'island' is fed by the original Copse Road sub-station within the depot. If the new scheme commences in November 1998, a new sub–station will be built next to the tram track at Stanley Road, while an in-fill one will be built at Broadwaters, which will need planning permission within the Wyre Borough – and a contribution!

The present contract by James Scott Ltd is complete – at the time of writing – and therefore phase four will have to go out to tender again. During my briefing by the James Scott staff, they pointed out work that needed be done in the Fleetwood section. The present poles at the Ferry support six span wires at the corners and this makes them lean under the weight. The sand bases, in which the poles are sited,

strings and protective cups, also in stainless steel, are fitted to joints. The span-wire, which is used at several three-track layouts, such as at Cabin, Bispham and Thornton Gate, is made from stainless steel which does not stretch, unlike the previous version which included parafil and did stretch. The frogs are suspended by an additional span wire above the level, and bars are inserted between the crossover and main-line wires to keep them level, for the safety of the pantographs.

Under the ground next to the tram track, there are twenty-eight miles of ducts, one free for the future and one wired for the present scheme. The substations will be centrally controlled from Kirby Road sub-station, within the Rigby Road depot compound, which has been re-equipped. Under this scheme nine sub-stations are to be connected to the tramway system, both new and old, increasing the number by three – at Metropole, Little Bispham and Broadwaters. The design of the equipment will be modified in existing sub-stations at Bispham and Thornton Gate, while completely new sub-stations were built at the Pleasure Beach, Metropole, Gynn Square and

allow the movement of the poles in various seasons – including heat or rain respectively! In the future a change in the design of the poles will be made, to provide greater strength at the curves and avoid them bending from the straight position. Along the main streets of Fleetwood, the poles will be slimmer and set-back from the edge of the pavement. On the reservation the new poles would be replaced in the same position between the track, since allowance for wider trams (like the Coronations) was made before 1952 in relaying. However the present Centenary cars of 3000 mm in width would raise no objection to the introduction of the new poles by the Railway Inspectors.

At the time of a conducted tour in November 1995, James Scott staff pointed out that the work on Cleveleys Square, which has a long web of span wires, would be delayed until the installation of a one-way traffic scheme. However, the contractors proceeded with new poles and rewiring during the winter of 1996, and could not wait any longer for the traffic scheme – in May 1997! Once the illuminations were finished in 1995, the traction and street lighting poles from Gynn Square to Pleasure Beach were replaced, and stainless

steel bracket-arms were used. One year later, the work on South Promenade continued with the same style of the bracket-arms – in new form – replacing the twin poles and span-wires. Fortunately rewiring on that section included the illuminations, which will be able to maintain their tradition from Starr Gate to Bispham. During the financial year, ending in March 1997, James Scott completed their contract by fitting the disused – and emergency – track along Princess Street and Blundell Street, together with Lytham Road, Hopton Road and the depot-fan overhead. Certainly the achievement of success in this electrical infrastructure scheme, leaves us in anxious anticipation of its completion in Fleetwood. The Tramroad Centenary celebrations in 1998 will remind Wyre Borough, along with Blackpool Borough, of the essential inter-urban activity of the trams, for the benefit of visitors, residents and commercial concerns too!

The Return of Blackpool & Fleetwood Box 40

In 1996, the approach of the Centenary was established by the welcome liaison between Blackpool Transport and the National Tramway Museum, in securing the return of No. 40 to its native system. Since there had been considerable restoration before its return in 1988, and subsequently work had been done to its motors while it was in Blackpool, it was felt that repainting the car was necessary, giving publicity to the Centenary. Therefore 'Friends of Forty' was reformed to provide financial support, along with the Fleetwood Tram Sunday Committee and the owners of North Euston Hotel. On 22nd April a quick journey was made from Clay Cross to Blackpool, with your author meeting it on the M55 and providing guidance back to the tram depot. Certainly I noticed that people at the bus-stops on Lytham Road were amazed at this sight, since 40 had

'Blackpool & Fleetwood' painted on each end. It only took a short time to unload 40 from the low-loader, with the aid of a rail-ramp, onto its native rails. It was then pushed by Brush 631 into the depot compound. Work soon began on fitting a new set of head and tail lights beneath the frame at each end, together with the indicator boxes surmounted on the roof. On Monday 6th June 40 was driven to Fleetwood in the evening, now complete with a lengthy trolley and rope, still retaining its advertisement for Fisherman's Friend. In Bold Street the press recorded the presentation of cheques to Blackpool Transport, and the participants were taken for a local journey to the appropriate Fisherman's Walk. Although 40 was used – along with Coronation 660 – on Market Day that week, it went into the paint shop for its appropriate repainting. During that time the paintwork was rubbed–down and painted in the traditional livery with intricate gold lining and full lettering BLACKPOOL & FLEETWOOD ELECTRIC TRAMROAD along the lower panel. The previous advertising on the display boards above the saloon windows was replaced by the historic date 1898 BLACKPOOL & FLEETWOOD TRAMROAD CENTENARY 1998 – and its sponsors, to establish the occasion!

Box 40 had been joined on 28th May by Stockport 5, which had been under restoration for several years at Mode Wheel, and which was a contrasting diminutive 4-wheel open-topper. In the red and white livery with gold lining, coat of arms and STOCKPORT CORPORATION TRAMWAYS on the rocker panels, 5 was formally handed-over by Stan Heaton on 11th June, alongside Bolton 66 which took its sponsors for a tour. Subsequently work on fitting air brakes was undertaken to fulfil the safety requirements of the Railway Inspectors, as had previously occurred with Bolton 66. However it should be mentioned that the relaying of the street track at the Metropole had been taking place during the winter months, following the dramatic derailment of Balloon 717 in the previous September – which had given a clear indication of its necessity. Work was completed by the end of March, when the trams returned to normal working after single-line operation between Gynn Square and North Pier. However the trams disappeared between 28th December and 2nd January 1997, when the intensely cold weather froze the braking of the Centenary cars once again. More interesting was the reconstruction of Balloon 719 as the Walls Ice Cream tram, which would publicise and sell the commodity on-board. The interior of the saloons were made very brightly cheerful with their colourful panelling, while the 44 seats in the upper saloon were well-spaced and, together with the 20 seats in one lower saloon, were of extravagant design. Of course the other saloon contained the servery for ice cream by Walls staff. When it appeared at Easter the striking 719 was very eye-catching, with a blue and cream livery surmounted by illuminated advertising panels. Undoubtedly the large cornets above the indicators and the reversed flare at each end with a star, added to the effect of being illuminated each evening. At first its operation was between North Pier and the Pleasure Beach, but it was occasionally seen at Fleetwood when it replaced a service car.

The 12th Fleetwood Tram Sunday occurred on 21st July 1997, when the parade of seven trams was greatly enhanced by the beautifully–restored B.& F. Box 40 leading the

and half-drop saloon windows which would ensure good fresh air in warm weather. Ventilation of the saloons at all times of the year, together with warm pipes at saloon floor level were originally fitted in 1934, but on this occasion 700 was only fitted with the external appearance of ventilators above the windows, in a purely ornamental capacity. However, it was pleasing that the traditional glass louvres were fitted to all windows which were designed originally for protecting passengers from rain when they were opened.

On the electrical side, an inverter unit was installed under the stairs (one of the original luggage compartments) to reduce the lighting circuit to 24 Volts. A ventilator was fitted to the fibreglass panel in the window frame, thus providing the appearance of the original frosted glass next to the stairs. In each driver's cab, the chrome surfaces of the EE Z6 controllers were restored, providing a very striking original appearance. The whole car was rewired, as is the standard procedure for all refurbished trams these days. In the saloons the original appearance was sought by fitting cream fibreglass panels to the ceilings, replacing the original alhambrinal. While it is unobtainable today, some of the Balloons are still fitted with the original alhambrinal, and panels were subsequently saved from 709. Certainly these could have been fitted to 700, in order to maintain its correct original appearance. The woodwork was enhanced by the appearance of the varnished teak in the saloons, especially the partition of the drivers cabs, the window frames and also the division of the ceiling panels.

Today the original linoleum floor with its coloured-grained appearance and a different colour in the aisle is not available, and thus had a mundane beige coloured 'Tarabus' anti–slip floor covering has been used. The fluorescent lighting panels were set in the curves of the lower saloon ceiling, and in the original style they alternated with grills for ventilation. In the upper saloon, lights were in semi-circular shades in the traditional position, and it was pleasing that the curved windows in the ceiling made a brighter interior, together with the curved forward-seeing corner windows. Reversible tram seats were installed throughout all saloons, with patterned green and cream moquette, whereas to be correct the traditional firm upper deck seats should have been fitted to restore the nature of the seating to that of a converted open-topper. Balloon 702 is the only one of this type which is still fitted with the original seats, and these could have been transferred to 700 for accuracy in its restoration to the 1942 style.

By November 1996, 700 entered the paint shop for completion of its appearance in the wartime and early post–war livery, and for the addition of the stainless steel facing to the fenders. While having the complete green livery painted first, the cream lines which had curvature at each end were added, together with a cream panel beneath the centre entrance – for safety! A darker shade of green lining

procession, surprisingly followed by Walls Ice Cream 719 and the inaugural appearance of Stockport 5. Bolton 66 had been recently repainted and therefore looked very smart, while the procession was completed by Vanguard 619, Boat 605 in vintage livery, and 607 in a publicity style. Since Stockport 5 had not yet been approved for passenger service, it carried its voluntary working party on the upper deck, in a lively–ride at speed. When it arrived at the Ferry, it was stored on the siding with its trolley removed from the overhead, since its resistances were heated. It was returned to the depot, but sadly broke–down at Thornton Gate and had to be rescued, subsequently leading to an investigation of the problem. Since it advertised Blackpool Pleasure Beach on its upper panels, they had contributed to the car's restoration, and it is hoped that Stockport 5 will become a popular feature of the Promenade tramway in future. While the other six trams taking part in Tram Sunday were popular features as a means of sightseeing, Chairman Jim Cowpe said "We have had the best selection of trams for many years, and we look forward especially to Fleetwood Tram Sunday in 1998 – Centenary Year!"

Towards the Centenary

Behind the scenes, work had begun on restoring the original Balloon 237 – now 700 – early in 1996, by fully stripping down the body to its wooden frame and removing the driver's cab from each end. The steel work of the centre platform was reinforced, and a new framework was installed at each end. Work on 700 proceeded in the body shop during the summer months, with new stairs and floors fitted, while the external panelling showed the traditional central indicators above the doors and the twin indicators matching the windscreens at the fronts. To facilitate the changing of the indicators from the driver's cab, the original type of winding–gears were obtained from 'Green Linnet' Works car 259. To enable the driver to change the display the provision of a viewing-hatch in each panel would have been necessary. In the event, conductors had to help the driver by standing in front of the car motioning with their hands as he changed the screen! Restoring the original 1942 appearance of Balloon 700, it became necessary to restore the shining metal windscreen frames to the drivers cabs, outlined the cream as well as the bottom of the green panels. This, together with the traditional Borough coat of arms surrounded by the garter scroll ensured that the appearance of 700 was correct externally. It was a bonus that the original metal fleet number 237 – supplied by Keith Terry – was fitted traditionally over the centre entrance. The discretely black number of 700 was situated above the headlamp – for the information of the staff. Unfortunately the one inaccuracy in its appearance was the fitting of only one windscreen in the absence of a matching pair, and it is hoped that this will be completed by the Centenary!

Entering service as a 'special' on the 1997 Easter weekend – complete with its trolley – 700 made its first journey to Fleetwood on Easter Sunday, setting the scene for a traditional Balloon in a flattering style. 700 looks better than the rest of the Balloons, and fortunately it is matched by 703 in the same livery. It does catch the eye of the public and the twin indicators are perfectly readable, although to be correct if should have black and white style lettering. 237 will represent trams of the thirties in the Centenary procession – although with its present number of 700!

Meanwhile work continued during 1997 on the track work between Cleveleys and Thornton Gate and also in the Fylde Borough area. While the track gang was busy relaying road-crossings, the tram service was operated as a single-line to facilitate progress. Beach Road was reached by the summer months and new railings were fitted alongside the location of the new track, while West Drive road crossing used street track laid upon sound concrete foundations, suitable for heavy traffic. It is appropriate here to look into the Track Service Section background, which today is based at the Layton Headquarters of the Operational Services Department and employs 22 men. While formerly there were 48 men, it is claimed that the present number achieves the same amount of work today, equipped with suitable vehicles including a JCB digger and lorries, and a Leyland PD3 bus as the workers rest room and facilities. The track is inspected monthly by the foreman, who uses a van to visit each section in turn. The track is owned by the Blackpool Borough and is leased to BTS, who pay 50% of their tramway profit as an access charge. The maintenance budget for track and the overhead amounts to the total of a £1 million. In 1997 the Lancashire County Council (LCC) grant was diminished to 10%, and will disappear in 1998 owing to the new status of Blackpool as an independent Borough. Consequently there has been concern about the finance of the section of the Tramroad in the Wyre Borough area the contribution LCC.

Liaison and planning of the Track Services Section involves an annual meeting with the Chief Engineer, Bill Gibson, and Fleet Engineer, Mike Francis, of BTS, at which the aim of their programme is discussed and notice given of the work. Plans during winter 1997–8 have included: the road crossings at Rossall Lane and Rossall Square before Christmas and Cleveleys Square in January. While the crossovers at Rossall, Broadwater and Stanley Road were unusable, the tram service terminated at Thornton Gate with buses completing the journey to Fleetwood Ferry, appropriately using the traditional service number 1. While these crossovers and much of the track in Fleetwood needs renewal, this will not be undertaken until the Wyre and Blackpool Borough Councils agree to share the renewal costs of EI Phase 4, which of course includes new sub–stations at Copse Road and Broadwater, feeder cables and new poles. With the Centenary pending it is felt that the future of the Tramroad has to be confirmed in the near future otherwise, sadly, 1998 may be the last year of trams in Fleetwood.

The two types of new rail are ordered from different suppliers. British Steel notifies appropriate operators when they have a special rolling of 95 lb/yd rail, from which Blackpool will usually order 50 rails of 60 ft lengths for usage in the current programme. The tramway street track RI 60 comes from three rail manufacturers in Germany, Austria and France, while Blackpool OSD orders 150 tons, and thus 150 rails, on each occasion. Incidentally the Metropole street track section, laid in winter 1995/6, came from France. The pointwork comes from Edgar Allen Ltd. Presently all the 1935 depot track–fan needs renewal at the cost of around £750 000, which has been proposed for the 1998 budget. The good news of spring 1998 is that SPENO is returning to grind the track between Talbot Square and Gynn Square and the new road crossings in Cleveleys and Rossall, and the Lord Street track again. Incidentally the old Grinder 752 was last used to grind the new rail in North Albert Street, which was good practice to smooth the new surface, which might involve surface ripples upon manufacture. Another priority during winter 1997 was the relaying of the track in Hopton Road – approaching the depot – which has suffered from heavy traffic during the construction of a new building on the former Coliseum site. The trams will then leave via Blundell Street and Princess Street, in an old tradition. The railway inspector – on board 754 – inspected the track in November 1997, and passed its use after a successful passage. Incidentally, it is planned to move the crossover at Broadwater to the north side of the Fleetwood Road crossing, to facilitate turning cars from Blackpool. Its use will be unlike the years of the Broadwater & Fleetwood local service. The trams presently travel to Fleetwood over track which is circa 30 years old – lighter than new rail and weighing only 85 lbs per yard – and greatly in need of renewal, especially on curves, where the swaying of the trams from side to side causes the pantographs to nearly miss the overhead, and may cause the passengers to feel sick. However, on 1st July 1898, the "official passenger" said "The feeling was grand". We hope that this feeling will be re-established for the safety and reliability of the system in the future – and certainly by the millenium!

Returning to the fleet in 1997, developments are always interesting, notably with the renovation of 707 in a new style of front ends. While 700 has been restored to its original appearance, it has at last been decided – after 63 years – that there should be better conditions for the driver in a cab, which improves visibility by having a full windscreen and an adjustable seat. Certainly the appearance of 707, with a wide–window being repeated on the upper deck for the benefit of the passengers, is reminiscent of the Twin cars in the sixties. While 707 will look like the start of a new generation, with an air–conditioned driver's cab and a fixed windscreen, the centre doors and stairs are in the same position, requiring two conductors. In effect, this will render 707 more expensive to operate than the Jubilee cars, of which 762 has the front entrance and centre exit in a more economical design. It will be interesting to see how 707 operates effectively, and thus whether this is how the Balloons will develop in the future. In contrast to such changes was the refitting of 706 with a trolley in June, which certainly restored its pre–war appearance and safety for its passengers. When 706 was being restored to its original open-top style in 1985 the elegant trolley gantry was re–created, but was sacrificed when a pantograph was installed, thus requiring a short protective roof for passengers. Subsequently, on wet days the passengers were showered with dirt from the sliding pantograph collectors, in a similar manner to the pantograph-fitted Boat cars in 1992. Thus a restoration was justified, albeit with the unnecessary short roof.

On the vintage front, problems with Stockport 5, notably its resistances not coping with its 50 h.p. motors, sadly left it in the depot during 1997, apart from TV appearances for the Antiques Roadshow on 14th April with Box 40, Boat 605 and Coronation 660. Happily in November, Stockport 5 passed its inspection for future operation, giving us two red and white open-toppers in 1998. In contrast, the arrival of the Trampower articulated car on 23rd July posed the hope for a new generation of fleet trams, if the trials were successful. It was given the fleet number 611, but it was not until 2nd June 1998 that a gauging trial was eventually carried out to Fleetwood. This is the UK Tram Consortium's low–floor demonstrator light rail vehicle, of which BTS supplies the facility of an operating tramway for important trials – with passengers. While we wait to see the results, one can reflect that a new generation of trams with a 200 passenger capacity should replace the small 60 year old

railcoaches with a crew of two. However in sheer contrast with this, on 10th September 1997, was the return of Marton Box car 31 from Beamish, which entered service on the 27th during the Illuminations. Having been restored since its last appearance here as 754 in 1984, it looks attractive with its red and white livery, classic bevelled windows and its traditional indicator boxes surmounted by tail lights. The passengers had the choice of the open-top deck seats or the comfort of the saloon, while they were seen aloft touring the Illuminations, even in the rain! Certainly it brings back the nostalgic memories of Dreadnought 59, which was always popular with the tourists as well as the enthusiasts. The latter should return by its own Centenary in the year 2002.

Finally, in the 99th year of the Tramroad history, it has been interesting to trace developments, including the planning for the Centenary. The BTS Committee has been meeting during the year, and finalising arrangements to recreate the first tram from Blackpool to Fleetwood – as on 1st July 1898. Blackpool & Fleetwood Crossbench car 2 has been loaned by the National Tramway Museum for the occasion, and work has been carried out to restore the body to the 1919 condition: with a K10 controller, removal of the indicator boxes, re–canvassing the roof and the replacement of the head and tail lights by battery operated oil lamps. An appeal was made to enthusiasts to financially support this restoration project, to ensure that the

Centenary would be enhanced by one of the original trams of 1898. Having made a first appearance at Crich, Crossbench 2 will feature on the BTS depot open day on 28th June. This will be followed by the historic trams like B&F 40 of 1914, Pantograph 167 of 1928, Coronation 660 of 1953 and Marton Box car 31 of 1901. Undoubtedly it is fortunate that 2 & 40 of the Tramroad Company fleet survived as Works cars and were restored in 1960 for the 75th Anniversary of the Blackpool Tramway. While they commenced the Crich public service in 1964, this will be the first occasion that the two Tramroad cars have appeared together – a momentous occasion! Since 40 will be staying at Blackpool for some time, Crossbench 2 is not today considered safe on our Promenade and so will return to be a prime historical tram at the National Tramway Museum. During the Centenary occasion, there will be tours for those enthusiasts who have supported the presence of 2, 40 and 167, having financially contributed to their presence on the Tramroad. During the the 1998 season it is expected that there will be a vintage service between Cabin & Harrowside, together with appropriate journeys to Fleetwood from North Pier – on market days.

Above left: Sections of the articulated "Tram Power" (later known as "Roadliner" car arrived at Rigby Road yard on Wednesday 23rd July, seen before unloading. **James Millington**

Left: A view sitting on the track without it's front grill. **Philip Higgs**

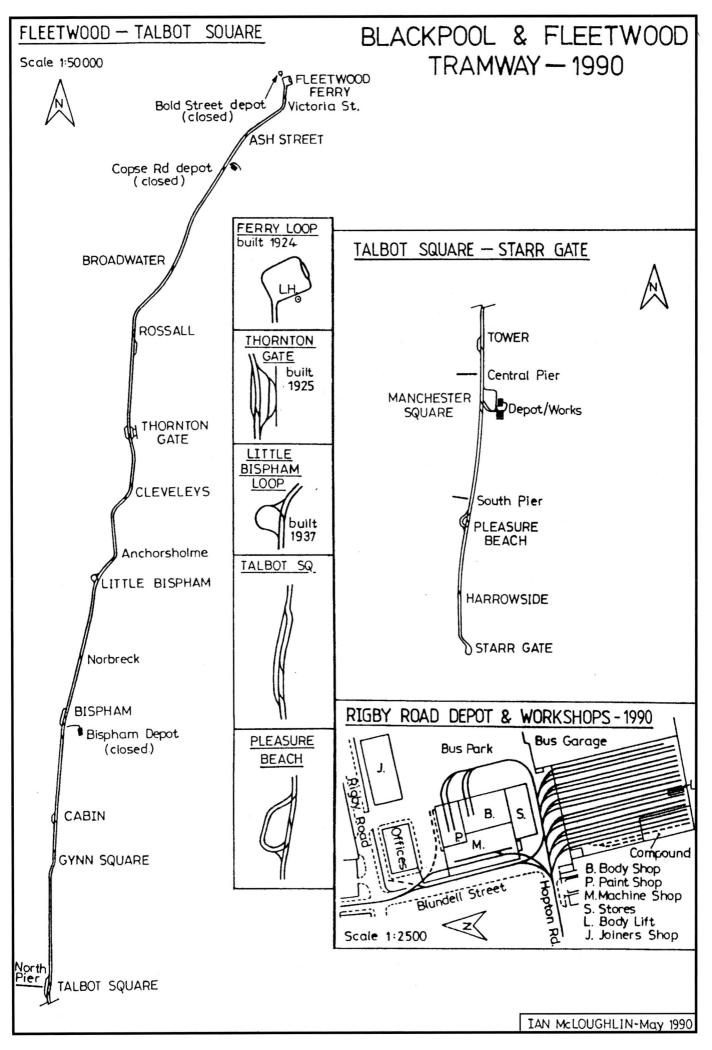

FLEETWOOD — TALBOT SQUARE

Scale 1:50 000

N

FLEETWOOD FERRY
Victoria St.
Bold Street depot (closed)
ASH STREET
Copse Rd depot (closed)
BROADWATER
ROSSALL
THORNTON GATE
CLEVELEYS
Anchorsholme
LITTLE BISPHAM
Norbreck
BISPHAM
Bispham Depot (closed)
CABIN
GYNN SQUARE
North Pier
TALBOT SQUARE

BLACKPOOL & FLEETWOOD TRAMWAY — 1990

FERRY LOOP built 1924
L.H.

THORNTON GATE built 1925

LITTLE BISPHAM LOOP built 1937

TALBOT SQ.

PLEASURE BEACH

TALBOT SQUARE — STARR GATE

N

TOWER
Central Pier
MANCHESTER SQUARE
Depot/Works
South Pier
PLEASURE BEACH
HARROWSIDE
STARR GATE

RIGBY ROAD DEPOT & WORKSHOPS - 1990

Bus Park
Bus Garage
Rigby Road
J.
Offices
B.
S.
P.
M.
Blundell Street
Hopton Rd.
Compound

B. Body Shop
P. Paint Shop
M. Machine Shop
S. Stores
L. Body Lift
J. Joiners Shop

Scale 1:2500

N

IAN McLOUGHLIN—May 1990

FLEET SUMMARY 1997

Number	Type	Date	Total	
600–607	Boat Cars	1934	6	600 on loan, 601 + 603 in USA.
700–726	Balloons	1934–35	24	700 restored as 237, 705 scrapped, 706 restored to open-topper in 1985.
678–680	Railcoaches	1936	3	Formerly towing cars in same style.
621–637	Brush Cars	1937	13	635 restored as 298, 629 scrapped, 624 + 628 used as Works cars.
671–677	Twin Cars	1936	7	In pairs with 681–7 (matching last digit).
681–687	Trailers	1960	7	
660	Coronation	1953	1	Vambac removed + EE Z4 fitted.
5, 8, 11	OMO	1972–74	3	Presently stored.
619	Vanguard	1987	1	Rebuilt from OMO 7 - Mode Wheel.
761–762	Jubilee	1979–82	2	Rebuilt from Balloons 725 & 714.
641–648	Centenary	1984–86	8	Controller: Brush Chopper. Bogie: BT.

Illuminated Cars:
These conversions generally have the equipment of their predecessors.

732	Rocket	1961	1	Seats: 46. Converted from Pantograph 168.
733	Western Train	1962	1	Seats: 35. Converted from EE Railcoach 209.
734	& Carriage		1	Seats: 60. Converted from Pantograph 174.
735	Hovertram	1963	1	Seats: 99. Converted from Railcoach 222.
736	Frigate	1965	1	Seats: 75. Converted from Pantograph 170.

Works Cars:

752	RailGrinder	1928	1	Brill -4-wheel truck. Controller: BTH B18. Motors: Two BTH/GE200 of 35 h.p.
753	Overhead-line	1958	1	Converted from Standard 143; stored after fire.
754	Overhead-line	1993	1	Built by E.L.C. with EE bogies + EE Z4 Controller. Motors: Two EE327 of 40 h.p. Diesel-generator unit for power.
259	Permanent way car	1971	1	(Brush 624) owned by the Borough.
260	Railcrane	1973	1	(Brush 628) owned by the Borough.

Vintage Cars:

Bolton 66	1901	1	Arrived June 1981. Restored at Back o' the Bank Power Station, Astley Bridge, Bolton. Bogies: Brill 21E. Motors: Metro-Vick 323. Controllers: EE DB1. Air-brakes fitted.
B & F Box 40	1914	1	Returned from NTM on 22 April 1996, repainted and fitted with platform doors. (see Chapter 1 list) Controllers: BTH B-510. Motors: Two BTH GE67 of 40 h.p.
Stockport 5	1901	1	Arrived 28 May 1996 from Mode Wheel where restored by Friends of 5. Truck: Brill 21E from Porto 67. Controller: EE DB1. Air-brakes fitted upon arrival in Blackpool.
Marton Box car 31	1901	1	Returned from N.E. Museum Beamish 30 September 1997 for the Centenary. Restored from Works car 4. Body: Midland R.C.& W. Co. Bogies: Preston McGuire. Motors: Two BTH 265 of 35 h.p. Controller: BTH B510.
Pantograph 167	1928	1	Loaned by NTM, for 1998 Season, in its 70th Year! (see Chapter 2). Motors now two BTH 265C of 35 h.p.
B & F Crossbench 2	1898	1	Loaned for the Centenary Celebration in July 1998, and now 100 years old! (see Chapter 1). Controllers: BTH B18. Motors: Two GEC 100 of 35 h.p.

Fleet Total: 91

TRAMCARS PRESERVED

A total of 22 Blackpool tram cars are preserved as follows:

No.	Type	Date Departed	Destination
144	Standard	11th March 1955	Seashore Electric Railway, Maine, USA [1]
167	Pantograph	17th May 1962	Crich Tramway Museum
49	Standard	13th December 1962	Crich Tramway Museum
1	1885 car (ex-conduit)	18th March 1963	Museum of British Transport, Clapham, London
2	Fleetwood Crossbench car	17th September 1963	Crich Tramway Museum
40	Standard	3rd October 1963	Crich Tramway Museum
40	Fleetwood Box car	4th October 1963	Crich Tramway Museum
48	Standard	24th August 1964	Oregon Electric Railway, Glenwood, Oregon, USA[2]
59	Dreadnought	18th March 1965	Crich Tramway Museum
11	Marton Vambac	9th September 1965	EATMS, Lowestoft
2	Grinder car	10th December 1965	NTM Crich, Derbyshire
-	Electric Locomotive	28th January 1966	NTM Crich, Derbyshire
153	Standard	18th April 1967	EATMS, Lowestoft
147	Standard	6th September 1967	Columbia Park, Ohio, USA
226	Boat car	19th August 1971	Rio Vista, California, USA[3]
166	Toastrack	9th June 1972	NTM Crich, Derbyshire
304	Coronation	16th July 1975	St. Helens Transport Museum
327	Coronation	19th August 1976	St. Helens Transport Museum[4]
298	Brush car	14th April 1977	Mode Wheel, Salford (NTM)
731	Blackpool Belle	18th March 1982	Glenwood Trolley Park, Oregon, USA
31	Marton Box car	17th July 1984	N.E. Open Air Museum, Beamish, Co. Durham [5]
228	Boat car	19th February 1985	San Francisco Municipal Railway, California, USA

Notes:

[1]   Shipped to Boston USA, from Liverpool by United States Lines ship "American Press", arrived Boston 28th March.

[2]   Shipped from King George Dock, Hull. On Thursday, 27th August, on East Asiatic Lines ship "Sibonga" and became the first British tram to travel through Panama Canal.

[3]   226 has operated in San Francisco for the Trolley Festival in 1984.

[4]   327 has been at Lytham Railway Museum, Steamport Southport and Bradford Transport Museum, as well!

[5]   31 is on loan to Beamish and will return to Blackpool for special occasions ... Centenary 1998!

Two trucks from Lifeboat and Gondola illuminated cars have also been preserved. Lifeboat truck left in August 1962 for Crich, and Gondola truck left in March 1963 for Nottingham.

To ensure safe operation in the best tradition of the Tramroad, there will be a team of drivers for vintage trams, as delegated by BTS for the season. The Centenary celebration will culminate by the Last Night of the Prom, with vintage trams commemorating the momentous events of 1998. As was sung in 1898 – a hundred years later:

'Now roit you are for Blackpool,
For Fleetwood roit you are,
And passengers sat viz–a–vee,
On the vintage electric car.'

Therefore 'an exhilarating ride' – after 100 years by Tram!

Right: The demise of the OMOs was stimulated by this accident on 22nd February 1977, when 6 was driven off the track and onto the new sleepers!
The Gazette, Blackpool

CHAPTER 6

THE OTHER FIRM – FARES PLEASE!

In the first chapter of this book, the history of the Tramroad Company showed how most of their trams operated from Bispham depot, with its power-station and the residence of the Manager, John Cameron. When Blackpool took over in 1920, its Promenade tramway was integrated while maintaining the original North Station and Fleetwood route. The Bispham depot trams maintained a distinction as 'the other firm', showing route '1' on their indicators complete with former Company employees.

Capturing the scene, the working experience is always interesting when recorded by tramway men – drivers and conductors – in the final years of Bispham depot and route 1. As a student, who worked on the tramway between 1959 and 1964, your author served as No. 3604, starting as a point-boy and continuing as a guard (conductor) for five years –most of it at Bispham depot. Thus I was able to record the tramway scene from the inside, giving a different perspective from an enthusiast, from which to enjoy the tramway and chronicle its day-to-day workings. I hope that you will find it interesting and amusing – so hold tight please!

Steve Palmer

Pulling the Points

I was 17 when I first joined the Transport Department – too young to be a guard – and so I became a point-boy.

When school was finished for the summer, I reported to the Traffic Superintendent, who sent me across to the tailor's shop to get my uniform. In those days, the tailor issued uniforms from a crowded upstairs room, reached by walking through the old Blundell Street depot. At the top of the stairs, next to the hatch where you rang for attention, was a faded framed photograph of the first Marton tram in 1901. The tailor had not got much time for students, and gave them cast-off garments which more-or-less fitted. Because I was working outdoors, I was issued with tunic and trousers, a mackintosh and a peaked hat. The uniform colour was navy blue, piped with green, and the silver buttons bore the Corporation crest and the Legend 'Blackpool Corporation Tramways'. Proudly clutching my bundle, I made my way to the tram stop at Manchester Square, and got a free ride home, I was now one of the staff!

At that time, there were eight point-boys: two regulars who manned the Royal Oak points in Lytham Road, and the rest of us, students, who were sent to the points at Central Station (Tower), Pleasure Beach, Talbot Square or Bispham. Our job was to ensure the smooth flow of cars by switching the points and pulling the overhead frog for cars reversing there. During the season, the points were fixed for the loop-lines used by the through-cars, while we switched the points for the short-workings. There was a certain art in swinging the points, to make sure that the blades went right over, and at that time the lever was inserted in a slot at the side of the track. This was moved to in-between the rails after an occasion when somebody pulled the points back when a car was half across, with disastrous results! In 1959, the number of cars in service was such that there was a car every few minutes along the Central Promenade. Sometimes huge queues would build-up at the Central Station points, while short-working cars waited for others to clear the centre track, thus delaying the service cars.

As a point-boy, it was important to strike-up a good friendship with your Inspector, who would often send you on messages to the depot, or into town to get his dinner. On one such occasion, when coming back from the depot canteen with a full brew-can, I ran for a railcoach at Manchester Square, slipped off the step and was showered with hot tea as I hit the Promenade. Sympathetic holiday makers picked me up, but my Inspector was not pleased when I returned to Pleasure Beach with cuts and bruises, but without the brew. I quite liked working at Pleasure Beach loop, where you could pull the points and then ride round the circle and chat to the crew. At lunch-time rows of cars in all shapes and sizes – would stack on the loop, while the crews had the half hour break in an eight hour shift. One day, I was sent down to Royal Oak to relieve the regular point-boy, while he went to the training school for guards. He showed me the times of the Marton cars scratched conveniently onto the pole, and warned me to pull the frog hard to avoid dewirement as cars turned into

Waterloo Road. It was his practice to jump onto a South Pier car as it turned into Lytham Road, ride with it to Station Road where he pulled the points, and jumped on the next car back. There was a car every nine minutes from South Pier to Marton, and a Squires Gate car every six minutes, with the occasional Circular Boat car turning right, via Marton. I used to stand fascinated while the Marton cars turning at Royal Oak automatically reversed their trolley, swept over the bridge and disappeared from view. While working at Bispham Top, I formed a particular attachment for Bispham depot crew, doing the points and trolley for the Squires Gate cars. The weary crews appreciated my help and I made many friends there, resolving to join them in the following year when I became a guard, and thus would join 'the other firm'!

Joining 'the Other Firm'

From 1960 to 1963, I worked mostly at Bispham Depot, which was always known within the Transport Department as 'the other firm': partly because it was originally a Company shed, and partly because the crews there were somewhat cliquish. If you belonged to Bispham you were accepted, otherwise you were an outsider. Even the cars were distinguished on the North Station service by showing the number '1' next to their destination indicator. This reputedly dated back to the days when the 'back-road cars' charged penny fares, while it was 2d minimum on the Promenade. Even the cars themselves were distinctive with Bispham Depot operating all twenty of the Brush Railcoaches 284–303 and the eight remaining Pantograph cars 168–175. The Depot itself was tucked away from public gaze down Red Bank Road, and only when a car trundled up or down the single track did the public realise that there was a tram shed there. Round the corner from the Bispham Hotel was a neat depot yard, where the single track fanned out into six and passed through the large green sliding doors, surmounted by a proud headstone: BLACKPOOL & FLEETWOOD TRAMROAD COMPANY 1898. The whole place had the air of a forgotten empire, with its deserted power station and outbuildings, the neat depot office adjoining the yard, and the nearby Bispham Conservative Club, once the home of the Cameron family, who had managed the Company. Until 1982, all the buildings still stood, even though the last tram had left in January 1966, and the running shed closed in 1963. While I worked there, I made a point of exploring this fascinating place and recording it for posterity.

The first impression you gained when entering, was of the low wooden roof supported by metal poles, pools of water on the floor and in the pits, and a general air of gloom and stillness. The original depot only extended to half the six-car depth, but in 1917 an extension had been built in reinforced concrete over the site of the power station reservoir. This was fed by a

Above: Author, Steve Palmer, dressed in the traditional blue uniform as a point-boy in 1959 at the Central Station Points.

supply of fresh running water, and may have accounted for the general dampness of the building. The roof in the rear section of the depot was so low that only single-deck cars could enter, and even their trolleys were bent lower. Traditionally, the old green Pantograph cars occupied pit 3, while pit 1, nearest the power station, was occupied by the overhead tower car 3 and an assortment of odd cars, which once included the ex-conduit car 4. By 1963, when Marton Depot had closed, six Boats had replaced the Pantographs, and track 1 housed two box-like track-

Right: The point boy at work at Royal Oak points with Pantograph 175 about to turn right for Marton during a tour on 23rd May 1959.

BLACKPOOL CORPORATION TRANSPORT

BISPHAM DEPOT TRAM DRIVERS & CONDUCTORS DUTIES COMMENCING 4th MARCH,1968

R4197

SERVICE.	Duty No.	Duty	Report at Depot	Route Duty	ON DUTY Time	ON DUTY Place	OFF DUTY Time	OFF DUTY Place	Time Worked	Day Off
			WEEKDAYS.					WEEKDAYS.		
Fleetwood.	501	E	4-46am.	1	4-56	Depot	10-14	Bisp;Stn		
Spl.			10-17am.	Spl	10-55	Depot	12-30	Depot	7¾ ¼	Sun
	502	Relief	Mon.508L Tues.O-P-L Wed.515L Thur.510L Fri.510L							Sun Sat
Fleetwood	503	E	5-52am.	3	6- 2	Depot	9-38	Bisp.Stn		
"				1	10-14	Bisp.Stn	11-38	Bisp.Stn		
Spl.			11-39am.	Spl	12-10	Depot	1-37	Depot	7¾	Sun Sat
Clev-N.Stn	504	L	4- 6pm.	9	4-16	Depot	6- 5	Depot		
Fleetwood				3	7- 2	Bispham Stn	12-12	Depot	8	Sun Sat
Reserve	505C	E	6-45am	Res	6-45	Depot	3- 0	Depot	8¼	Sun Wed
Reserve	505M	E	4-45am.	Res	4-45	Depot	1- 0	Depot	8¼ ¼	Sun Wed
Fleetwood	506	L	3- 4pm.	3	3-14	Bisp.Stn	7- 2	Bisp.Stn		
"				1	8- 4	Bisp.Stn	11-40	Depot	8½	Tues
	507	Relief	Mon.520E Tues.520E Wed.509E Thur.516E Fri.516E Sat.518E							Sun
Fleetwood	508	L	2-40pm.	1	2-50	Bisp.Stn	8- 4	Bisp.Stn		
"				7	8-48	Bisp.Stn	11-24	Depot	8¾	Sun Mon
"	509	E	6-49am.	2	6-59	Depot	10-26	Bisp.Stn		
"				5	11- 2	Bisp.Stn	3-38	Bisp.Stn	9	Sun Wed
Clev-N.Stn	510	L	3-56pm.	8	4- 6	Depot	6-15	Depot		
Fleetwood				2	6-50	Bisp.Stn	11-59	Depot	8	Thur Fri
Clev.N.Stn	511	E	7-52am.	10	8- 2	Depot	9- 5	Depot		
Fleetwood				6	9-50	Bisp.Stn	3-50	Bisp.Stn	8¼	Fri
	512	Relief.	Sun.501E Mon.514E Tue.514E Wed.505E Thur.O-P-L Fri.511E							Sat
Clev-N.Stn	513	L	11-52am.	8	12- 2	Depot	2-47	Depot		
Fleetwood				5	3-38	Bisp.Stn	7-26	Bisp.Stn	7¾	Sun
"	514	E	6- 9am.	4	6-19	Depot	9-50	Bisp.Stn		
"				7	10-26	Bisp.Stn	11-26	Bisp.Stn		
"				2	11-50	Bisp.Stn	3- 2	Bisp.Stn	9	Sun Mon Tue
Clev.N.Stn	515	L	12- 2pm.	9	12-12	Depot	2-26	Depot		
Fleetwood				4	3-26	Bisp.Stn	7-57	Depot	8	Wed
"	516	E	6-38am.	7	6-48	Depot	10-26	Bisp.Stn		
"				3	11- 2	Bisp.Stn	3-14	Bisp.Stn	8¾	Thur Fri
"	517	L	2-52pm.	2	3- 2	Bisp.Stn	6-50	Bisp.Stn		
"				5	7-26	Bisp.Stn	8-52	Bisp.Stn		
Clev.N.Stn			8-55pm.	8	9-30	Depot	11-29	Depot	8¾	Fri
"	518	E	7-53am.	9	8- 3	Depot	9-14	Depot		
Fleetwood				4	9-50	Bisp.Stn	11-14	Bisp.Stn		
"				7	11-26	Bisp.Stn	3-38	Bisp. Stn	8	Sat
"	519	L	3-28pm.	7	3-38	Bisp Stn	8-48	Bisp Sth		
Clev.N.Stn			8-51pm.	9	9-40	Depot	11-50	Depot	8½	Sun Mon
Fleetwood	520	E	6-38am.	5	6-48	Depot	11- 2	Bisp.Stn.		
"				1	11-36	Bisp.Stn	2-50	Bispham Stn	8½	Mon Tues
	521	Relief	Sun.504L Mon.519L Tue.506L Thu .523L Fri.517L Sat.O-P-L							Wed
Clev.N.Stn	522	E	6-52am.	8	7- 2	Depot	9- 3	Depot		
Fleetwood				3	9-38	Bisp.Stn	11- 2	Bisp.Stn.		
"				4	11-14	Bisp.Stn	3-26	Bisp.Stn	8¾	Wed Thur
"	523	L	3-40pm.	6	3-50	Bisp.Stn	7-39	Depot		
"				5	8-52	Bisp.Stn	11-54	Depot	8¼	Thur
"	524	E	5-51am.	6	6- 1	Depot	9-50	Bisp.Stn		
"				2	10-26	Bisp.Stn	11-50	Bisp.Stn		
Spl			11-51am.	Spl	12-10	Depot	1-36	Depot.	7¾	Tues
Reserve	525C	L	2-45pm.	Res	2-45	Depot	11- 0	Depot	8¼	Sun
Reserve	525M	L	4- 0pm.	Res	4- 0	Depot	12-15	Depot	8¼	Sun
	526	Relief.	Tues.524E Wed.522E Thur.522E Fri.O-P-L Sat.504L							Sun Mon
			SUNDAYS					SUNDAYS		
Fleetwood	501	E	7-33am.	5	7-43	Depot	10- 4	Bisp.Stn		
"				3	10-44	Bisp.Stn	11-44	Bisp.Stn		
Spl			11-47am.	Spl	12- 0	Depot	2-33	Depot	7	
Fleetwood	504	L	4-50pm.	5	5- 0	Bisp.Stn	12- 4	Depot	7¼	
"	506	L	4- 2pm.	3	4-12	Bisp.Stn	11-16	Depot	7¼	
Reserve	510C	L	3-45pm.	Res	3-45	Depot	11- 0	Depot	7¼	
Reserve	510M	L	4-45pm.	Res	4-45	Depot	12- 0	Depot	7¼	
Fleetwood	511	E	9-54am.	5	10- 4	Bisp.Stn	5- 0	Bisp.Stn	7¼	
"	515	L	3-46pm.	2	3-56	Bisp.Stn	11- 0	Depot	7¼	
Reserve	516C	E	8-15am.	Res	8-15	Depot	3-30	Depot	7¼	
Reserve	516M	E	7- 0am.	Res	7- 0	Depot	2-15	Depot	7¼	
Fleetwood	517	L	3-58pm.	1	4- 8	Bisp.Stn	11-30	Depot	7½	
"	518	E	8-37am.	4	8-47	Depot.	11-16	Bisp.Stn		
"				3	11-44	Bisp.Stn	4-12	Bisp.Stn	7¾	
"	520	E	8-53am.	2	9- 3	Depot	3-56	Bisp.Stn	7¼	
"	522	E	9- 6am.	3	9-16	Depot	10- 44	Bisp.Stn		
"				4	11-16	Bisp.Stn	4-44	Bisp.Stn	7¾	
"	523	L	4-34pm.	4	4-44	Bisp.Stn	11-48	Depot	7¼	
"	524	E	8-36am	1	8-46	Depot	4- 8	Bisp.Stn	7¼	

grinding cars the track-gang car 170, the last-remaining Marton Vambac 11, and the small green electric locomotive. My feet echoed in the still building, as I moved along the silent lines of cars, covered with a thin layer of dust. Halfway down pit 1, I mounted the stone steps which led to the former power station, to peer through the glass door into the cavernous interior reminiscent of a Victorian public bath, then housing only a mercury-arc rectifier. The back wall of the depot was punctuated by six large arched windows running the full height of the building, and shedding some light on the scene. At the far side, adjacent to pit 6, were a series of low doorways into small workshops and storerooms, where once the heavy engineering was carried out on the Company cars. By this time, they were mainly used for storing spare controllers, glass, seats, cushions, sand-bags, brake blocks, timetable frames, trolley-heads, and a thousand-and-one other things to keep the cars running. Although heavy overhauls and bodywork were done at Rigby Road, the depot did its own running-repairs and partial repaints, and as such had a team of brake-fitters, electricians, and body-makers. Near to the doors at the front of the shed, were mounted two glass cases containing the painted discs with the numbers of the cars: ready for service and those under repair. I carefully undid the brass catch, and turned over the Pantograph car discs. On the reverse side I found some even older numbers: 168's disc originally belonged to car 16 and 174's to car 19, the numbers of old Company cars. The whole place was reminiscent of history and haunted by ghosts of the past; I was quite glad to step out into the sunshine and cross the yard to the crew room, where the late-turn crews were reporting for duty and watching a game of bowls on the green.

Learning the "Wrinkles"

As I locked up my bike in the outhouse of the crew-room on my first day in 1960, I felt that I was entering a completely new world, known only to those who work on the trams. As a probationer I had to spend twenty hours with another guard 'on the road', and since I was still at school, I used to cycle there in the evenings, draw out my TIM (ticket issuing machine) from the office, and board a car at Bispham Top. I usually chose a Pantograph car on the North Station route, simply

The traditional Bispham Depot with the Pantograph cars, showing the B&F Company headstone and the original power station joining at the side. Over the large sliding doors are the numbers of the six pits, each taking six trams. Notice the pull-frogs on each pole and the point-work of the Fifties. **W.G.S. Hyde**

A view of the depot interior, showing the row of Pantograph cars and the line of roof pillars, together with the large windows of the workshops at the side. **R.P. Fergusson**

An interesting scene in 1963 – the final year of operation – showing two grinder cars 1 and 2, preserved Marton Vambac 11, the electric locomotive, Permanent Way 170 and a Boat car. The ladder against the Brush car in the foreground belonged to the cleaners. **Author**

Above: The Author's favourite tram Pantograph 170 seen in 1960 at Gynn Square, with passengers boarding from the island shelter while the new Ford Zephyr is waiting to cross the track. **Author**

because I liked them and found them easier to work, with their one saloon, rather than two on the centre-entrance cars. The first thing you had to learn was to separate the cash in your leather bag: ha'pennies and three-penny bits in the front pouch, pennies in the middle, and silver in the back. The TIM was a science in itself – you had to keep turning the fare-stage indicator as you passed along the route, and then dial the fare, before turning the handle. The paper ticket issued, had printed on it the date, stage, and fare, so that any inspector could check whether you were efficient, or needed booking for a mistake. If you were booked you might get a note to see the Traffic Superintendent, and that could be an uncomfortable experience. At each terminus, the guard filled-in the total tickets sold on the waybill, and at a very early stage I discovered that this was no easy task on a moving tram. One of the guards at the depot made waybill boards, with your staff number stencilled on, and I ordered one, which solved the problem. The other essential piece of equipment was a brew-can, an enamelled jug with a tin cup for a lid. I soon discovered that the mark of a respected guard was a good brew, and that the hot-water geyser was situated at Bispham Station. If the driver wanted you to brew going north, he would hold-up the cup in the cab window, and once at Bispham you would collect it through the open windscreen. While the impatient passengers waited, the guard would disappear through the little green door, and re-emerge a few minutes later, swinging the can round his head to give the brew a good mixing.

My probation taught me many other wrinkles learned from the regulars, and also the language of the job, which is explained in a glossary at the end of this chapter. I learned that you should never ring-off with the doors open, and to give one bell for stop, two for start and three for a full-load. You had to clock at each terminus, and at Cleveleys in both directions on service 1. Last cars going north had also to clock at Bispham, and if you were found to have clocked 'early' the time-keeper would report you. However you could 'bang the clock' and get an extra minute out if it, which could be useful at busy times. At the end of the shift, guards had to enter the total of each ticket-value on to the

waybill from the TIM, and pay in their money at the depot. If your money and tickets did not balance, then your staff number would appear on a huge print-out, pinned-up in the depot office and showing how much was to be deducted from your wages. If you were seen paying in a large amount, other guards would say that you must 'have been running with your doors open'.

There was a code of honour amongst the tram-men, and anyone who broke the rules soon became disliked: thus a Promenade car should always give-way to a car coming from North Station on to the Promenade at Gynn Square. If two cars were going to the depot at the same time, the first car should always go down for two at Bispham Station. A car should never leave passengers for the car behind, or miss-out stops unless it was carrying a three-bell load. Drivers liked their guards to be quick on-the-bell and careful with the doors: if a guard rang-off from the saloon, a passenger who was still boarding could be dragged along the track, and this did occasionally happen. The older tramway men were very keen on good time-keeping, and many carried a large fob-watch on a chain, which they consulted when time was getting tight. Many guards and drivers worked as teams, and shared a turn, which gave them early and late shifts in alternate weeks. Students either replaced regular guards who were having a day-off, or worked on specials which each depot sent to supplement the service cars on the Promenade. When a student had worked a full season, the next year he might be offered a turn with a regular driver. I always refused this because I enjoyed working with different drivers each day; at Bispham there were some real 'characters' and some who had driven trams in other towns, including Salford, Stockport, the Stalybridge, Hyde, Mossley & Dukinfield Joint Board (SHMD) and Leeds. The senior driver at the Depot was 632 Tommy Leeming, who had joined the Blackpool & Fleetwood Tramroad Company at Bispham in 1917, and could remember the old manager John Cameron, who was a real martinet. Tommy still had his Company driver's badge as well as his Blackpool licence, which he wore on an enamelled plate, buttoned on to his breast pocket by a leather strap. All the older drivers had these, but students merely paid their shilling and got a

'Conductor's Licence for A Carriage Using a Tramway'. If you worked on buses you had to wear the PSV plastic licence discs, red for drivers and green for guards. Few of these were seen at Bispham when I first started, but as the years passed, more of the younger men got their badge, ready for the time when the inland tram routes were to be replaced by buses.

Such morbid thoughts were quite unknown when I first arrived at the Depot in 1960. Bispham was then quite a busy shed, operating a 12 minute North Station & Fleetwood service with an intermediate 12 minutes to Thornton Gate. The latter routes were known as whiz-bangs, because you were straight in-and-out again with only 2 minutes layover time at the terminus. Much more loathed were the Squires Gate duties, where we operated a 12 minute service to Bispham using seven cars. On some shifts you worked exclusively on the Back Road route – as North Station was known, and on others you did half on Squires Gate. The duty rosters were prepared by the depot inspector each day, and were posted both at Bispham Station and in the depot crew-room, twenty-four hours before. The sheets – as they were known – told you the duty number, the routes, starting and finishing times, the driver's number, and your own. When you reported for duty, you ticked-off on the sheets, and drew your TIM from the office. If a guard or driver missed, the depot reserves would have to turn-out, but this was a rare event at Bispham.

Crews liked the Back Road service because the pattern was completely predictable: regulars on the early cars going to the Station, all with the right change, quiet in the mid-morning, except on market days, and busy at teatime from the Station. On Tuesdays and Fridays, large queues developed for Fleetwood Market, and 'specials' were sent up to North Station to clear the crowds. Saturdays were busy, with holidaymakers departing and arriving at the Station: we used to stack luggage high on the platform – the old Pantograph cars were specially useful, with their commodious platforms. In those days we unloaded right in front of the station, and the traffic was held-up while all the cases were unloaded into the road. On one memorable occasion we were running late, so I left the passengers passing-out their cases while I went to turn the trolley.

The terminus outside North Station, as the conductor raises his arm to stop the traffic and allow the passengers to disembark from the tram. **R.P. Fergusson**

Outside the Odeon, a fully loaded Pantograph 173 is about to leave while the next tram Brush 291 arrives. The queue barrier is empty and we can see the Bundy clock on the tram stop pole. **Author**

The conductor's view of the Pantograph 175 saloon, showing the standing driver, the worn seats, bare light bulbs, ceiling clerestories – and the clear centre passage. **Author**

Forgetting that our car was a Brush-car with air-operated sliding doors, I pulled the trolley off the wire, upon which the doors closed and trapped one man half-in and half-out of the car! Fortunately he didn't suffer from any ill-effects, and we were soon off to collect the next load of newcomers, with their pound notes for penny fares. They always asked for their hotel by name, and expected you to know them all. Saturdays were really hard work on the Back Road, and guards were heard to mutter that, "it would be a good job, if it wasn't for the passengers."

The Pantograph Cars

My personal favourites were the old green Pantograph cars, which were pressed into service on the Back Road during the height of the season. However I have to admit that they had their drawbacks; since no seat was provided for the driver this meant standing-up while driving, and the platforms were draughty. Elderly passengers sometimes refused to board them because of the two high steps which folded down from the platform, or if they did, they had to be helped on, which made for slow-loading. Once inside, many passengers protested about the lumpy seats, where the springs protruded through the faded red moquette. Letters appeared in the local press every year when the veterans reappeared on the road, but the Department doggedly turned them out each season until 1961. Guards were the only people who liked the Pantographs, because they had the privacy of the back platform, where on a sunny day you could sit on the step and enjoy the sunshine, Another distinctive feature was – paradoxically – the trolley rope, which was hooked through a 'pig's tail' over the windscreen and looped over the handbrake on the rear platform. On a windy day, it was very difficult to get the trolley on to the overhead wire, but experience taught that you had to aim slightly up-wind to succeed. My worst experience with a Pantograph car happened on a wet day in 1960, when I bent down to pick up my waybill from the platform floor, and all my change cascaded in every direction. Somebody thoughtfully rang the bell, and the car set-off down Dickson Road with me scrabbling in every corner to retrieve my cash. The passengers got a free ride on that trip, and I was on the short-list next week!

During the quiet evenings on Fleetwoods, I explored the titles on the side destination box in the saloon, which was normally used to display service number 1. I found some interesting destinations: STOPPING CAR TO BISPHAM, ALL STAGES TO CLEVELEYS, FLEETWOOD ONLY, ALL STATIONS – TO BLACKPOOL. When I experimentally tried introducing these to the travelling public, the Bispham inspector told me to turn the blind back to show the usual unimaginative '1'. Of course the Pantographs were never used on any other route because of their restricted indicator blinds and their slow-loading. I also expect that the Department were somewhat ashamed of them, when compared with the sleek Coronations. However in 1960, Pantograph 170 ventured down to the Pleasure Beach, in order to take part in the 75th Anniversary procession on 29th September. Since it had no Promenade destinations, 170 showed a blank display and carried free passengers. Of course it was distinct in its green livery, in contrast to all the other cars. Being built in 1928, Pantograph 170 was sixth in the historic procession, undoubtedly finally establishing a unique reputation in the fleet!

The 1961 Season & Nostalgia

The 1961 Season was a gloomy one in many ways, with the threat of change in the air. The local press was full of controversy about the trams, which they alleged were a source of traffic congestion in the Town Centre. The Squires Gate route was already doomed in that year, the Marton route seemed likely to follow and even down at the Bispham depot 'the writing was on the wall'. The long-familiar Pantographs were in decline and the depot inspector told me that only 170, 172 and 175 were available for use in an emergency. Following the fitting of the new trolley reverser outside the Odeon in Dickson Road, they had been fitted with longer trolleys and lost their characteristic ropes. These last remaining Pantographs cars ran during the Easter weekend 1961, but never ventured into regular service again, despite my best endeavours. On one Sunday, when I started at 9 a.m., I found myself working with one of the old drivers Bill Crag, and I was overjoyed when the shed-man had booked Pantograph 170 for us. However Bill said: 'I'll go home rather than stand-up for seven hours driving that thing', and the shed-man found us railcoach 213, and there was no compensation for me!

I seemed to spend a lot of time on stand-by that year, but it was a very interesting way of looking behind the scenes and finding out what was going on. We had several visitors in late July, two open buses – old Leyland Cheetahs – were stored in the yard, decorated with flags and bunting for Bispham Gala Day on the Saturday. On the following day, Grinder car 2 arrived from Marton Depot, by way of Royal Oak and Lytham Road, to do some night-grinding of the Lord Street track in Fleetwood. One of our old cars – Pantograph 168 – was seen out on-test in July, in the guise of a Rocket – with an inclined saloon and an entrance through the fiery rocket tail at the back. On August 1st we sent two 'specials' to Rossall School to carry the end-of-term school boys to North Station, in a traditional way. One day that month I was sent up to Bispham Station on Engineering Car 3, which was going to repair the overhead wire at Cavendish Road. My job was to stand at the track-side several poles away and warn the tram drivers to reduce their speed, till the job was complete.

At that time the traditional Standard cars were very much in evidence on the Promenade, although they did not usually work up to Bispham apart from taking their lunchtime breaks. Then you could see them together, 40, 48 & 49 making a fine sight at Bispham Station! Each morning the Standards would work from Marton depot and reach the Promenade by way of Waterloo Road, Royal Oak junction and Lytham Road. Sometimes, in order to spread them out, the Depot Inspector would send them first to Highfield Road or Squires Gate. While working on a service-car on 8th August, we passed 40 and 49 bound for Squires Gate, and this was such an unusual sight that even the passengers turned round and admired them! During 1961 all seven available standards (40, 48, 49, 147, 158, 159 & 160) were in use at the height of the Season, on the Promenade where their 78-seat capacity was a great advantage.

Many of the Bispham crews had worked on trams in other towns: Jack Bendelow from Leeds, Inspector Charlie Andrews and guard Stan Pollit from SHMD depot at Hyde. One day when I was waiting for my driver to return from delivering a tram to Rigby Road Depot, I listened to them reminisce about the old days. The depot at Hyde was apparently right next to the river, and crews had trouble turning the trolleys outside the shed and next to the river. One day during the War, a tiny conductress who pulled the trolley rope down to swing the boom, was lifted right off her feet and was left dangling over the river! The shed-man had to retrieve her back to the depot yard, so that the tram could depart with a conductress! Towards the end of my season on the trams in 1961, I worked with Arnold Mitchell, who had been a tram driver in Stockport, and he told me how each driver used to carry his own maintenance kit. During the Second World War blitz in Manchester, Stockport cars were turned round at the Levenshulme boundary for safety. Sometimes drivers had to continue with their service-car to the centre of Manchester, with the threat of an air-raid imminent, then it was the aim to get in-and-out as quickly as possible, ensuring some fast running! Compared with that, even the rigours of Squires Gate seemed safely familiar in 1961!

Squires Gate

If you were booked to work on routes 51–57, you knew that you were in for a pasting on the Gate. I once punched 140 tickets on a round trip with a 48-seat Brush car, and it was rumoured by the crews that the passengers dropped out of the trees on Lytham Road. The main problem with Squires Gate was Central Promenade, where you were delayed by the Promenade specials. Despite the separate shelters for Squires Gate passengers at Cabin, Gynn, Talbot & Central, there was considerable confusion amongst the visitors, as to where Squires Gate was. Most of them thought that it was at the end of the Promenade, and used to run from that shelter to catch the Lytham Road car. When it turned off the Prom at Manchester Square, there was consternation amongst the visitors and a mad scramble for the doors. The Department contributed to this confusion by displaying a neat board at the stops, which stated 'WATSON ROAD for the PLEASURE BEACH'. The locals who lived along Lytham Road resented this, and the crews discouraged passengers who wanted Pleasure Beach. There was a lot of short-stage riding between Squires Gate and Manchester Square, which kept the guard busy all the way down. Alternate cars – double-deck Balloons from Rigby Road –provided a service as far as the Cabin. There was no love lost between the crews of the rival depots: Rigby Road crews were known to turn short at Highfield Road when they were running late or getting near their break. We would then have to take their passengers on to Squires Gate, and on the return journey we could have a three-bell load by the time we got to Highfield Road. Once, I was so busy collecting fares, that I did not notice that one of the passengers was trapped in the sliding doors all the way from Royal Oak to Station Road. The route seemed to have more than its fair share of cantankerous old ladies with dogs, and I can't say that I was sorry when the green bus stop poles appeared during the summer of 1961, in readiness for the changeover at the end of the season. For once, the professional overcame the enthusiast in me.

A Journey Into The Past!

By 1962, when I reported to the Transport Offices once more, and paid my shilling licence, things had changed quite a lot. There were now less tram jobs, and many ex-patriots from Bispham were sporting bus badges. Much of my time that season was spent at Rigby Road, because there were now only 14 service cars running out of Bispham Depot. In contrast to the other firm, Rigby Road operated all the bus services and the Promenade trams, and so it was a very busy and cosmopolitan place. Instead of a single output sheet to tick-off, you had to search for your number on a row of them, and then go round to the depot, where the shed-man was despatching the cars. The service cars left first, and then the specials, a process which could last until 10.00 a.m. as the cars left in convoys for different destinations. The shed-man that Year was 'Little Billy' Howarth, who reputedly had to give up bus driving because he couldn't reach the pedals! One day, I was booked to work with him, and he sent me back to the canteen while he got all the cars away.

I used the opportunity to visit the works, where the Western Train illuminated car was being built from Railcoach 209 and one of our old Pantograph cars 174. Eventually Billy and I went out on a Boat car, and because he was well-known to the inspectors, we were given a circular tour. Loading at the Tower, where the tour advertising-boards stood, we waited until the car was full before we set off for Little Bispham. Unfortunately the loop there was closed for repairs, and so we had to reverse at Bispham and confusion reigned as the passengers had to turn-over their wooden seats. In compensation, Billy took them to Starr Gate instead of Pleasure Beach, where tours usually turned round. That – as Billy announced – was the Circular bit this time! Working at Rigby Road was certainly varied; one day you might be relieving a regular guard on a Coronation car operating the Fleetwood service, and spend the next 'topping' on a Balloon.

Right: A unique opportunity – when the Author worked as the conductor of Crossbench car 2, photographed by a holidaymaker in 1962 at Pleasure Beach loop.

NORTH STATION-FLEETWOOD. 1st. Oct. 1962 to 28th. Oct. 1962.

ROUTE NO.4. Leave Depot Weekdays..4-56am. Sundays..7-43am.

	SUNS START a.m.	WEEKDAYS a.m.	*WAIT FOR BUS FROM LAYTON SER.22* a.m.	a.m.	a.m.	p.m.	p.m.	p.m.	p.m.	SUNS FIN p.m.
North Station......	-	-	6-25	8-59	11-47	2-35	5-23	8-11	10-59	11- 0
Bispham...........	7-48	5- 1	6-36	9-10	11-58	2-46	5-34	8-22	11-10	11-11
Cleveleys........	7-55	5- 8	6-43	9-17	12- 5	2-53	5-41	8-29	11-17	11-18
Broadwater.......	8- 4	5-15	6-51	9-27	12-15	3- 3	5-51	8-39	11-27	11-26
ASH STREET.......		5-21								
Fleetwood........	8-14	-	7- 1	9-37	12-25	3-13	6- 1	8-49	11-37	11-38
Fleetwood........	8-15	-	7- 2	9-43	12-31	3-19	6- 7	8-55	11-37	11-38
ASH STREET.......		5-23								
Broadwater.......	8-25	5-28	7-11	9-53	12-41	3-29	6-17	9- 5	11-47	11-48
Cleveleys........	8-34	5-36	7-20	10- 2	12-50	3-38	6-26	9-14	11-56	11-57
Bispham..........	8-41	5-43	7-27	10-10	12-58	3-46	6-34	9-22	12- 4	12- 5
North Station....	8-52	5-53	7-38	10-21	1- 9	3-57	6-45	9-33	To Depot Weekdays.	To Depot Sundays.
North Station....	9- 3	5-55	7-39	10-23	1-11	3-59	6-47	9-35		
Bispham..........	9-14	6- 7	7-50	10-34	1-22	4-10	6-58	9-46		
Cleveleys........	9-21	-	7-57	10-41	1-29	4-17	7- 5	9-53		
Broadwater.......	9-31	-	8- 7	10-51	1-39	4-27	7-15	10- 3		
Fleetwood........	9-41	-	8-17	11- 1	1-49	4-37	7-25	10-13		
Fleetwood........	9-43	-	8-19	11- 7	1-55	4-43	7-31	10-19		
Broadwater.......	9-53	-	8-29	11-17	2- 5	4-53	7-41	10-29		
Cleveleys........	10- 2	-	8-38	11-26	2-14	5- 2	7-50	10-38		
Bispham..........	10-10	6-12	8-46	11-34	2-22	5-10	7-58	10-46		
North Station....	10-21	6-23	8-57	11-45	2-33	5-21	8- 9	10-57		

then
as Weekdays.

9

TROLLEY LEAVING WIRE

Blackpool Corporation Transport

TRAFFIC EMPLOYEE'S REPORT.

FOR OFFICE USE ONLY.

Date Received :   Referred To :

Depot. BISPHAM   Car No. 294   Date 5/8/1963

To the General Manager.

Sir,

When travelling from BISPHAM

to NORTH STATION the trolley left the wire at

Pole No. .... situate at LOWTHER AVE.

time 8-53 a.m. Damage caused OVERHEAD BROUGHT DOWN + POLE BENT   Delay to Traffic 10 MINUTES

Mtn. BROWN W.   Staff No. 1234

Cdr. PALMER S.   Staff No. 3604

NEWSPAPER PARCEL STAMP — BLACKPOOL CORPORATION TRANSPORT — 4d. — W. LUFF GENERAL MANAGER — AT OWNER'S RISK

NEWSPAPER PARCEL STAMP — BLACKPOOL CORPORATION TRANSPORT — 6d. — W. LUFF GENERAL MANAGER — AT OWNER'S RISK

A 6301 — Blackpool Corporation Transport — 9d. PARCEL TICKET — To cover Carriage of Parcel up to 28 lbs. — This Parcel is carried subject to Corporation's Regulations thereon.

A 7953 — Blackpool Corporation Transport — 1/- PARCEL TICKET — To cover Carriage of Parcel up to 56 lbs. — This Parcel is carried subject to Corporation's Regulations thereon.

Right: Short workings in Fleetwood always turned at the Ash Street crossover, and Coronation 319 is seen with it's conductor armed with the trolley pole.
David Packer Collection

Below right: The traditional saloon of Brush car 290, showing the original decor including the lamp shade panels, the half-drop windows with handrails and the sliding platform doors.   **Author**

Undoubtedly the high-point of my career as a guard came on 2nd August 1962, when I had the privilege of guarding No. 2, the 1898 open-sided Fleetwood crossbench car. Following the 75th Anniversary celebrations of the Tramway in 1960, No. 2 had been stored at Copse Road depot, out of service. Suddenly in August 1962, it had returned to Rigby Road depot, and was cleaned ready for service. On that day, I was booked to work on a Boat-car with Tommy Bradshaw – an old Salford driver. Being a hand-brake man, he agreed to my idea for persuading Gilly Potter – the shed-man – to let us have No. 2 instead. Eventually he agreed, and after a tangle with the dirty trolley rope, we swept down Central Promenade in style. The time-keeper at Central Station was speechless with amazement, but the passengers in the circular tour queue were more enthusiastic. The bell-system on the car was rather primitive, so I borrowed the point-boy's whistle. For the first time I had the experience of standing on the running-board for collecting fares, with one arm wrapped round the stanchion. Issuing 2/6d tickets from a TIM was not easy, while holding on at the same time, and you had to watch out for those projecting road signs along North Promenade. Older crews to whom we chatted at the terminus, could recall dreadful stories of guards who had been injured while collecting fares on the old Racks. I was extra careful, but when at lunchtime we had to do a service journey between Bispham and Pleasure Beach, things were decidedly hectic. Tommy seemed to enjoy driving the car, tapping the gong and standing upright to the controls, hand poised on the hand-brake column. The passengers enjoyed it also, and it was lucky that the day was fine and sunny. Whenever the car passed, cameras were raised to capture the moment for posterity, and we must have been the most-photographed tram crew in town. We stayed out with No. 2 until it started to go dark, and then exchanged it for a mundane warmer railcoach for the rest of the turn. The old car was out several times that week with Tommy at the control – in fact I think he got a liking for it – but after that, it went back into store and never ran again in service at Blackpool. Happily, it is now operating at the National Tramway Museum, but it has returned to its native Tramroad in 1998, for its 100th Birthday to celebrate the Centenary!

Early turn at Bispham

Most of my career as a guard was spent at Bispham Depot, where the daily routine seemed commonplace at the time, but in perspective had gained a new interest. The early-turn shifts were headed by duty 590, which entailed bringing out the first tram of the morning at 4.56 a.m. I worked this turn for several days in 1963, and travelled to the depot by the night-tram, which left Fleetwood at 4.19 a.m. Standing at Rossall Beach tram stop in the first flush of dawn, I could hear the regular tapping of the wheels on the rail-joints as soon as the car left Broadwater and crossed the open fields towards Rossall School. The unblinking glow of the twin-headlamps appeared round the corner, and the howl of the gears indicated that the car was travelling at full speed. These night cars were staffed by three-badge men, who were bus and tram drivers so that they could crew either type of vehicle, as the occasion demanded. The car rarely slowed-down enough for me to jump on, and wave to the crew, both of whom were talking in the front cab. I have never had such a fast journey to Bispham, no compulsory stops, and running in full parallel for most of the way. Subsequently, one of these night cars, travelling at speeds in excess of 40 m.p.h., brought down the overhead line at Norbreck, and did such damage that all future night-cars were changed to buses!

Down at the silent depot, nothing stirred in the yard, and all the doors were closed, except on pit 5, where the first car waited for us with its lights on and compressor running. I drew my TIM from the night-man, and found that my mate was Tommy Leeming, whose mate Betty Rose was having the day off. We walked across to the Depot together, and while I filled-in my waybill, he checked the car. First, he knocked-off the main switch, and rattled the controllers through all the notches of power, and back through the brake-notches. Having already turned on the compressor, he checked the lights for dead bulbs and the windows for cracks, before sounding the hooter and drawing the car out into the yard. While I turned the trolley, Tom lifted the seats over the sand-hoppers and made sure that they were filled and working – you never knew when you would need them if the rail was greasy. Having operated the sand-hopper from both ends, Tom got out and checked that there was a neat pile of sand in front of each wheel. Thus satisfied, he released the air brake with a hiss, and put on one notch of power, calling to me 'in the street'. I had to jump off the car as we turned into Red Bank Road, and hold the wooden handle to operate the frog in the overhead. As we rumbled up the street, passing an early morning milk float, I turned the back indicator to ASH ST. FLEETWOOD, where the car was due at 5.21 a.m. Having crossed the deserted Promenade, I had to push-over the points with a rusty point-iron, and swing the trolley arm, so that we could cross to the northbound track, We were two minutes late already, but at that time of the morning it was soon made-up. There were no passengers on the first part of the journey to Cleveleys, so I had plenty of time to make-up my waybill and put my cash-float into my bag. As we rolled down the cutting towards Anchorsholme, Tom warned that he was going to apply Jimmy, the emergency electric brake. This was standard procedure on the first trip of the morning, and I held on tight to the stanchion as the car jerked to a halt with noisy protests from the motors beneath.

Once in Fleetwood, we picked-up a few passengers along Radcliffe Road, but nobody said much at this time of the morning. As we approached each stop, Tom drew level with the pole and switched the lights off without ever leaving the cab (today they operate on a time-switch). On the first trip we turned at Ash Street, on the old crossover at Styan Street, just past Woolworths and this meant trolleying the car, since no crossover wire was provided. You could either trolley the pole from behind, swinging it onto the other line as the car crossed-over, or – more daringly – trolley-leading, which meant the car driving towards you before you ducked the pole and let it swing round with the momentum of the car. Several crews were waiting for us at Ash Street, bound either for our depot or Rigby Road. Our time card told us to connect with the Central Station car at Bispham, and while our passengers transferred, I took the opportunity to switch-on the water geyser in the station, ready for our first brew when we returned.

The Parcels Trade

Up at North Station, we had to wait for the Layton bus at 6.25 a.m., and pick-up passengers at the end of the track, instead of the usual tram stop. This was probably a relic of the Layton tram service before the war. Another interesting ritual on these early morning duties, was carrying newspapers up to Fleetwood. A W.H. Smith van would draw-up alongside the tram, and the guard would help in stacking the bundles of papers on the platform. In return for his help, the Smith's driver would give the tram crew a couple of morning papers to read. The Transport Department had its own newspaper stamp for this service, which was affixed to each bundle, and bore the value and the manager's name. I once saw a stamp bearing the name of Walter Luff, the previous manager, and I managed to peel it off the parcel. When we arrived in Cleveleys Square, a newsagent was usually waiting with a van, and his bundles were passed out from the platform. At Fleetwood, we pulled-up in Albert Square outside Coppock's wholesale newsagents, Tom gave two pips on the hooter and a boy ran out to collect the papers. Later the same morning, Tom stopped the car outside a small sweet shop in North Albert Street, near to the Ferry, and pointed to a sign with a letter 'P' hanging outside. They had a parcel ready for collection, I went inside, collected the package, signed for it, filled-in my staff number and the car number on a small receipt, and returned to the car. "To be collected at North Station" read the label, and there was a small blue 6d stamp attached. At Cleveleys, Tom told the time-keeper to ring through to the bus station at Talbot Road, and warn them that we had the parcel, so that they could collect it when we arrived at North Station. A messenger was duly waiting there: "Have you got a parcel?" he said, collected it, and in return gave me a tin of paint, bound for Cleveleys. This parcels service (up to 56 lbs), which died with the North Station service in 1963, was a relic of the old Company days, and an interesting link with the past.

The Evening Volunteers

When you finish the morning early-turn, it is possible to sign the list for 'Evening Volunteers' – known by the crews as 'Grabbing'. After a short lunch break I reported back to the depot and found that my mate was the depot's *'Bête noir'* - a noisy Cockney who had been sent down from Rigby Road depot. "We're all right on this – if we play it right" he confides. We motor-up Red Bank Road in a Brush car, and the Inspector at Bispham Top sends us to Cleveleys for our first trip. There are several passengers, including some well-dressed ladies, and Tony decides to take them on a lively ride. Once clear of the points at Bispham, he opens-up the car, which on the badly-maintained track starts to swing and jazz violently from side-to-side. The passengers are nearly thrown-off their seats, and Tony grins round to me. "Guard tell the driver to stop doing that!" says a lady imperiously, "Sorry Madam, it's the bad track causing it", I replied, "Nonsense – he is doing it deliberately", she replies, and gets off at Cleveleys, threatening to report us for this insubordination. We spend the rest of the shift drifting up and down the Promenade, until we are sent to Bispham. Before we arrive there Tony puts-up CLEVELEYS on the windscreen, and later changes it to FLEETWOOD – to ensure a longer ride. At the Ferry we go on the Loop and brew-up, before putting PLEASURE BEACH upon the screen, and carrying the first-house passengers in the town centre. Of course the aim was to stay out for as long as possible, but by 9.00 p.m. we are caught without any passengers and sent back to the depot at the end of a long day. For me this adds up to more than fourteen hours working on the platform, and boosts the pay packet for that week.

Boating on Sunday

After Marton Depot closed, we acquired a fleet of open Boat-cars, which were sent out each fine Sunday to operate the Circular Tours. These were staffed by crews working their days off, at double-time rates of pay. When I arrived at the crew-room one Sunday morning in July, it was full of unfamiliar faces from Rigby Road, mostly sporting bus badges on their uniforms. The chatter of conversation died-down as the depot inspector 'Tot' Thompson put his head round the door and gave the order, 'Take to the boats'. The depot resounded with unaccustomed laughter, the ringing of bells and testing of hooters before, one by one, we were summoned out to the depot yard. Here, one of the depot reserves, Albert Brown, whose highly-polished straps were rarely worn in-action, stood waiting with the bamboo pole. My driver, somewhat unkindly, asked what would become of Albert when the depot closed, suggesting that

he be mounted on a pedestal at Bispham Station. However, Albert swung the pole with dignity, and we were on our way up Red Bank Road.

Once we left Bispham and were on the open track, the driver opened up the controller, and the wind ruffled the crew's usually smart appearance. Guarding a Boat was fun, but had its disadvantages when your tickets blew-out like streamers and could be lost overboard, and when you had to shout to the driver or use a whistle, because there are only two bells on the platform. If you were given a circular tour, the minor disadvantages were heavily outweighed, especially on a sunny day. Once the tour passengers had been loaded, and the fares collected, the guard could enjoy the passing scene, apart from his duty of swinging the points at Little Bispham and the Pleasure Beach. I used to take a camera with me in my TIM box, and standing at the back of the car, sneaked some interesting pictures, which included the Dreadnought and the new Western Train, also running on circulars. There was a special waybill for tours, which had recently included the Marton circular, the Prom circular, the coastal tour and the tour of the illuminations. It was usual to pay-in at Bispham Station, where a cash-clerk was in attendance during office hours.

We did two tours in the morning, and a busy service-run to the Pleasure Beach at lunchtime, where we stacked for half an hour, before starting the afternoon tour. The passing kaleidoscope of faces and places were all seen to an advantage from a Boat car, and other crews, battling on the service cars, looked at you in envy. Later in the afternoon, the clouds gathered ominously over the sea and rain was threatening. We were then glad it was our last tour of the day, since nothing could be worse than being caught by a shower when only halfway round the Tour. The passengers could always get off, but the crew were not allowed to leave the sinking ship! We were heading for Bispham when the rains came, but to my amazement, people actually still wanted to board the car. I concluded that there must be some truth in the old Lancashire saying: "There's nowt as queer as folk".

A Chapter of Accidents

The thing that makes a tram interesting, is when it fails to follow its predictable path, and I include incidents which happened to me during the Seasons 1960–1964.

Left: Turning the trolley is always good for exercise, and I am seen here at the Tower about to swing 227 round for its return.

Right: Collecting the fares on Boat 227, with the tickets blowing in the wind and the passengers joking about wallpaper!
John Minor (2)

The early turn on 23rd July started normally enough, I was working with Jack Tonge on railcoach 221, and it was Market Day. We found ourselves following a Balloon along Dickson Road to the Station, and Jack opened the cab door to tell me that we should go down for two, so that we could come out of the terminus ahead of it. This would not delay us on our trip to Fleetwood. Accordingly, I turned the rear indicators, pulled-over the seat-backs, and made-up my waybill as we approached the terminal track. Because we would reverse outside the Odeon, and the trolley could not use the automatic-reverser, which was positioned nearer the station, I would have to turn the trolley by hand, using the bamboo pole. When I coaxed it out of its rack in front of the Odeon and reached for the trolley, I found that it

Top left: Railcoach 221 resting on the siding at Rossall with it's passengers, having damaged it's life guards and being photographed by the guard!

Left: A guard's view from the cab of the service car, as he turns the indicators and captured this scene of the terminus and Dickson Road in 1963.

Below: Brush car 285 at the new loading barrier since 1961, with the lunchtime queue boarding it. Notice the TRAM STOP warning painted on the road for traffic. **Author**

BLACKPOOL CORPORATION TRAMWAYS.

CONDUCTORS' DON'TS.

1. **DON'T** " Ring On " until Passengers are safely aboard.
2. **DON'T** " Ring Off " until Passengers are quite clear of Car.
3. **DON'T** turn your back on prospective Passengers.
4. **DON'T** lose your temper.
5. **DON'T** forget it is just as easy to be courteous and civil as brusque in manner.
6. **DON'T** forget **respect** begets **respect**.
7. **DON'T** neglect to register your **Commencing** and **Finishing Numbers**.
8. **DON'T** **neglect** paying in promptly (each trip when possible).
9. **DON'T** lose time ; your smartness in assisting to **maintain good time** is appreciated both by the Public and the Management.
10. **DON'T** hesitate to courteously challenge Passengers for tickets or contracts when in doubt.
11. **DON'T** **MISS FARES.** (Missed fares reflect on your smartness and endanger your position).
12. **DON'T** allow " **Over-riding.** "
13. **DON'T** fail to look out for " would-be Passengers " at Stopping Places.
14. **DON'T** forget to call out all stopping places in a loud and distinct voice.
15. **DON'T** forget to place **Reversible Seats** in the **Direction in which the Car is going,** and care must be taken to see that **before leaving Termini** that the **Seats are placed correctly.** Also en route Conductors must see that passengers do not turn the seats back.
16. **DON'T** fail to give passengers their change promptly.
17. **DON'T** dress in half Uniform ; better without than one incomplete, and keep your buttons and bright parts well polished.
18. **DON'T** ride on Car Platform Steps when passing through depot doorways, and beware of the Car Pits when alighting.
19. **DON'T** neglect to read all posted Notices and Regulations issued for the efficiency of the Tramway Service.
20. **DON'T** let the above points escape your memory ; they are necessary qualifications which the General Manager requires and which he appreciates.

MOTORMEN'S DON'TS.

1. **DON'T** Switch on Power until proper signal has been given by Conductor.
2. **DON'T** neglect to sign after first journey as to state of Brakes, Life Guards, and to report any irregularities.
3. **DON'T** fail to stop at " Compulsory Stops."
4. **DON'T** miss Passengers at Request Stops (missed fares reflect on your smartness and endanger your position).
5. **DON'T** hesitate to pull up when in doubt regarding clear way.
6. **DON'T** forget the duty is yours to warn by signal any obstruction.
7. **DON'T** lose time between Compulsory Stops. A **quick service to time** is appreciated both by the Public and the Management.
8. **DON'T** allow any unauthorised person on your platform.
9. **DON'T** fail to always keep a sharp look out for intending Passengers.
10. **DON'T** forget **respect** begets **respect.**
11. **DON'T** dress in half Uniform ; better without than one incomplete, and keep your buttons and bright parts well polished.
12. **DON'T** neglect to give necessary warning when approaching and passing the rear of a standing Car.
13. **DON'T** neglect to report immediately any defects observed on your Car or line.
14. **DON'T** run too close to the preceding car (See Rule No. 5), also Bye-law No. 3, which reads : " The Driver of every Car shall so drive the same that it shall follow a preceding Car at not less than twenty yards distance." Any Motorman offending against this Bye-law is liable to prosecution, and dismissal.
15. **DON'T** fail to report immediately all accidents, no matter how trivial.
16. **DON'T** ride on Car Platform Steps when passing through depot doorways, and beware of the Car Pits when alighting.
17. **DON'T** neglect to read all posted Notices and Regulations issued for the efficiency of the Tramway Service.
18. **DON'T** let the above points escape your memory ; they are necessary qualifications which the General Manager requires and which he appreciates.

---

was rotten, and drooped like a wilting flower. A passing bus driver found it highly amusing, and I had to resort to raising the offending pole by leaning it against the side of the car and raising it slowly, like a periscope. Having overcome that trauma, we loaded at the barrier, and set off at a spanking pace for Fleetwood. At Gynn Square, the Promenade car was waiting for us, and we swept on our way with panache, and a three-bell load.

We reached Rossall School without incident, and I rang-off the car which started forward and then was halted by a series of bumps and lurches, Jack jumped down from his cab, and I joined him to inspect the front of the car: he pointed to the lifeguard, which had dropped and hit the road crossing. The slats of wood had broken-off, and we had run over them, Jack decided that the car could not be driven forward, and looking at the large queue of trams behind, I suggested that we reversed over the crossover and stacked on the old siding. He was a bit dubious, but bowed to my superior knowledge as I declared that we had used the siding on a tram tour the previous year. I swung the huge point-lever or the railway-type points, which moved easily in their black grease, and trolleyed the car as it swung onto the other track. Then we found a snag; the leading points into the siding were locked. We decided to proceed to the points at the other end of the loop-line, and reverse in. This accomplished, Jack lit a cigarette, I took a photograph for posterity, and the passengers looked bewildered.

When the next car came passed heading to Blackpool, we flagged it down, and sent a message to the Cleveleys time-keeper Len Wright. Soon the reply came with a Fleetwood bound car; we were to put our passengers on that car and proceed with our normal time-card, leaving the relief crew on 221. By the time we were back at Bispham, we were only twenty minutes late, but had missed taking over our Squires Gate duty. The depot reserves had taken the car, and we sat in the sunshine on the cliffs and had a lunch break until they came back. Every cloud had a silver lining!

The second incident happened on August Bank Holiday Monday 1963, and true to form, it was raining. My driver that morning was called Bill – he had been late reporting for duty and, in fact, I had been sent round to his house to 'knock him up'. Accordingly, we were late, and Bill had the handle round as we left Bispham and headed for the Cabin. The car was pitching and swaying over the poor track, when suddenly there was a bumping and banging from overhead, which Bill had not heard. I tried ringing the bell, which obviously didn't work, and eventually got his attention by banging on the cab door. He stopped the car, and we got out to look: "Oh bloody hell", he exclaimed as he surveyed the bent and twisted trolley pole, and the overhead line, which was hanging loose. We tried putting the trolley back on the overhead, but it was so contorted that the wind blew it off again. In the end an Inspector, who had been travelling as a passenger, suggested that I travel in the back cab, and hold the pole down, while we were pushed clear of the track.

The next car behind was a Coronation, driven by Harry Likeover, known as 'Happy Harry' because of his antics in the cab. He entertained me through the cab window all the way to the Cabin, where we were uncoupled, and rolled down to the Gynn ourselves. The inspector jumped out, and pulled a handle on the side of the automatic-point box, as we rolled across Gynn Square, and waited at the bottom of the hill for the next North Station car. By the time it came, my arms were getting very tired, and very wet, as the water ran down my sleeve. We were pushed up Dickson Road by another Brush-car and on to the terminal stub, where the motor tower-wagon was waiting, to lash, down the offending trolley with rope. Bill and I sat in the saloon and read the paper, until we were told to leave the car, and travel back to Bispham, where another car would be brought out of the depot. As we returned along Dickson Road, we passed the Engineering car No. 3, sent to recover 294, and I was sorry that this time I had missed a photographic scoop.

The conductor always had to be imaginative and even energetic when dealing with unexpected situations on a tram. On 29th July 1960, I was working on Pantograph 173 and we were heading for Fleetwood at Rossall, when the driver slowed down and stopped the car in the middle of countryside. He opened the sliding doors at the end of the saloon and pointed out to me that the overhead was hanging down ahead, because it was loose from the bracket-arm. I had to get out onto the reservation and hold the trolley rope tightly, thus taking the pressure off the overhead and maintaining contact. While the driver motored the car through the problem to the overhead, I had to stumble along behind, keeping my feet on the ballast! We did succeed in getting through and I was glad to get back on to the platform again – the real location of the conductor!

Finally – on 29th June 1964 – we left the Ferry with a fairly full load on railcoach 270 and when we got to Ash Street, there was a crowd of workers waiting for us. They were busy boarding the platform, when a child clutching a large tin of paint let it slip from her hand. The tin fell to the floor on its side and the lid opened, with white paint spreading all over the platform. I told the child to scoop it back into the tin

Night scene at North Station on the last day of Service 1, as Brush car 288 is about to reverse at 8.25 p.m.

Trams entering track 2 pause to have their trolley wheel greased, and the conductor leaves the car to pay in his takings at the office.

The final paying in at Bispham Depot on 27th October 1963 by the crew of last tram 290: Driver Bill Bracewell, Guard Stan Pollitt and Inspector 'Tot' Thompson. The finale of Bispham Depot! **Author (3)**

with the lid, while the tram set off along Radcliffe Road and I tried to collect the fares in. At each stop I had to give a warning 'mind where you put your feet', and the child got off at Broadwaters with the remaining tin of white paint. One of the passengers gave his newspaper to cover the white paint and mop it up, while at Cleveleys the Inspector inspected it and decided to 'phone Bispham Depot. Here we changed onto Brush car 302, while 270 with its white platform was taken down to the Depot for cleaning.

Certainly the conductor's life is full of surprises - and they should always 'Be Prepared'!

Late Turn at the Depot

Amongst the regulars, late-turn was a shift to be endured rather than enjoyed, but I quite enjoyed it because the night scene showed the trams in a different perspective. One late-turn duty stands out in my memory: No. 504, the last Fleetwood from the town centre. My mate that night was Bernard Crossley, who worked permanent lates much to the amazement of his colleagues. He confided in me that he didn't like getting up in the morning. The shift started down at the depot, where some of the drivers were watching a game of bowls on the green at the back of the crew room. We found that there was a special going out on evening volunteers, so we all hitched a ride up Red Bank Road. Suddenly we were thrown off our feet as the car screeched to a halt just out of the depot yard, head-on to a 15A bus. "Why didn't someone tell me that was there?" laughed Frank, the driver. He motored-up again, frightening the visiting motorists who strayed across the road-centre track, and were confronted by this tram. As we reached the Promenade, Annie – the guard – blew her whistle and shouted, "Everybody out!"

We took-over our car going north, and true to form when we got to Fleetwood, Bernard pulled up outside a sweet shop and went inside to buy a bag of toffees, which we consumed during the shift. Our break-time companion in the tiny crew-room at Bispham Station was a character called Dick Barton, the depot-lawyer, who was always good for a laugh. Taking his pipe out of his mouth, he jabbed it in my direction: "How much did you pay-in last night son?" When I told him, he went on, "There you are, you see, when these were penny fares, yes penny fares, I used to take as much as that in copper. No, things aren't what they were, son, and they'll get worse – you mark my words." How right he proved to be, Dick probably never found out, but that night we ran almost empty on 'Fleetwoods', which gave me cause to reflect on his words.

I used to enjoy those quiet evening trips across the fields of Rossall to Fleetwood, followed by a rumble down Lord Street, our lights reflecting in the shop windows. At the Ferry loop, the lights of Morcambe Bay shone across the still water, although the peace was usually shattered on the later trips when the pubs turned out. Trawlermen were hard drinkers, and there was much shouting

and singing, at least as far as Broadwater. Normally, you would have a quiet run up to Bispham, so that you could get your change bagged-up ready for paying-in, but when you were on duty 504, things were different.

A special ritual was followed for the last Fleetwood car. After a night on Squires Gate (Promenade duties after 1961), you would put CABIN on your indicator blinds, turn there, and proceed slowly to North Pier for 11.30 p.m., Here, you would turn the buck, and wait on the centre track with blank indicators, until the last Thornton Gate car arrived from Starr Gate. While it was loading at the shelter, we put FLEETWOOD on our blinds, and drew alongside. Once it accelerated away into the night, as only a Spiv could, the crowd rushed forward, and you had to make sure that you took no more than your three-bell load. Many were left behind to get a taxi, or to wait for the night tram. Here, I must pause to tell the apocryphal tale of the last Fleetwood tram driver, who saw a chap trudging along the track towards Fleetwood. Drawing level with him, the driver opened the windscreen and enquired, "Fleetwood?" "Yes," said the chap, "straight on."

At Bispham Station we clocked on our last trip, and the Inspector turned out the station lights and locked-up for the night. On the way to Fleetwood, all the cars we passed were rushing back to their respective depots; showing MANCHESTER SQUARE for the Rigby Road cars, and 1 - BISPHAM for ours. Soon we were bound for depot too, and at Bispham Top, I swung the trolley and set the points, before the driver sent the car flying down Red Bank Road, the rumble of its wheels echoing from the shop fronts. The shed-man was waiting at the bottom: "On two," he shouted, and we screeched round the curve, into the depot yard. I jumped off and pulled the frog, and the driver took the car into the brightly-lit world of the depot, where the night cleaners were already busily at work. The car stopped in the doorway and the lights went out, as the trolley was hooked and swung over to be greased by a fitter mounted on the top deck of No. 3. The driver went to sign-off in the depot, and I went to the office to pay-in. There was a quiet intense atmosphere, as the queuing guards pushed their waybills piled with change, round the counter towards the hatch where the Depot Inspector checked it, and entered it on the waybill. Everyone was quiet, tired at the end of a

Right: In the following year, 1964, the Brush cars, and the Author, had to move to Rigby Road. The Author is seen here at Fleetwood on 301, along with driver Harold Holden, this being his finale as a guard.

MEMORABLE TOURS OF THE ROUTE

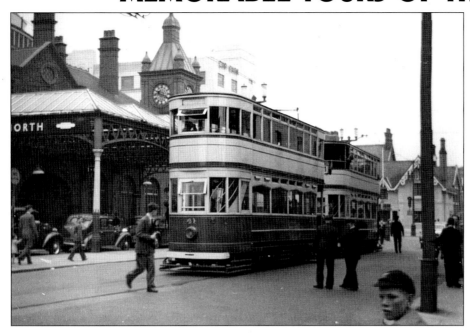

An interesting scene of two Standards, 41 & 40, at North Station during a tour organised by Keith Terry and Keith Pearson in June 1958.

A Sun Saloon – in the form of Marton Vambac 11 – returns to its wartime location at Rossall sidings, during a unique tour to Fleetwood by Keith Terry in July 1962.

On the final weekend of the trams at North Station, an unusual sight of Boat 225 (600) was made by a tour on Saturday morning. Here it is seen outside the Odeon and driven by senior driver Tommy Leeming. **Author (3)**

hard shift and nobody wanted to spoil each other's concentration. Behind the glass partition, the night TIM man checked each machine, and put a new waybill into its box, ready for the next day. Out in the clear night air, all was quiet, the last tram was safely away and the big green doors were shut. The ribbons of steel shone brightly, if forlornly, out of the depot yard and into the deserted street beyond. Another day was finished, and on 26th October that year, the scene was enacted for the last time, when the depot closed for good, now living only in the memory of those, like me, who worked for 'The Other Firm'.

Conclusion

I would like to pay special tribute to all members of Bispham Depot still living, who helped to make my time there so happy. I hope that this chapter brings back some memories for them, even though seen through the eyes of a student-conductor.

Tramway Terminology used in this chapter

back-road cars	trams operating to North Station via Dickson Road – i.e. behind the Promenade.
blue cars	trams operated by Lytham St. Annes, until 1937.
booking	reporting to the management for a misdemeanour.
clocking	punching the time on the waybill by a Bundy time clock.
demic	broken down car.
duck	the trolley-head containing the wheel which runs along the overhead wire.
ducking the pole	pulling the trolley down.
evening or morning volunteers	crews doing overtime.
frog	overhead switch for moving the trolley to another wire.
full parallel	(also getting the handle round) – running at top speed.
guard	tram conductor.
Jimmy	the emergency rheostatic brake.
motor-up	accelerate.
pasting on the Gate	heavy loadings on Squires Gate service.
pig's tail	curly strip of metal mounted on the canopy, used for trapping the trolley rope.
point-iron	a lever used for moving point-blades.
probationer	learner conductor.
shed-man	a driver who directed the cars in and out of the depot.
shower-baths	open-fronted cars, which exposed the driver to the elements.
specials	cars operating without time-cards at the discretion of the time-keepers.
stacking	lining cars up on a siding for later use.
swivelling-duck	a trolley-head which turns round to facilitate using an automatic trolley reverser.
the copper canyon	the Marton route, so named after its penny fares.
the other firm	Bispham Depot and its staff, originating from Company days before 1920, when it was another firm.
the sheets	duty rosters for the next day.
three-badge men	platform staff who were bus driver, tram driver and bus guard – hence the three licence badges.
to go down for two	one car leaves room for another to pull-up behind it.
topping	acting as a top guard, upstairs on a double-decker.
trolleying	swinging the trolley arm while the car crosses-over.
turn	a regular rota of shifts.
turning short	reversing at a crossover before the terminus to make-up time when running late.
whiz-bangs	term used to describe North Station & Thornton Gate service.
wrinkles	tricks of the trade.

Names of Tram-Types used in this chapter

Balloons	Double-deckers built by English Electric in 1935, so named from their bulbous appearance. Nos. 237–263.
Boats	Open cars of this shape, built 1934 by English Electric. Nos. 225–236.
Brush-cars	Cars built by the Brush Company of Loughborough in 1937. Nos. 284–303.
Coronations	Cars built at the time of the 1953 Coronation. Also known by the staff as Spivs. Nos. 304–328.
Marton Vambacs	Cars 10–21, running on Marton with 'silent' bogies.
Pantographs	Single-deck saloons in green livery, built in 1928 for the Fleetwood route, and originally having a pantograph collector instead of a trolley. Nos. 167–176.
Rack	An open-sided car with rows of pillars and seats – hence the full name toastrack – usually applied to completely open cars. The Fleetwood cars had a roof.
Railcoach	A modern single-deck saloon car built in the thirties, by English Electric, usually applied to: 200–224 & 264–283.
Standards	Traditional double-deck cars, some with open balconies and some totally enclosed.

OTHER LIGHT RAIL TRANSIT AND TRAMWAY TITLES FROM PLATFORM 5

LIGHT RAIL REVIEW

Light Rail Review is the ongoing series from Platform 5 Publishing examining Light Rail developments around the world. The editorial content of each volume consists of topical articles by recognised authorities in the Light Rail field, devoted to important issues in this growth area. Much use is made of illustrations, a high proportion in colour, making Light Rail Review an informative source of reference for enthusiasts and transport professionals alike. Each book includes a round-up of UK developments and a full world list of existing LRT systems at time of publication. The following is a list of the main features included in each volume:

LIGHT RAIL REVIEW 3 (Published November 1991) £7.50 + P&P.
Greater Manchester - The Meaning of Metrolink. Amsterdam Sets The Pattern For The Future. Zürich - A Model System. South Yorkshire Supertram - Construction Under Way. Croydon - Public Boost for Tramlink. Midland Metro Awaits Decision. Photo Feature - Europe in 1991. House of Commons Select Committee LRT Report. Hiroshima Leads The Way in Japan. Consultation - Winning Ways. Mixing Light Rail with Heavy Rail.

LIGHT RAIL REVIEW 4 (Published March 1993) £7.50 + P&P.
Midland Metro Funding Fiasco. Nantes - France's First Modern LRT System. Guided Buses - A Credible Alternative? LRT for Cardiff Bay. Melbourne - Tramway in Transition. Manchester Metrolink - Nine Months of Success. Photo Feature - France, Germany & Switzerland. USA - The West Coast Experience. South Yorkshire Supertram - Construction Continues. Romania - Seven New Tramways in Seven Years.

LIGHT RAIL REVIEW 5 (Published November 1993) £7.50 + P&P.
South Yorkshire Supertram - Progress on All Fronts. France - Current Developments. Manchester Metrolink Forges Ahead. Land Use, Transport & Environment Study. Low-Floor Cars Come of Age. Shared Track Running in the UK. A Light Rail System for Saarbrücken. Leeds Supertram - An LRT System for Leeds. German Miscellany. USA - Light Rail Success in St Louis. Lille - Revival of the 'Mongy'. Photo Feature - LRT Around the World.

LIGHT RAIL REVIEW 6 (Published November 1994) £7.50 + P&P.
Tuen Mun - The World's Busiest Light Rail System. Current Progress in Blackpool. LRT Chosen for Gosport-Portsmouth. USA - The Tandy Subway, Fort Worth. France - Current Developments. Strathclyde Tram - Glasgow's Transport Strategy. Nantes Opens Line 2 Northern Section. Strasbourg's Futuristic Tramway. Photo Feature - LRT in Europe. South Yorkshire Supertram - Tramway Operation. US Light Rail Success.

LIGHT RAIL REVIEW 7 (Published July 1996) £8.95 + P&P.
Ultra Light Rail. LRT Plays an Important Role in Japan. Midland Metro Under Construction. Transport Policy in European Cities. Low-Floor Trams - Manufacturers' Initiatives. France - Current Developments. Photo Feature - LRT Around the World. Germany - The Kassel-Baunatal Extension. Manchester Metrolink Airport Extension Public Enquiry. South Yorkshire Supertram - Progress, Problems and a Crisis.

LIGHT RAIL REVIEW 8 (Published June 1998) £9.50 + P&P.
Amsterdam - A Tottering Giant. Midland Metro Prepares for Tramway Operation. Saarbrücken's Light Rail System Opens. Trams Return to Sydney. Siemens LRVs in the United States. Croydon Tramlink - Trams Return to London. The Return of the Conductor. France - Current Developments. South Yorkshire Supertram - Progress & Privatisation. Photo Feature - Portland, Oregon.

- -

TRAM TO SUPERTRAM by Peter Fox, Paul Jackson & Roger Benton

The official publication concerning the South Yorkshire Supertram system traces the history of Sheffield's old street tramway and tells the story behind the development of the new modern tramway network. It is lavishly illustrated in colour throughout, and includes maps of both old & new systems. The book is divided into three main sections:

1. SHEFFIELD'S FORMER TRAM SYSTEM. From horse-drawn trams to early electric trams and later the cream and blue double-deckers familiar to Sheffield's residents. The development of the early system, 20th century progress and post war decline. Sheffield's tramcars in preservation.

2. SUPERTRAM. The largest section of the book covers why the light rail option was chosen; Funding and implementation of the pioneering scheme; Construction - track, power supply, overhead line equipment, tramstops, Nunnery depot; The new trams; Operations and ticketing. Each of the three lines to Meadowhall, Halfway and Middlewood is described in detail.

3. SHEFFIELD TRAMWAY PICTORIAL. A combination of high quality photographs from both tramway eras.

48 pages. A4 size. 75 colour illustrations. £4.95 + P&P.

- -

MANX ELECTRIC

Manx Electric is the story of the Manx Electric Railway and the Snaefell Mountain Railway. It traces the history of the systems in detail and charts the development of the lines and their rolling stock to the present day. The book examines the wide variety of options available to builders of the lines and explains why particular options were chosen. It is interesting as a text book on tramway construction and operating methods, as well as being important reference work. As well as a comprehensive history of the two lines, there are detailed chapters on the Rolling Stock, Ticketing, Overhead Equipment, Traffic, Buildings and the Training of Motormen. Author Mike Goodwyn is chairman of the Manx Electric Railway Society and his knowledge of the subject is unsurpassed.

A4 size. Thread sewn. 112 pages including 12 in colour. £8.95 + P&P.

- -

HOW TO ORDER:

Telephone your order and credit card details to 0114-255-2625 (overseas +44-114-255-2625), or fax to 0114-255-2471 (overseas +44-114-255-2471).
or: Send your order and credit card details, sterling cheque, money order, Eurocheque or British postal order payable to 'Platform 5 Publishing Ltd.' to:

Mail Order Department (BFT), Platform 5 Publishing Ltd., 3 Wyvern House, Sark Road, SHEFFIELD, S2 4HG, ENGLAND.

If paying by credit card, please state type of card, card number, expiry date and full name and address of card holder.
Please add postage and packing: 10% UK; 20% Europe; 30% Rest of World.
Many other tramway and railway books are available from the Platform 5 Mail Order Department. For a full list of titles available, please send SAE to the above address.